HOLIDAYS
THAT DON'T
COST THE EARTH

John Elkington is one of Europe's leading authorities on environmental strategies for business and a founder-director of SustainAbility Ltd. He is a director of the Association of Environmental Consultancies, and an adviser for several associations and councils, including the BioIndustry Association, the Merlin Ecology Fund, the Business Council for Sustainable Development and Business in the Environment. He is author or co-author of around thirty books and published reports, and writes for a range of publications, including a regular column in the *Guardian*. During the course of his work over the last twenty years he has visited hundreds of companies in countries all over the world. John Elkington is married with two children.

Julia Hailes is a founder-director of SustainAbility Ltd and is a member of several environment-related committees, including the UK Department of the Environment's National Advisory Group on Eco-Labelling. She has acted as an environmental consultant for companies such as Dow Europe, Gardner Merchant, ICI, and Procter & Gamble. She has organised a variety of 'green consumer' events, including the hugely successful Green Consumer Week in 1988 and a 'Green Kitchen' stand at the Ideal Home Exhibition, and several events relating to tourism and the environment. She has travelled extensively, both through her work and as an individual. Julia Hailes is married and lives in London.

John Elkington and Julia Hailes are co-authors of the No. 1 bestselling *Green Consumer Guide*, *The Green Consumer's Supermarket Shopping Guide*, *The Young Green Consumer Guide* and *The Green Business Guide*. In 1989 they were elected to the United Nations Global 500 Roll of Honour for their 'outstanding environmental achievements'. Both have made many appearances on television and radio and in the press, and regularly speak at conferences associated with the environment.

HOLIDAYS
THAT DON'T
COST THE EARTH

John Elkington & Julia Hailes

LONDON
VICTOR GOLLANCZ LTD
1992

First published in Great Britain 1992
by Victor Gollancz Ltd
14 Henrietta Street, London WC2E 8QJ

A Gollancz Paperback Original

A catalogue record for this book is available
from the British Library.

ISBN 0 575 05111 6

Photoset in Great Britain by
Rowland Phototypesetting Ltd, Bury St Edmunds, Suffolk
Printed and bound in Great Britain by
Mackays of Chatham PLC, Chatham, Kent

CONTENTS

ACKNOWLEDGEMENTS

Holidays that Don't Cost the Earth has been a long time in the making. We started the research for the book as long ago as 1987 – and some of our early thinking appeared in earlier books, including *Green Pages* and *The Green Consumer Guide*, both published in 1988.

We owe a huge debt of gratitude to Amanda Pratt, of SustainAbility, our 'green growth' company, who has played a key role in putting this book together; she has helped us enormously with our thinking and has co-ordinated the main bulk of the research for the book. We should also like to thank Emma Scobie, who helped to pull together information on tourism initiatives in Africa, Asia and North America, and Anne Dimmock for her continuing support on many fronts.

Our publishers, Gollancz, have been reassuringly and fully committed to the project during the long lead-up time to publication. Liz Knights and Katrina Whone in particular have been consistently enthusiastic whilst steering us towards a better final product.

In the run-up to the launch of the book, SustainAbility co-hosted a workshop in London on tourism and the environment with Tourism Concern. We are grateful to Tricia Barnett and Alison Stancliffe of Tourism Concern for their help both then and since.

We should also like to thank those people who attended for their support and ideas. These included people from the tourism business, among them ABTA, British Airways and P & O; tour operators Janet Cochrane of Detours, Travers Cox of Explore Worldwide, Hedda Lyons of Twickers World and Richard Watrous of the Greek Islands Club; and environmental campaigning or educational groups Ark, Earthwatch Europe, Friends of the Earth International, Friends of the Ionian, the RSPB and the World Wide Fund for Nature.

Hilary Bradt, author of a number of travel guides, has been helpful in a number of ways, talking through some of her experiences and contributing ideas. Tony Lloyd of Kodak's Environmental Advisory Service kindly looked through the section on photography and made comments.

Thanks also to Clive Stacey from Arctic Experience; Julie Cray from TRAFFIC; Andrew Mitchell from Earthwatch; Mark Samuelson, our world traveller; Brian Johnson; Neil Rock of Friends of the Earth Europe; Eve Henley-Welch; Eggie, Kathy and Mike Kock; and James Skinner who has orchestrated a number of tourism and environment projects.

Many tour operators, hotel chains and transport companies helped by responding either to questionnaires or to telephone enquiries, and we very much appreciate the time they spared to contribute to our book.

It is inevitable in producing a guide like this that we will have overlooked some types of holiday and some environmentally conscious companies and organisations. If you would like to help fill any such gaps, to make any other comments or to participate in our on-going 'green tourism' campaign, please write to us at: SustainAbility Ltd, The People's Hall, 91–7 Freston Road, London W11 4BD.

1
INTRODUCTION: PROMISED LANDS

From the shimmering sands of the Caribbean to the shining peaks of the Himalayas, the tourism industry insists on locating its operations in the heart of the choicest landscapes. In so doing, it changes them – and these changes are rarely for the better.

Countries, regions and resorts that have embraced this rapidly growing industry are finding that it brings profound social and cultural impacts in its wake. And while some of these impacts are welcomed by local people, many wonder whether they have allowed a Trojan Horse to be wheeled into their cities, towns and villages.

Tourism certainly can deliver some nasty surprises. Who would have expected to hear the Archbishop of Canterbury dub tourism a 'new religion', warning that mass tourism is a prime cause of pollution, prostitution, economic exploitation and the devastation of indigenous lifestyles?

The world's no. 1 moneyspinner

Most of the people affected by such problems are not blind to the fact that they are getting more than they bargained for; indeed, in many cases they are responsible for actively encouraging tourism. But it is difficult for them to turn back the clock, particularly when the tourism business has allowed them to throw off the economic shackles that had previously kept them in poverty, and had denied them the Western lifestyles they saw in the latest TV soap operas.

Whatever you may think of the business, tourism is rapidly turning into the world's largest industry. American Express recently reported that the industry enjoys annual sales of more than $2 trillion (million million) and employs over 100 million people (one in fifty people worldwide).

The scale and pace of change has been extraordinary. Before the Second World War about one million people worldwide travelled abroad each year. By the early 1990s, however, this figure had exploded to 400 million a year, with another billion-and-a-half people travelling within their own countries.

And still, it seems, there is enormous untapped demand for travel. The opening up of Central and Eastern Europe –

and of the erstwhile Soviet Union – will not simply put new holiday destinations on the map for Westerners. It will also eventually unleash a tide of new travellers.

The Japanese, meanwhile, have only just begun to get into their stride as tourists, while the Chinese are not even at the starting blocks. Imagine what would happen if Beijing were to follow the trail blazed by Berlin, Prague and Moscow. In the summer months the planet would rock on its axis as hundreds of millions of tourists migrated across its surface in pursuit of sun, snow, new people, new places and new excitements.

Getting away from it all

As more and more of us exercise our new-found freedom, so our tastes in travel – where we go, how we get there, and what we do once there – have undergone incredible changes.

The cheap, convenient 'package tour', for example, was invented to take people away from it all. But as the south of France and the Spanish Costas filled up with package holidaymakers, the tour operators were forced to look for new 'paradises' to colonise.

Greece, Cyprus, the Gambia and – more recently – Turkey all came under siege as they were picked up by the fickle spotlight of fashion. In Turkey alone the number of tourists grew from 80,000 to 450,000 in the space of just three years. Now, even more remote destinations are open to mass tourism. Kenya, India, Thailand and Bali are just four of the destinations facing problems of overload. Their very success in attracting tourists threatens to be their undoing.

In America, the density of visitors to California's Yosemite National Park on some summer days is greater than it would be on Manhattan Island in New York. On the other side of the Atlantic, in York, England, the city is visited by thirty times its population every year – and some local residents have taken to wearing anti-tourist badges.

The more tourists a resort attracts, the more water and sewage-treatment plants, power plants, roads and hotels it has to build. If you consider that every tourist in Hawaii or

Barbados uses about six to ten times more water and electricity than a local resident, you get some idea of the size of the problems facing such destinations. And the problems are likely to be much worse in world regions that have little experience of handling tourism. In 1965 Nepal welcomed less than 10,000 tourists. By 1987 it had to cope with nearly 250,000 – all with an insatiable appetite for scarce firewood.

The sheer number of people wanting to travel, almost always at peak periods, guarantees problems. And in this case friction does not make the pearl; it threatens to sand it away.

Close encounters of the unpleasant kind

Unabashed, the travel brochures wax lyrical about the brilliant, bronzing sun. The sparkling waves. The glistening, golden sands. And, between the lines, the endless opportunities for romance – and, safe or not, sex.

But once we get to our holiday destinations, particularly if we pick a beach holiday, we can find ourselves face to face with the same problems we thought we had left behind us at home. In one world region after another, the rapid growth of 'battery tourism' is causing concrete costas to devastate once-beautiful coastlines, the sky to be filled with roaring jets and new motorways to cut across the countryside, devastating the landscape in their wake.

The brochure writers all too often turn a blind eye to the traffic jams, the crowded beaches and the polluted sea – glazed with oil, foamed with sewage and glistening with a carpet of plastic and other litter. Just as brochure designers use an air-brush to mask eyesores in the brochure photographs, so some brochure writers use a mental air-brush to gloss over anything that might put off potential customers. Of course, once the customer is face to face with the problem it's too late. The money's in the bank.

And these are just some of the obvious problems. There are many others which are invisible to most ordinary holidaymakers, among them the economic, social and cultural impacts of tourism. Even most tour operators and travel agents are blind to such problems – indeed they are blinded by their belief that their industry does nothing but good for the destinations it favours with its custom.

Unfortunately, the tourism industry has turned out to be a difficult target for environmentalists to get to grips with. But it must be tackled. Highly fragmented and used to intense, cut-throat competition, the industry is remarkably short-sighted. It tends to 'quarry' environmental quality, with little or no interest in re-investing in the areas that it exploits. If one Shangri-La is wrecked, the industry's boom town mentality suggests that another can always be found.

The guilty ones

So who is to blame? The easy answer is the tour operator, who puts together our holiday package – and the travel agent, who sells it to us. Our survey of tour operators (see page 309) shows that many are waking up to the fact that they will need to do something to protect the environments to which they send their clients – but precious few have concrete plans to move beyond words to action. Ultimately, too, the honest answer is that we are all to blame, whether we are holiday-makers, travel agents, tour operators, resort managers or working for the ferry companies, airlines, car rental firms or hotel chains.

How many of us, as holidaymakers, have heard – and responded to – that siren call of the tourism industry: 'Come and see this extraordinary, untouched paradise before it disappears for ever'? How often have we heard family, friends or colleagues urge: 'You really ought to go to Turkey (or whatever the latest flavour of the month may be) before the rest of the world wakes up to its attractions and turns them to ashes'? *See it before it's gone*, is the invisible copyline on the holiday posters.

Without realising it, we have been infected with the late-twentieth-century equivalent of the Midas Touch – but in reverse. Our money lines the pockets of the very developers who pave Paradise and put up a parking lot – so people like us can mill around with other people like us in search of whatever it was the brochures promised us before we came.

Green consumers on holiday

What can we as consumers do to turn the tide? Must we simply accept what the tourism industry is prepared to offer us because we have no option? Of course not, no more than we would let manufacturers of environment-unfriendly detergents, cars or washing machines off the hook. Instead, we can help persuade travel agents to learn about some of the greener holiday options now on offer. We can ask the airlines, ferry companies, car rental firms and hotels what they are doing to clean up their act. And we can give our support to initiatives that are helping to green the places we visit.

As consumers, we have tremendous power to push for change. The rise of the Green Consumer has shown that many ordinary people do want to do the right thing. Until recently, however, they have not known how.

The publication of *The Green Consumer Guide* in 1988, and subsequently around the world, helped to launch a market revolution in high streets and shopping malls in country after country. The central message learnt was that if we as consumers demand products and services that are more environmentally friendly, they are much more likely to be offered. If we buy green we help to push unacceptable products off the shelves – and create completely new markets for more acceptable alternatives. People who had assumed that they were powerless, that their decisions to buy or not to buy scarcely registered on the commercial scales, have found they have the world of business by the ear.

This is not simply power to say STOP, but also to say DO SOMETHING DIFFERENT. As the supermarkets and other retailers have come under pressure, they in turn have challenged manufacturers, growers and other suppliers to produce better products and clean up *their* act. The message has thundered back up the supply chain. It is even beginning to penetrate the world of money, as growing numbers of ethical and green investment trusts have raised money to invest in companies with a good or improving environmental track record.

Enter the Green Tourist

It is perfectly possible for consumer pressure to turn the tourism industry around. *Holidays that Don't Cost the Earth* reveals some of the ways in which our decisions on where and how to go on holiday – and on what we do when we get there – already affect the environment. But it doesn't stop there. You will find the following chapters full of information on how to make things better.

Whether you pass your leisure hours on land, in the air, or in or alongside water, whether you ski, cycle, hunt or play golf, we give practical advice on how to make sure the places and sights you travel so far to see don't just live on in your photograph album or video rack.

Green – or environmentally sustainable – tourism may be an unattainable idyll for most as yet, but greener tourism is now becoming a reality, if you know where to look. In the following pages you should find all the information you need to start booking holidays that won't cost the Earth.

KEY ISSUES FOR THE GREEN HOLIDAYMAKER

As individuals concerned about the environmental impact of our leisure and holiday activities, Green Holidaymakers aim to:

- Book holidays through travel agents, tour operators, carriers, car rental firms, hotel chains and other businesses that adopt a responsible attitude to the environment and act on it.

- Favour organisations and firms that put back part of the money we pay into conservation and other environmental initiatives designed to ensure the long-term protection of the resources we have enjoyed.

- Favour countries, regions, resorts or localities where proper conservation measures are in force – even 'soft' forms of tourism can become 'hard' if too many people take part.

- Find out about the culture, customs and environment of the places we plan to visit before going, and behave as sensitively as possible towards the surroundings and local people.

- Be aware of issues and particular problems of particular regions and behave responsibly – for example, conserving water in an arid country where water is urgently needed for irrigation and other local priorities.

- Avoid – and encourage others to avoid – products based on endangered species of wildlife or which involve cruelty to animals, or which use materials whose production causes unacceptable environmental damage, especially to endangered habitats.

- Minimise waste products and favour destinations where adequate recycling (or, at worst, properly managed waste disposal) facilities are available.

- Leave a holiday location as clean – or cleaner – as before tourists arrived; and report pollution and litter problems to the local tourism authorities. No area wants to lose its tourism trade.

- Travel light – remembering, for example, that roof racks increase a car's fuel consumption by nearly 10 per cent.

- Join the consumer and environmental organisations that are doing most in this area – and keep them informed of the problems we have encountered on our holidays.

2
THE TRAVEL
BUG

At times it seems as if everybody has caught the travel bug. Millions of us are on the move, seeking new and more thrilling adventures. In fact people on the move are very much like locusts. A farmer may ignore one or two locusts, but a swarm can lay waste to both farms and landscape.

Most of us are unaware of the impact we have as tourists. We consider that travel, even foreign travel, is not so much a privilege as a god-given right; and every year, or even more often, we exercise this right, without thinking of the consequences. So before you reach for the pile of brochures for your next holiday, reflect on your motives for travelling in the first place.

Faced with bulging airports, congested motorways, hotels where the concrete is still setting and elbow-to-elbow crowds on beaches, many people are already wondering whether it is worth the effort. Perhaps we should all stay at home?

To Go or Not to Go?

Some 'deep green' environmentalists argue that 'truly aware' people would spurn holidays altogether. One leading critic of mass tourism, a Swiss professor called Jost Krippendorf, argues that the desperate urge to seek pastures new for two weeks in the year is an inevitable consequence of our pressure-cooker cities, monotonous working lives and the constant bombardment of seductive advertising. It may be crowded and dirty when you get to your holiday destination, but it's not as bad as it was at home!

The green logic is easy to follow. Persuade people to stay at home and they will put more effort into cleaning up their own environment – and less time trampling over other people's.

Ironically, however, many of those who make the most noise about the problems of tourism continue to travel at every possible opportunity. And, even as many parts of the planet teeter on the brink of tourist overload, most people who can travel still feel that a year without a holiday away would be a year not worth living.

In our increasingly hectic, fast-paced lives, many of us travel simply to break the pattern of our demanding working environments – but do we really need to fly to the other side of the world to achieve this? Sometimes, too, we travel somewhere because we have been told that it is *the* place to go. Yet when we get there, we find that almost everyone else we know has already been, is planning to go shortly or is staying in the same hotel when we arrive. Green holidays, in contrast, are easy to put together if you are independently minded and prepared to branch out on your own. Sometimes this may mean you decide to stay at home or to visit local areas you have never had the time to enjoy.

Ultimately, we may find that some of the decisions about whether or not we travel – and what we should do while on holiday – will be made for us. Around the world, planners are struggling to work out new ways of taming the golden hordes that are descending on over-taxed resorts.

Price is obviously an effective way to stop tourists from visiting already overcrowded attractions – and it seems inevitable that more and more attractions will switch to a 'pay-as-you-enjoy' system. But if charging for museums and churches is already unpopular, imagine the reaction if we were asked to pay for scenic walks along the coast or for a stroll in the hills.

Restricting access is another obvious but sometimes controversial solution. If the car-parks were sited further away from beauty spots, fewer people would take the trouble to visit. Another option is to limit the number of hotel beds. Some countries, like Bhutan and Nepal, have already imposed quotas on the number of tourists they allow in each year, and many tourist attractions regulate visiting times to keep the number of tourists down.

Some attractions, such as England's Stonehenge, Italy's Leaning Tower of Pisa and Greece's Parthenon, perched high atop Athens' Acropolis, already restrict access *and* charge a fee for entry. If present trends continue, it is quite possible that some of the more popular churches, among them Notre

Dame in Paris and St Paul's in London (which both receive about 11 million visitors every year), may have to introduce a means of discriminating between genuine worshippers and tourists.

What Sort of Holidaymaker Are You?

Before looking at the impact of different types of holiday in Chapter 4, try putting yourself under the green spotlight. You might be surprised by what you see!

It's amazing how most of us go through life thinking that *other people* are causing the world's problems. We devised seven main tourist types and tested them out on a number of people, and discovered that most people found it very difficult to fit themselves into any one category – but seemed to have no difficulty at all in labelling friends and colleagues!

One of the commonest misconceptions we have come across is the belief that the real troublemakers are the people who go on package tours, in contrast to nature lovers and assorted wildlife watchers who are seen as totally 'environment-friendly'. But this is far from the truth. Certainly, wildlife watchers are often described as 'eco-tourists', which many take to mean that they are not damaging the environment, but the fact is that they are even better placed to damage the natural environment, because they are in such close touch with it. It may even be that some package tour holidays impose less strain on the environment, per head, because the tourists are concentrated in one place built to cater for their needs.

Whatever type of tourist you are, remember that – for better or worse – we all have an impact on the environment. But *Holidays that Don't Cost the Earth* is not simply a complicated way of saying don't go on holiday. Instead, we show how every one of us can get more out of our holidays without taking more out of the environment in the process.

So what sort of holidaymaker are you?

Trailblazer

We recognise them almost immediately when we see them – but these types are few and far between.

Whether they are explorers, pioneering scientists or missionaries, Trailblazers like to be first on the scene. In the early days of the American frontier, these were the Davy Crocketts and Daniel Boones who chipped trees in the thick forests to mark out the trail others would follow. Today they write the books and film the TV programmes, mapping out the routes that the rest of the world will follow. Typical Trailblazers in recent times have included Thor Heyerdahl, Gavin Young, Tim Severin, Paul Theroux, Colin Thubron and Bruce Chatwin. Such people give thousands of readers and viewers real insights into the places they travel through – and the people they meet on their way.

Then there are the Trailblazers who climb Everest without oxygen or sail single-handed around the world. They may tell you they have gone riding – but then they tell you they were aboard an elephant alongside the Venezuelan wife of the Rajah of wherever. When it comes to meeting people from their own culture, though, most Trailblazers are usually hypersensitive. Livingstone may have welcomed Stanley's company in the dark heart of Africa, but probably also resented the journalist's appearance as a sign that the outside world was catching up with him. Many Trailblazers get on well with the natives, or like to think they do, not least because they are much more dependent on their goodwill than those who will follow. Some are seen – and treated – as demi-gods from the outside world.

Often extraordinary people in their own right – and one thinks of people like Wilfred Thesiger, the first white man to cross the Arabian Desert – they can bring new perspectives to the communities they pass through. Often, they are welcomed as great teachers. By the time the rest of the world catches up with them, however, the true Trailblazers have long since packed their bags and left. But like disease-carrying insects, some may already have infected their hosts with the seeds of their own destruction.

Missionaries have been particularly disruptive Trailblazers, arriving in remote parts of the world utterly convinced that other people's religions, cultures and lifestyles were 'wrong', if not actually heretical. By hook or by crook, they were out to add to their flock – or to die in the attempt. Indeed, many quite liked the idea of sacrificing themselves on the altars of Empire, Church, Science or just plain Adventure.

Some Trailblazers have been remarkably destructive. Even Audubon, now a patron saint of bird conservation, shot tens of thousands of birds to paint his masterpieces of American wildlife.

The early explorers rarely had any concept of conservation, hunting for furs, trophies or the sheer fun of it. Indeed some early conservationists – among them Teddy Roosevelt – were such relentless hunters that even they could see the animals were running out.

Late-twentieth-century Trailblazers have to work pretty hard to find new places to go, new things to do. Virgin's Richard Branson, for example, had to cross the Pacific in a hot-air balloon to get into the record books.

Today, however, many of these explorers and adventurers are distinctly green. Branson, to take the case in point, dedicated his trans-Pacific balloon flight to the cause of preventing ozone depletion.

Traveller
The independent Traveller is less likely to make a career out of travelling – and is also unlikely to be the first on the scene. But these people are adventurous spirits, often taking to the road for months – or even years – at a time.

And time is one thing they have plenty of. The Traveller embarks on the late-twentieth-century equivalent of the Grand Tour. Once the idea was that a young man of good family went to Europe to sow his wild oats and soak up a little classical culture. Now Travellers, of either sex, are still likely to return with broader cultural horizons, though the arrival of AIDS may have curbed some of their other expectations.

Travellers typically carry little money, even though many

come from well-heeled backgrounds. Kitted out with back-packs, hiking boots, pen-knives and other survival aids, they wouldn't be seen dead around ordinary tourists. Although they often travel in pairs, they generally like to have the place to themselves.

Naturally, most Travellers take an intelligent interest in the out-of-the-way regions they pass through, but some can be bores on the subject of how little they paid to get from A to B. Indeed, because Travellers are keen to see how far they can stretch their money, they are unlikely to help fund large-scale tourism development. They rely on local transport and accommodation, but may still be the objects of envy, high-lighting the huge chasm between the lifestyles of the developed and less developed worlds.

Travellers may not like to think so, but they too pave the way for more popular forms of tourism. The hippies of the sixties, for example, opened up places like Goa to mass tour-ism. They returned home extolling the virtues of the exotic and beautiful places they had visited and, as a result, others followed in their footsteps.

Some Travellers are now returning to their original stamp-ing grounds as Trekkers or even as Tourists – and are shocked to see how Paradise has changed.

Trekker

Trekkers are a relatively new breed – and seen by the special-ised tour operators as a growth market for the future.

Instead of travelling on their own, they opt for an organised journey with a small group, be it a safari, a hike through the Himalayas or a boat-trip down the Amazon. Often deeply interested in the environment, they are natural targets for eco-tour operators.

Indeed, some of today's Trekkers are likely to be yester-day's Travellers in middle age, with less time but more money. They are constrained by jobs, mortgages and chil-dren. This is likely to be 'quality time' for them and they will want to pack the experiences of a lifetime into the week or two available.

Not surprisingly, the main problems with Trekkers stem

from the fact that they are trying to do too much in too short a space of time. They want to get off the beaten track, but the fact that they move in groups may mean that they effectively put remote communities on the tourist trail.

Unlike the best of the Trailblazers and Travellers, Trekkers will rarely have time to work their way deep into a culture. So, for example, they are more likely to want to photograph the hilltribesmen of Thailand than to settle in for a while and learn the language. They are also prepared to treat themselves, which can cause problems if they find that they are having to 'rough it'. Many will insist on having a hot shower, for example, even if it means that some of the few remaining trees have to be cut down to provide the fuel for the water heaters.

More positively, Trekkers are willing – and able – to plough money into the areas they visit. Unlike many Trailblazers or Travellers, these people will not be staying with someone they happened to meet on the road. They are also very likely to report problems they encounter, join environmental groups and support conservation projects. Some of the more public-spirited ones may even be happy to join in a litter clean-up or similar project – as long as the environment is sufficiently exotic.

Tourer

Tourers often travel in family groups, taking their own transport – usually a car, but sometimes cycles – to ensure total mobility while they explore a region.

They are keen on rural areas, hill-top villages, old towns such as Avignon in France or Sienna in Italy, and are usually found in self-catering villas, small hotels or pensions with character. Many have friends in foreign parts and stay with them *en route*.

Generally at least thirtysomething, Tourers like to get into the spirit of a place, but are generally as time-constrained as Trekkers. They are constantly on the move, driving in easy stages from one place to the next. In France, they will brandish guides published by Michelin or Richard Binns. Soon, they will be streaming into Central and Eastern Europe. What used to be the Soviet Union is still a bit too tough for Tourers – and they tend not to be as keen on Third World countries as Trailblazers, Travellers and Trekkers.

Tourers love maps and also try to steer well clear of tourist-traps, although in most countries they will find that they inevitably collide with the rest of the world on holiday at some point. They seek out the local cuisine and pump a fair amount of money into local economies. They will also visit attractions like Disneyland – purely for the children, you understand.

Like all other tourists, Tourers confronted with tourist over-load tend to see the rest of the world as the problem – even though, for example, they contribute a disproportionate amount to air pollution, through emissions from the cars they drive. Although we are seeing the rise of the Green Tourer, most Tourers would still prefer to buy a compact disc player for their car than a catalytic converter.

Tourist

Almost anyone on holiday can be described as a tourist, but the Tourist is a migratory animal with very pronounced habits.

Almost always bedding down in a hotel, he or she likes to see the sights. Most feel that they have not really visited a tourist attraction, whether it be the Statue of Liberty or the Taj Mahal, until they have been photographed inside, along-side or on top of it.

They prefer to travel in groups and – because of their sheer numbers – tend to wear away the places they visit. Not so keen on talking to the locals, they make a bee-line for racks of picturesque postcards to rouse the envy of their friends and colleagues.

Tourists love to soak up the sun – indeed, some make an art of monopolising the best sun-beds, whether by the swimming pool or on the beach. Younger Tourists are often disco enthusiasts and some of these night-lifers have given their breed a bad name for rowdy behaviour and inappropri-ate attire.

But Tourists are usually welcomed with open arms by local

traders and developers like the first swallows of an English summer. Indeed, it often seems as if developers throw up new high-rise hotels even faster than swallows build their nests under the eaves.

The Tourist's insistence on every mod con, including air conditioning and familiar food, can mean that very little of their money reaches the host country – instead most of it will go to the airlines, hotels, tour operators and travel agents that organised their holiday, looked after them and carried them to and fro.

Tourists are often oblivious to local environmental or social problems, partly because they only catch a 'snapshot' view of the resort, community or local environment. But, like all species, Tourists have their environmental virtues. They tend to concentrate in purpose-built resort towns, which – in an ideal world – could mean that their waste and sewage is recycled or treated more efficiently. And, because they like to travel *en masse* in buses, coaches or on charter flights, rather than in convoys of motor cars, they may cause less air pollution and congestion per head.

Despite the disdain in which they are held by many other holidaymakers, and by some environmentalists, Tourists may well become the shock troops of 'green tourism'. Because of their numbers and spending power, their changing interests and habits are a subject of compulsive interest to the tourism business.

Tripper
A good natter, a lungful or two of sea air and a stop-off for a picnic at a nice pub or restaurant are essential ingredients in the successful day trip.

During the Industrial Revolution, most people working in highly polluted towns considered themselves extraordinarily lucky to get even a day in a resort like Blackpool. Nowadays, Trippers are everywhere – and have more time on their hands, particularly the older generation.

Trippers are not always welcomed, though. In the south-west of England they are sometimes referred to disparagingly as 'grockles'. Some travel by train or by car, but the ordinary

Tripper generally arrives by coach.

If Trippers emerge from their vehicles many of them will not stray further than a few hundred metres to find a picnic spot. They are great users of 'facilities', needing public lavatories, car-parks and shops close to hand. They produce mountains of rubbish and can be litter-bugs if bins are not readily available. They also spend much of their time collecting trinkets and other souvenirs.

Like columns of army ants, Trippers crawl along the world's motorways in great, nose-to-tail traffic jams. Their exhausts pump noxious fumes and greenhouse gases into the air and green fields are coated with tarmac to provide them with coach- and car-parking spaces.

Because Trippers are short-stay creatures, they are not particularly energy-efficient. On the plus side, they do not require monstrous sprawling hotel developments, nor do they turn up in the world's really remote areas. So, even though they encourage developers to opt for cheap and tacky buildings, the Tripper's impact is generally localised and temporary.

If Trippers could be persuaded to go 'tripping' by train, or even by bike, and to stay a little longer in one place, they might be rather more popular both with the communities they visit – and with environmentalists.

Termite

OK, so we invented the term, but it's easy to understand. The Termite is the holidaymaker for whom battery tourism was invented.

The stereotype Termite does not like going far from the termitary and is often keen on all the comforts of home – with a good measure of sun, sea and sand, too.

In the not-too-distant future they may not even need to stir far from home. We are seeing a boom in new-style holiday camp developments such as resort villages around the Mediterranean and Center Parcs, dome-based villages around Britain and Holland.

Termites want a complete, hassle-free break organised for them and their families. Some can be quite sporty, taking part in everything from crazy golf to windsurfing – as long as everything is laid on.

Inevitably, Termite nests can gobble up land. As a result, many communities have greeted the news of a planned Termitary in their area much as they would news of Armageddon. And the vast termitaries built along the shores of the Mediterranean may justify such fears.

But home-grown eco-domes (see page 174) may fill a gap in the market in a more environmentally acceptable way. Termites can get there without flying, could save on heating bills by staying close together and won't need to drive anywhere – since most of their needs will be gratified on the spot.

Indeed, if the world's population continues to soar we may all have no choice but to holiday in termite fashion as every corner of the Earth will have been developed.

Planning a Holiday that Doesn't Cost the Earth

Family holidays, solo adventures, business trips: the options open to you in planning your time away will obviously vary with your circumstances. Listed below are some key points that you should always bear in mind, remembering that the more flexible you are about what you want the easier it is to take the most environment-friendly option. Be sure to read also Chapter 3 which focuses on the major issues and then turn to Chapter 5 for particular considerations in different parts of the world.

- The further you travel – and the faster you go – the greater your environmental impact is likely to be (see pages 34–50).

- If you can travel in off-peak periods, out of season, so much the better. You will be helping to cut congestion and generally helping to spread the load.

- Remember, using public transport is almost always less damaging than using your own transport. If you have to have a car, rent one rather than taking your own – and insist on a diesel-run car or one fitted with a catalytic converter.

- The lighter your load, the more energy efficient you will be, so plan carefully and leave at home things you suspect you may not need.

- Staying in local, independently run accommodation will almost always put more back into the economy than staying in multinational hotels.

- The more you insist on having what you are accustomed to, the more likely it is that your food and other needs will have to be shipped in – and the less likely it is that local people will benefit.

- The bigger the group you travel with, the more resource efficient travelling will be. But, at the same time, the more intrusive your group may seem to small local communities and the less likely you are to adapt to their ways – rather than forcing them to adapt to yours. If you do travel with a group, work that much harder to ensure you fit in and take local people's feelings into account.

- The more you understand or learn about the places you plan to visit, the more likely you are to help – rather than hinder – their own greening.

- The better you understand the issues, which are the subject of the next chapter, the easier it will be to ask the right questions of the travel agents, tour operators and others who help you on your way.

- And the more (sensible) questions you ask – and the more information you require – the more likely it is that the tourism business will feel it has no option but to provide holidays that don't cost the Earth.

3
PRESSURE
POINTS

Like so many serpents in Eden, tour operators, travel agents, airlines, hoteliers and timeshare agents promise us that we will be happier, wiser and wealthier if only we would bite into their apple. But, like it or not, each time we succumb to temptation and book a holiday in a particular resort, area or country, we are effectively voting for further tourism-related development there.

We can't wriggle off the hook by switching our holidays from the busiest areas to less-known ones. All we are doing is shifting the problem from today's pressure points to tomorrow's. But what we can do is keep the tourism business under constant vigilance and pressure and learn how we can put together a low-impact holiday.

From the planet's point of view, the impact meter is running from the moment we decide to travel. It clocks up our environmental bill just like an electricity meter, registering the implications of our choices on:

- *how far we travel – and how we get there*
- *the type of accommodation we choose*
- *where and what we eat and drink*
- *the activities we pursue while on holiday*
- *what we buy, and where we buy it*
- *how we behave*

This section of the book tells you what the key issues are at every stage of your holiday – with suggestions on what you can do to make sure the impact meter doesn't clock up the sort of bills that could bankrupt the environment.

GETTING THERE

If you add up all the miles you have travelled while on holiday over the years, the chances are that you will end up with a figure that will take you many times around this small planet. Wherever we live, we are now travelling further afield for our holidays. As we do so, we are increasingly likely to make at least part of the journey by air. Today, nearly a third of holidaymakers fly.

Whichever form of transport we use, it is likely to have become more energy efficient in recent years. But the sheer volume of people wanting to travel – whether by air, water, rail or road – means that world tourism is consuming ever-more non-renewable fossil fuel and other resources, and, at the same time, causing growing congestion at peak times of the year.

Let's start by looking at the airways, before coming back down to earth.

By air

When air passenger travel first began, the aircraft of the day carried twelve to fifteen people and needed to refuel every 500–650 kilometres or so. By contrast, today's jumbo jets can carry 500 or more people over thousands of kilometres.

Worldwide, over one billion people – or about a fifth of the world's population – now travel by air every year, a figure which is expected to double by the year 2000. The scale of the coming boom in air travel shows up clearly in the forecasts for Europe alone. A 1988 figure of 267 million air travellers was expected to nearly double to 500 million by 2000 and then almost triple to 740 million by the year 2010!

Even so, this is an intensely competitive market. Many airlines operate on precariously slim profit margins and their fortunes were not helped by the Gulf War and simultaneous recession. Happily, however, the association which represents most of the world's airlines acknowledges their inescapable responsibility to minimise their environmental impacts.

The damage starts long before you get into the air. Unless you are flying by helicopter or vertical take-off plane, you will take off from a sizable airport. As ever-larger hordes of passengers fly off to exotic locations, new multi-terminal airports have had to be built or expanded to cope with the volume of aircraft – about 1,100 planes take off from Heathrow Airport on the average day!

In some countries, there have actually been hand-to-hand battles between those wanting to build new airports and those wanting to stop them. In Japan the battles between students and police were like something out of medieval warfare.

The scale of the destruction can certainly be very substantial. In Germany, for example, the building of Frankfurt's third runway resulted in the felling of half a million trees. Elsewhere in the world, airports threaten key ecosystems – Japan's Shiraho blue coral reef is just one of the Pacific reefs threatened by airport construction plans.

Once an airport has been built, noise is often the most politically pressing problem. During the 1970s, various airports – in London, New York City and California, for example – tried to control noisy aircraft, particularly at night.

The worst problems by far have come from Concorde, although mercifully few planes of this type have been built. There are currently thirteen Concordes, a very small number compared with other planes, but they are the worst culprits in the noise and pollution stakes. The plane has always been a loss-maker, guzzles far too much fuel and is so noisy that thirty countries have restricted its use. But as the Pacific Rim economy booms, aircraft companies around the world are now racing to develop the next generation of supersonic transports (or High Speed Civil Transports, as they are known). A plane of this sort could halve the flying time between Los Angeles and Tokyo. If such planes are ever to succeed, though, they must use less fuel, run more quietly and produce much less pollution. And, with warnings from German scientists that the new generation of 'Super Concordes' could significantly accelerate ozone destruction, we will need to keep a close eye on the stratospheric ozone layer.

But most of us have never travelled in a Concorde – and never will. So what about the everyday airliners we do use?

Have you ever wondered how much pollution is produced by a modern commercial jet? A single Jumbo burns 16,000 litres of fuel an hour. As a result, aircraft now account for large quantities of nitrogen oxide, relatively smaller amounts of carbon monoxide and soot and quite large quantities of carbon dioxide.

It is estimated that as much as 10 per cent of US carbon dioxide emissions comes from their aeroplanes, with the UK figure much lower – but still significant – at around 2 per cent. Nitrogen oxides, on the other hand, contribute to the thinning of the earth's protective ozone layer and, paradoxically, also add to low-level ozone, which can represent a serious pollution problem. The environmental impact of nitrogen oxides when released at high altitude by jet aircraft remains a major uncertainty for the industry.

There has also been concern about the impact of the water vapour emitted by high-flying aircraft. The typical cruising height of aeroplanes is between 10 and 12 kilometres from the ground. Research has not yet been done to assess the impact of aircraft vapour trails, but whatever it is it will be worse when twice as many planes are criss-crossing the globe.

Unfortunately, there is no way that a catalytic converter can be fitted to a jet engine. But there are some hopeful trends. The older, noisier aircraft are being phased out – and cleaner, quieter and more fuel-efficient ones introduced. Over the last twenty years most of the industry has managed to at least halve the amount of fuel needed to carry a passenger over 100 kilometres.

German research suggests that the most modern jets produce less pollution per passenger than a medium-sized car fitted with the latest catalytic converter technology. Indeed, it is important not to overlook the achievements of aircraft designers and manufacturers. Compared with the earliest Boeing 727s, for example, the latest Airbus A-320-200 consumes 40 per cent less fuel, produces 78 per cent less carbon monoxide emissions (an air pollutant and very toxic) as well as almost eliminating hydrocarbon emissions (which cause smog at ground level).

Some high-profile airlines are taking the lead in environmental issues, and implementing improvements. These include:

- careful assessment of the environmental impact caused by aircraft
- the use of new, less harmful chemicals to clean aircraft and to clear snow from runways
- better disposal of sewage, which is now collected in sealed systems and discharged to sewers on arrival at the airport, rather than raining out of the sky as it once did
- the use of 'safer' chemicals in chemical loos – many airlines have switched away from formaldehyde, because it is thought to be carcinogenic, but no one has yet revealed that they have a better alternative than ammonium salts (which can irritate the skin)
- reducing wastage by switching away from disposable cutlery and crockery to materials that can be re-used
- the introduction of recycling schemes
- the banning of smoking on many internal flights
- in-cabin measures to save on fuel consumption, such as the stocking and sale of duty-free spirits bottled in lightweight plastic, rather than glass

Remember, though, that the airlines will need constant consumer pressure to ensure they keep on track. If you think further smoking bans are guaranteed, for example, think how much money the airlines earn from cigarettes! And we still have the question of how we can green the smaller airlines, particularly those flying from Eastern European and Third World countries.

But even small things that we do as airline passengers can have an unexpectedly large impact if enough of us act in the same way. Travelling light does not just make carrying your bags from A to B easier. Indeed Lufthansa estimates that a 747 aeroplane flying over the North Atlantic requires about 0.27 kg of fuel for every kilo of extra weight. Interestingly, just fifteen years ago one extra kilo on a 707 would have meant about 0.4 kg of fuel.

An enormous amount of fuel is wasted in carrying unnecessary cargo around the world. Even though lighter plastic bottles are now used for many drinks, *Flight International* estimated that more than 70,000 tonnes of duty-free alcohol are flown back and forth across the North Atlantic annually, wasting more than 27 million litres of fuel a year. British Airways told us that the environmental effects of such fuel consumption are relatively small. BA reckons that airborne duty-free goods add around 0.05 per cent to their annual carbon dioxide emissions. Nevertheless, the small effects all add up.

The airlines achieve a fair proportion of their profit in this area, which makes them loath to change, but one obvious solution would be to allow passengers to buy their duty-free goods when they arrive at their destination, rather than before they board the plane. The European Commission is planning to phase out duty-free altogether – which, at least in environmental terms, would be a positive step.

Overall, however, and despite the expected growth in its markets, the airline industry is clearly worried about its longer-term prospects. 'Hostility towards air travel could suddenly reach levels currently directed against sections of the nuclear and chemical industry,' warned a UN climate adviser at a recent aviation conference.

The airlines are clearly alert to the challenge, with British Airways and Swissair among those carrying out environmental audits of their operations. British Airways also launched a 'Greenwaves' scheme, to encourage staff to come up with practical ideas on ways the airline could make real environmental improvements.

Worried by the success of environmentalists, the airlines have also been working on a 'love your local airport' campaign. 'The Green movement has been kicking sand in our face for too long and making us look like idiots,' said one airline chief. But, even if they do get their defensive campaign airborne, the airlines know the pressures will continue to build around the world.

SHARKS HELP SAVE FUEL

No airline is green, or ever will be. But the response we got from Lufthansa – based in Germany, land of *die Grünen*, the original Greens – impressed us.

The airline's switch to new Airbus A320s means a 90 per cent smaller noise 'footprint' on take-off than with the older Boeing 727, while fuel consumption is cut by 40 per cent. Thanks to the latest engine technology, the exhaust emissions contain – per tonne of kerosene burned – 90 per cent fewer unburned hydrocarbons, 78 per cent less carbon monoxide and 10 per cent fewer nitrogen oxides.

The airline has taken an innovative approach to catering on domestic flights. To reduce the amount of waste generated, Lufthansa has introduced what it calls a 'gate buffet' to replace the plastic box of food dished out once on board. A selection of food and drinks is offered in the final departure lounge, from which passengers can choose what they want and either eat it there or take it on board the aircraft. So far, around 60 per cent of passengers take nothing or at most a piece of fruit – and Lufthansa has reduced its rubbish by 1,700 tonnes a year.

Lufthansa's efforts are not just a superficial gloss. They have also turned their attention to paint and solvents. Lufthansa aircraft are repainted every six to eight years, with more than a tonne of paint needed

WHAT YOU CAN DO

- First, consider whether you really need to fly. It may be possible to go by boat or by train – or to take a holiday closer to hand. In Germany, Lufthansa advises passengers to travel on its Airport Express train, where possible, rather than go by plane.

- If you do fly, write to the airline and ask what environmental initiatives it is taking – and keep an

for a single A320 fuselage. These paints have to be astonishingly tough: they must withstand temperature differ-
ences of far more than 100°C, between burning heat on
the ground and −60°C around 122,000 metres up. So they
are also tough to get off.

Lufthansa is now using a new process, 'Aquastrip', to
remove the paint from some parts of their aeroplanes – and
plan to use it for the whole body when they have built the
necessary facilities. Instead of using toxic dichloromethane
and phenol, this process uses high-pressure water. And
Lufthansa, among other airlines, has moved to electro-
static spraying for the final painting – which cuts paint and
smog-forming solvent losses by two-thirds.

The company is also learning energy efficiency from
sharks. The skin of the fastest-moving sharks has fine
grooves running down the length of the shark's body.
These grooves were emulated using plastic 'riblets' which
were stuck to model aircraft to make them more stream-
lined, and tested in windtunnels. The results were so
good that a Lufthansa A320 was fitted with the artificial
sharkskin, resulting in a likely saving of 70 tonnes of fuel
per aircraft per year.

Good news, but can the airlines keep up this rate of
climb? Lufthansa expects that its fleet will double in size
by the year 2000. If all the other airlines get involved in
this great frenzy above our heads, any hopes of clean
skies are likely to fade into the haze.

eye out for airlines that are taking a real interest in
their environmental performance.

- Remember, every question helps. Since very few
  people ever quiz airlines about their environmental
  performance, even a few polite questions can
  have a major impact. Airlines like British Airways
  and Lufthansa (see box above) will move even
  faster if you give their efforts a following wind.

- Ask your favourite airline for a copy of its environment policy. See if you can spot any gaps. If you can, tell them.

- Ask your flight attendants what the airline is doing for the environment. If it is using disposable cutlery, cups and plates, for example, suggest a switch to 'rotable' equipment – which can be washed and re-used.

- Ask the flight attendants if they have any magazines or in-flight videos on what the airline is doing to clean up its act, as well as information on how to be a green tourist.

- Encourage airlines to adopt a total no-smoking policy. Air Canada was the first to do this in North America – let's make sure the idea spreads.

- Encourage competition by mentioning what other airlines are doing. Virgin, for example, now plants a tree in its 'Virgin Forest' for every passenger flying its new Los Angeles–London route.

By water

 Ships and ferries are much more energy-efficient than are aircraft. So if you can travel by sea do. But remember that the environmental impact of individual ships will depend on how they are designed and run. One of the newly designed Brittany Ferries ships, the *Bretagne*, for example, is twice as big as the ship it has replaced – yet uses the same amount of fuel. Cutting fuel consumption once a ship is built can be extremely expensive, but when Cunard fitted its *QE2* with new engines in 1987 it cut its fuel consumption by nearly a third. Interestingly, too, the ship's propellers were polished, resulting in a further saving of 40 tonnes of fuel a day.

But even the best-designed ship will only be as good as its

captain and crew. As a rule of thumb, the best-run ships are also likely to be the most environmentally sound. As the *Herald of Free Enterprise* disaster showed, the competence and skill of the captain and crew are critically important even on the most modern ships. It is not simply a question of passenger safety. Many passenger ferries carry other cargoes like toxic chemicals, which could cause extensive ecological damage if lost at sea.

And there have been a number of worrying examples of well-known ships – among them the *QE2* – dumping rubbish at sea. Five tonnes of rubbish build up on the *QE2* alone every day. In fact, Cunard has now invested more than £1 million in bringing its waste-handling facilities up to date.

According to the latest laws of the sea, all rubbish produced aboard such ships must be collected at a central point. In certain areas, the Baltic, North Sea, Mediterranean and Red Sea, for example, all glass, metal and plastic must be compacted and brought back to shore. Only food waste can be discharged – and then only 20 kilometres or more from the nearest coast. In other areas, though the better companies would bring compacted glass, metal and plastic back to shore, it is still legal to dump glass and metal uncompacted more than 20 kilometres from shore!

Another area of concern is the use of tributyl tin (TBT) anti-fouling paints. The importance of keeping a ship's hull free of barnacles and weed is illustrated by the benefits of polishing the *QE2's* propellers. The problem is that TBT paints have been shown to endanger marine wildlife. Female dogwhelks, for example, were recently found to have grown penises after having been exposed to TBT.

These dogwhelks act like the miner's canary, warning of problems before our own senses – or sensing systems – pick them up. Surely any chemical that strikes at the reproductive systems of a living creature should be banned without further ado? For pleasure boats under 25 metres TBTs are banned (see page 104) and the more environmentally aware lines are testing alternative paints which keep the whelks and barnacles at bay without ruining their sex-lives! But are they acting fast enough?

Most, if not all, ships still use ozone-destroying CFCs in their cooling and refrigeration systems, including those used to chill the rubbish stores. P&O European Ferries admitted that they still used CFCs, like other lines, but argued that the shipping industry's total consumption of CFCs accounts for less than one per cent of annual world production. With a problem of this scale, however, even percentage points count. And the message seems to be going home. P&O, for example, say that most of their ships have their own CFC-leak detectors and equipment is regularly checked for leaks.

Whichever line you sail with, show a healthy interest in the intimate workings of your ship. Even the most sea-sick passenger can do something to help treat the planet's sick-sea syndrome.

WHAT YOU CAN DO

- Follow the guidelines for 'Cruising', on pages 98–9.

- Check whether the line you intend to sail with abides by an appropriate international environmental code – or perhaps it has its own?

- Ask about the use of CFCs and TBT paints.

- If you have any reason to suspect that waste is not being handled properly, report it to the captain. If you get no satisfaction, contact the authorities – or environmental campaigning groups.

By rail

Once, trains were the most exciting form of transport imaginable. They still are in some parts of the world, although not always for the right reasons. In Brazil, for example, some young people have found a new amusement which they call 'railway surfing'. This involves riding on the roof of a train with arms outstretched, leaning into the wind. There are safer ways to travel: fifty railway surfers were killed in a single year and yet the 'sport' later spread to Britain.

If you are travelling overland – and are content to ride inside, rather than on the roof – trains often represent the greenest form of motorised transport available. The Green Party, calling for a cut-back in the use of aircraft for holiday travel in Europe, pointed out that trains use 20–50 times less energy than aircraft.

It's possible, of course, to criticise even the greener forms of transport. In the early days, when Britain's first railways were built, farmers protested that the monstrous machines would make their animals abort, and parts of many major cities were turned black by the coal used to power early trains and other steam engines. Though today's trains are much cleaner, anyone who has stood near a diesel train in a station will know that they can produce clouds of noxious black smoke. Electric trains produce less local pollution, but do contribute to the environmental problems associated with producing electricity.

Many trains still discharge sewage straight on to the track. In the railway authorities' defence, they point out that storage tanks for sewage mean that their trains use more fuel to get you to your destination, but an increasing number of modern trains are now fitted with them – and some have low-flush lavatories, which save 35 million litres of water a year.

New railway lines also pose serious problems for people whose fields, gardens and even homes they must pass through – as the controversy surrounding the proposed lines linking London to the Channel Tunnel has shown.

Overall, however, rail travel's environmental performance is still better than that of a fleet of cars transporting the same number of people over the same distance.

Although in Britain the recent trend has been to expand road networks at the expense of railways, in the rest of Europe a great deal of investment is being poured into railway networks. In Germany, for example, the money is going into intercity expresses where some passengers will have access to cordless telephones, faxes and photocopiers. Instead of thinking how it can invest more in rail, the government of the country that invented railways is now thinking how it can sell them off.

In France, meanwhile, the TGV – the *Train à Grande Vitesse* – has been running successfully for a number of years, despite the considerable controversy it caused when first introduced. To their credit, the French railways have sometimes shown a capacity for compromise. When one track threatened to cut through the much-revered vineyard of Vouvray, for example, it was decided to run a tunnel underneath the vines. Unimpressed, the *vignerons* complained that the TGVs passing underground would still shake the bottles as they lay in their racks. So the engineers laid the lines on rubber to cushion the great trains as they thundered through.

Even high-speed trains are more energy efficient than private cars, using about two litres of fuel for every 100 passenger-kilometres, compared to more than nine litres for a private commuting car. On high-speed trains, three-quarters of the energy used is to overcome the resistance of the air through which the train speeds – so train designers are constantly trying to cut the drag factor.

Unfortunately, however, while some new lines are being built, many older and uneconomic railways are being shut down. Occasionally, as on the Settle–Carlisle line, a hard-fought campaign may keep open a much-loved line, but in many parts of the world trains are fighting a losing battle against the motor car. It is up to the traveller to keep them going – although we should always criticise the railways if the service is inadequate.

WHAT YOU CAN DO

- Leave the car and travel by train whenever possible. Use park-and-ride schemes where they exist: lobby for them where they do not.

- Don't plan your holiday and *then* see if you can get there by train. Plan your holiday around the train. In Switzerland, for example, you can travel across almost the entire country by train, tram, trolleybus and funicular railway.

- Stay in hotels that will arrange to collect you from the local station.

- Wherever you are, if you see heavily littered areas along the track, call the railway manager and complain.

- Never throw a lighted cigarette out of a train window, particularly in the summer months.

By road

Even if most of your journey is by air, water or rail, at some stage you will almost certainly have to take to the road. Environmentally, of course, the best way to travel by road is to use a cycle. Failing that, a bus or coach.

If you assume that the average car carries 1.5 people and is around four metres long, then a coach, taking up perhaps three times more road space and carrying over thirty times more people, obviously makes a great deal of sense.

This is not to say that buses and coaches are totally environmentally sound. If you have walked in the streets of Third World cities like Bangkok, for example, you will have seen battered buses emitting oily black smoke-screens worthy of a World War II destroyer. Exhaust emissions from tourist coaches are also now known to be causing damage to historic monuments as far apart as Notre Dame in Paris and the Mayan ruins of Central America. Coach-parks also consume a good deal of land that would be better left wild.

Cars, unfortunately, are more popular, more convenient and likely to be one of the biggest environmental headaches of the future, whether they are used for ordinary trips or for holidays. They kill people, clog up the roads, pollute the air, consume considerable quantities of fossil fuel and require the building of ever-extending road and motorway networks. But the convenience that the car – and heavy lorries – offers has meant that road transport is given a high priority when it comes to government funding.

There are already too many cars, with an estimated 350 million worldwide. Smog is becoming almost an everyday occurrence in some cities. In Chiang Mai, northern Thailand, the nearby sacred mountain and its monastery are often invisible behind traffic smog. In Mexico City the authorities have warned joggers to do their running indoors, with the windows closed. Doctors say that breathing Mexico City air is the equivalent of smoking forty cigarettes a day. And in Athens smog often wreathes the Parthenon, eating away at stonework which until recently had survived more or less unscathed for more than two thousand years. 'It is a recorded fact that 80 per cent of pollutants forming the photochemical smog in Athens comes from cars,' said the Greek environment minister.

As the smogs hit cities as far apart as Berlin and Beijing, cars are also emerging as a major contributor to the greenhouse effect. An average motor vehicle, for example, takes the energy equivalent of 1,500 litres of oil to make and uses at least 10,000 litres of fuel before it is scrapped or dumped.

The mind-boggling statistics do not end there. For every 3.8 litres of fuel the average vehicle consumes, it pumps out around 8.6 kilos of carbon dioxide. In other words, a single 55-litre fill-up at the petrol station results in the eventual release of about 125 kilos of carbon dioxide into the atmosphere.

Congestion simply makes matters worse. When the Japanese go on holiday, as during Golden Week in April and May, they form traffic jams which are worthy of the *Guinness Book of Records*. In 1991, a 134-kilometre jam kept drivers and their families tied up for 12 hours on their way to their holidays – and another 12 hours on the way back! And there can't be many of us who have not been caught up in 'bank holiday madness' traffic jams.

Many parts of the world have started trying to limit car numbers, particularly in town or city centres. A variety of methods have been or are being tried from toll roads to car pooling and even trying to enforce rules stopping drivers using their cars on particular days of the week. As the pressures from cars intensify, these and other schemes are likely to become the norm and we will all have to accept restrictions on this ultimate convenience.

The car, in short, is a disease, undermining the beauty and health of many of the places we have travelled so far to see. Think of some of the world's most-loved cities, like Venice, and eccentric places like the island of Sark, in the English Channel, and you will see the link between the absence of the car and urban environments which it is a pleasure to walk or cycle through. Pedestrianisation is one of the great challenges now facing the world's cities and towns.

WHAT YOU CAN DO

- If you can, leave the car and take the bus or train, walk, ride or cycle.

- Welcome pedestrianisation – indeed, lobby for it where you have a chance.

- If you use a coach, make sure you travel with a reputable operator. Be prepared to criticise the driver, particularly if he or she keeps the engine on while parked.

- If you have to drive, do so at a fuel-efficient pace and always fill up with unleaded fuel. If you travel by coach, suggest to the driver that he keeps to a safe, fuel-efficient speed, rather than pushing the throttle to the floor.

- And if you rent a car insist that it should run on unleaded fuel and be fitted with a catalytic converter. Alternatively ask for a modern diesel, which can be just as clean. Avis claims to have been the first car rental firm to introduce 'cat cars' wherever unleaded petrol was available, but other firms also now say they offer the cat car option in a growing number of cities. Try them out.

By foot or cycle

Walking and cycling are undoubtedly the greenest ways of getting around. But as the tourist hordes sweep around the world, even those on foot can prove too much for local people in some places.

On the island of Capri, for example, traffic wardens can now fine package tourists – *turisti di massa* – who dawdle too long in the central square or alleyways of Capri town anywhere between £100 and £400! The island plans to control mass tourism by raising prices, controlling the number of ferry crossings and even closing its doors entirely at peak periods.

Anyone wanting to know how to leave greener footprints or tyre-tracks should turn to our sections on walking (page 149) and cycling (page 126).

ONCE THERE

Where to stay

The young are prepared to stay just about anywhere. Hotels are often beyond their pocket and they sleep where they happen to be when it gets dark. Millions of adults around the world also love to sleep in the open, under canvas (see page 116), but most tourists still prefer to sleep in a bed. In some areas, this may actually become a requirement. Worried that too many young travellers are entering the country with little money and intent on sleeping rough, the Greek government has been tightening controls on flight-only tickets.

The most environmentally sound – and often the cheapest – way of finding a bed is to make use of long-established buildings, whether in someone's home, perhaps with family or friends, or in a bed and breakfast. By doing this you are not encouraging the construction of new buildings – and your money finds its way into the pockets of local people.

There will be occasions, however, when you may have no option but to stay in a multinational hotel. An awareness of the issues will help you to ask the right questions of the hotel management – and encourage them to put an environmental policy into action, or improve on an existing one.

Holiday homes and timeshares

Thousands of people are now buying second homes here and abroad to which they retreat for a few weeks during the year. This worrying trend can turn once-lively villages into ghost-towns, because the houses will be standing empty for much of the year and can price local people out of the housing market.

Timeshare developments are also increasingly popular, thanks in part to the timeshare agents, best known for their hard-sell tactics, who offer huge prizes if you come and expose yourself to their blandishments for several hours. Timeshares basically enable holidaymakers to buy their holidays in bulk by joining a club with holiday facilities in many different areas or countries. They have been causing growing concern in vulnerable areas: in Britain's Lake District, for example, some towns already report that up to 40 per cent of houses are being used as second homes, and timeshare developments are seen as another turn of the screw.

The one thing to be said in favour of timeshares is that the properties are used much more intensively than are most second homes. But other, greener alternatives are also emerging. In Britain there is already a Green Theme Home Exchange Holiday Service. And in France the long-established self-catering *gîtes* system helps to preserve the rural economy by putting money directly into the pockets of the local people.

Hotels and B & Bs

However much we may like sleeping under our own roof or under the stars, most of us also find that we need to book into a hotel or B & B at some stage.

B & Bs frequently provide the best alternative as they are often run from people's homes. Many historic houses also now offer bed and breakfast. By staying in these you will not only be contributing to local people's pockets but also to the conservation of the national heritage. Without tourism and the money it generates, many old houses might have become derelict without funds for maintenance and up-keep.

The hotel business, meanwhile, is seeing new pressures emerging. Until recently, the press focused any criticism on such issues as whether hotels are fire-traps or whether their kitchens are fertile breeding grounds for cockroaches and food-poisoning organisms. Now a range of environmental issues are becoming important, too.

The desperate rush to cash in on the booming tourist trade led developers and hotel groups to build too many hotels too quickly and with little consideration for wider issues. In the heart of Guatemala's Lake Atitlan National Park, for example, next to a clear blue lake surrounded by volcanoes, stand three unfinished tower-blocks, resembling giant broken teeth. Part of a planned luxury tourism complex, they have been await-ing completion for fifteen years, stalled – after many bitterly disputed rounds – by environmentalists.

In most parts of the world, however, the pillars of concrete, steel and glass continue to spring up with alarming speed. Along the Mediterranean coast, where a third of the world's tourists settle like an annual locust swarm, the UN warns that tourism development is proceeding at such a pace that as much as 95 per cent of the coast could be urbanised within a generation. From space, astronauts report that it already looks like a continuous holiday town. Meanwhile, the Chinese are planning to copy Spain's monstrous Benidorm, hoping that its 'Manhattan skyline' will attract the Japanese with their yen.

In a tragi-comic example of the rush to cash in on tourists eager for the sunshine experience, developers in Crete managed to get themselves in a fix. High-rise hotels were built cheek-by-jowl right along the beach front, all with spectacular sea-views. The result was that by noon the buildings blocked the sun from reaching the beach and the resort lost its main attraction!

In the Dalyan region of Turkey, meanwhile, hoteliers have found themselves on a collision course with conservationists keen to protect the area's turtle population – and subjected to considerable media attention (page 254). When challenged on this point, Turkey's tourism minister retorted that the country's ambitious tourism programme 'cannot be sacrificed just for a few tortoises'. But the Turkish government have since had to shift their position on this.

The concrete wave that is sweeping around the globe has caused ecological havoc in country after country. Coral reefs have been dynamited to provide construction materials for airfields and hotels in Kenya, Tanzania, Mozambique, Madagascar, Reunion, Mauritius, the Seychelles, Sri Lanka, Malaysia and Thailand. Mangrove swamps in many parts of the world are being filled in to create new holiday resorts. Fishermen and farmers in Goa have been evicted – without compensation – from land soon to bear a crop of hotels. And beaches are being dug up in the Philippines and the Caribbean and their sand tossed into churning cement mixers.

Key issues for the future will include the importance of proper sewage disposal facilities. This will be even more critical if the hotel sits in or on a vulnerable ecosystem, as was the case with Australia's first floating hotel, the Four Seasons Barrier Reef Resort (see page 199), moored alongside Great Barrier Reef.

But the situation is not all bad. Indeed, some hotel chains have been looking at ways to 'go green' for a long time. The Inter-Continental Hotel Group, for example, produced its first energy management manual in 1977 and more recently has produced an extensive manual on the environmental impact of hotel management which it has circulated, even to rival hotel chains, apparently to encourage their greening!

As the pressures to go green have grown, however, some chains, among them Ramada, have been taken to task by environmentalists for claiming green credentials on the basis of relatively minor achievements – switching to 'biodegradable' detergents, for example.

The more expensive hotels, which tend to be the ones calling the most attention to their green projects, often fail to make the grade on the most basic green criteria. Writer Miles Kington recently carried out an 'audit' on the 'free' items in his hotel room. His list included the following: one chocolate, wrapped in gold paper; one set of stationery; two cakes of soap, in plastic boxes; one mini-canister of shampoo and another of shower gel; one very small bowl of fruit; one courtesy shower cap; one regulation helping of shoe cleaning paper; one large bag marked 'For Your Laundry'; one bag for the disposal of sanitary towels; and one hotel magazine.

None of these 'gifts' is actually free and the waste produced in the process scarcely bears thinking about. Smaller hotels are very unlikely to offer you such a profusion of fripperies, which is one more reason for favouring them over the bang-up-to-date concrete and glass eggboxes.

Anyone looking for an idea of what greener forms of tourism development might look like, should check into the Hotel Ucliva in Waltensburg, Switzerland. The hotel's developers gave priority to local construction firms and insisted on a simple, vernacular style. The clean-burning fires use wood grown locally – and, they say, sustainably. Food is prepared in-house wherever possible, using traditional recipes. Branded international drinks are avoided. And the greener guests are well catered for with a wide range of activities, from cycling to visits to wildlife reserves.

Sadly, though, thus far the large hotels that have responded to the environmental challenge are such rare birds that they stand out a mile. One such is the ITT Sheraton (see opposite). Another is the Cheeca Lodge, in the Florida Keys (see page 267), which received the 1990 Gold Key Environmental Achievement Award from the American Hotel and Motel Association – and hosted President George Bush's Earth Day '90 speech to the nation.

Another green tourism project is being planned for Tanzania, just outside the capital, Dar es Salaam, in the form of

THE OPTIONAL DOLLAR

When the nine hotels in ITT Sheraton's Africa and Indian Ocean division launched their 1990 'Going Green' project, it suggested that guests gave at least a dollar to conservation when paying their bills – an astounding 86 per cent of guests paid.

The hotel chain then matched the guest's donation in local currency and gave the money to projects picked with the help of the World Society for the Protection of Animals (WSPA) and the Marine Conservation Society (MCS). One of the projects funded by the Sheratons in the Seychelles and Djibouti was the MCS *Let Coral Reefs Live* campaign. The Harare Sheraton, in Zimbabwe, channelled its support into *Operation Stronghold* at the Kariba game reserve. The money was used to build game-viewing stands, camp-sites and wilderness trails. In Nigeria, two reconditioned Land-Rovers were given to the game protection unit at the Yankari Game Park to help the Nigerian Conservation Foundation in its fight against poachers.

A good start. But if you are staying at an ITT Sheraton hotel, ask if the Going Green campaign can be extended to the group's global network of nearly 500 business hotels, luxury hotels, inns and resorts.

an *Ecopolis* (or environmental city). The plan is very ambitious, based on the creation of 'a sustainable tourist resort which makes the minimum demand on resources and aims to be as self-sufficient as possible'. Some of the ideas include:

- using local materials for the buildings, ranging from luxury suites to self-service chalets
- developing research facilities and farms to provide daily organic produce and sea-food within the complex
- offering exhibition space for innovative cleaner, greener technologies

- opening an information and education centre on African ecology
- basing the whole complex around a specially designed transport system, which – if all goes well – will be mainly solar-powered

Camping and caravanning
Camping and caravanning clearly do not require as much development or infrastructure as hotels, but they can bring some fairly significant environmental problems in their wake (see pages 116–19).

WHAT YOU CAN DO

- Stay with friends, family or local people wherever you can – or arrange 'house-swaps'.

- Don't turn countryside communities into ghost-towns by buying a second home and then keeping it closed up for most of the year.

- If you are considering buying into a timeshare scheme, ask the organisers about the site (what have the buildings replaced, for example) and what they are doing to make sure that their developments are environmentally acceptable.

- If you are considering checking into a hotel, write and ask whether it has an environmental policy and whether it provides environmental training for staff members.

- Ask, too, whether the hotel supports any local environmental projects or organisations.

- Beware of green marketing gimmicks. At least one UK hotel has offered a 'Green Christmas', involving five nights in unheated rooms, a green-clad Father Christmas and a video of Prince Charles speaking about the environment – instead of the traditional Queen's speech. Amusing, but it isn't really going to do much for the environment.

- Look out for developments that are putting green tourism ethics into practice and try them out.

- Don't take the hotel's printed literature at face value. Ask staff – and local people – for their own views on what the hotel or resort is doing.

- When you check out – or when you get home – let the hotel know how you rate its environmental performance.

Signs of overload

 New developments of hotels, holiday complexes and tourist attractions invariably put pressure on local infrastructures. Vital services – water, energy, waste disposal, sewage and water treatment facilities, and roads – must be provided, and subsidiary services such as car-parks, shops and entertainment are all needed if tourist appetites are to be catered for.

It is not only the dramatic increase in numbers that tourism imposes on communities; tourists often consume a great deal more resources than do the locals. Many countries have inadequate water supplies before tourists even arrive for the holiday season; so when the hotels get priority it puts a serious squeeze on local farmers and villages.

In North Africa, for example, large tourist developments are being built in the desert. Where a hundred nomads and their flocks once survived for three years on the average year's rainfall, the same number of tourists will consume this amount in less than six weeks. And in Hawaii and Barbados each tourist uses between six and ten times as much water and electricity as does the average Hawaiian or Barbadian.

Equally, areas that are unused to providing energy for influxes of tourists will experience a considerable drain on their services. The more energy we use on holiday the more likely it is that new power stations will be needed to cope with the extra demand. Not only do these gobble land, but every commercially useful form of electricity generation known to man causes major environmental problems. Coal and oil contribute to acid rain, and the dangers of nuclear power are now well known across the globe. Even hydropower, which is a genuinely renewable form of energy, involves the flooding of valleys, destroying their vegetation and wildlife and forcing out those who lived there.

Another way in which we are flooding the valleys is with our waste. In many countries the waste disposal facilities are totally inadequate. It is often dumped at sea or on land ill-suited for the purpose. In many countries you can get an eyeful of the problem simply by looking up valleys, over cliff edges or out to sea.

Sewage pollution is an even more serious headache, causing outbreaks of dysentery, hepatitis, typhoid and even cholera around the Mediterranean and other seas. The population of tourist areas explodes during peak periods, placing a huge strain on already groaning sewage systems. You can smell the problem in the streets and you may come face to face with it in the sea.

One in five Spanish beaches failed the latest EEC tests and the worst Spanish black-spots were in Andalusia and Valencia. In France, the figure was 17 per cent, in Italy 16 per cent and in Greece 22 per cent. And environmental groups warn that the local authorities that take the water samples often pick areas they know are relatively clean. The European Commission agrees that sewage disposal is inadequate along much of the coastline from the Atlantic to the Mediterranean.

The local people in these areas are so worried that they have staged protests over sewage dumping plans in both Corfu and the Greek part of Cyprus. In Corfu, they managed to close the international airport, stranding tourists, whilst in Cyprus they staged a three-day general strike, closing shops and offices.

Now the bad news is getting through to tourists, too. Faced with a fall-off in demand, the Spanish tourism industry has been trying to attract more of the millions of tourists who visit each year to areas well away from the ravaged Costas.

Instead, tourists are being encouraged to visit areas such as the Covadonga park in the mountain region of Asturias and Coto Doñana, Spain's largest bird sanctuary, near Seville, both of which are vulnerable areas and are already suffering from intensifying tourism pressures.

At Covadonga, the traffic jams now stretch for many miles, raising the threat of more roads and more traffic, all of which will frighten away the area's wildlife. 'There is a real danger that noise, pollution and people will simply drive the birds away for ever,' said one Spanish conservationist. Further south, at Coto Doñana, a vast area of dunes, woods and salt-water swamp which serves as a breeding ground for pink flamingos, rare Imperial eagles, lynx and wild boar, the pressures are also mounting rapidly. Already threatened by water extraction for agriculture and the run-off of pesticides, the area is now further threatened by plans for what the developers call 'Costa Doñana', based around another tourist complex and golf course.

More positively, there are occasional signs that the tide may be on the point of turning in some areas. Governments and local authorities in many areas are beginning to realise that if they are going to keep their custom they must listen to complaints from tourists and tour operators. The recent appointment of an environmental officer for Benidorm (page 247) was one example of this embryonic trend – while in other places the authorities are beginning to plan more carefully and to look at schemes to limit visitor numbers.

WHAT YOU CAN DO

- If you are staying at a commercial hotel or resort, write to the management to ask about its commitment to:
  - carrying out environmental impact assessments for new developments
  - conserving, enhancing and interpreting the environment for both visitors and local people
  - saving energy
  - minimising the use of any potentially harmful chemicals, either inside or outside the hotel

- reducing waste by cutting back on over-packaging and unnecessary gifts
- recycling waste
- using only timber from properly managed forests
- planting only native species in any landscaping.

● Wherever you are, economise on the energy and water you use when on holiday.

● If you stay in undeveloped rural areas, remember that heating your water may send your impact meter whizzing round.

● Carry out your non-food rubbish from the rural areas of Third World countries. In some parts of Africa, poisonous chemicals from batteries have been used as make-up by local people. Wildlife is at even greater risk.

● Write polite letters to the tourist agencies or local authorities in the countries you have visited to tell them about environmental problems you have encountered – and support whatever achievements they have made so far.

● Spread the good news about places where people were doing the right thing.

What the menu doesn't say

Some people are happy to eat almost anything, while others will eat only what they are accustomed to eating at home. Inevitably, both ends of this dietary spectrum are catered for by the tourism industry, together with most tastes in between.

At the eccentric end of the culinary spectrum, South African hunters recently shot a giraffe, lifted it with a mobile crane and stuck it on a five-metre spit for what was believed to be the world's first giraffe barbecue. Less ambitiously, regulars at one Florida bar drink live gold-fish with their tequila. But when China's Donghu Hotel tried to serve pangolin (a scaly ant-eater) to a group of Singaporean businessmen, they refused to eat the dish – and the hotel was fined for serving an endangered species.

Tour operators occasionally cater specifically for people's taste for ultra-exotic food, as in the case of one firm which offers treks in the Belize rainforest. The intrepid trekkers live off a diet of centipede stew, worm mash, mouse deer and monkey. In Australia, at least one tribe of Aborigines has also opened its homelands to tourists who are prepared to 'go native'. Visitors eat kangaroo meat, honey ants and Witchetty grubs while they listen to stories around the camp-fire.

Whatever our preferences, however, we should look into the environmental shadows cast by our holiday menu. While some of us may rebel against the idea of barbecued giraffe, or gargling with goldfish, one dead giraffe – or three dozen goldfish a week – cannot be described as a major ecological problem. By contrast, there is no question that tourist demand for some types of food is helping to decimate some species.

In Bali, for example, turtle meat is still sold in restaurants and from street stalls, despite a Greenpeace campaign and a decree outlawing the practice. In the Caribbean, the pressure is on conches and spiny lobsters, while coconut crabs are a threatened menu item in the South Pacific.

Most tourists, however, are much more conservative, which is why Spain's Costas are now infested with egg-and-bacon bars. Ironically, one of the products of international tourism is 'international cuisine' – with good cooks every-where cooking other peoples' dishes badly – or, worse, a bland, characterless style of hotel cooking that attempts to appeal to all nationalities and tastes.

Frequently, imported tourists insist on eating imported food. In the Gambia, for example, 60 per cent of the food and 40 per cent of the drinks served in resort hotels are imported. Because of this trend, only half of the money tourists spend in a country like Kenya actually remains in the country. In addition, imported or foreign-style foods often involve more transport and refrigeration, with all that implies for energy use and the leakage of ozone-depleting CFCs.

Drinking local fizzy drinks, rather than imported ones, will mean putting more money into the local economy – but even drinking Coke or Pepsi need not mean that all the money you pay will be exported. Local bottlers will generally have licensed or franchised the brand. The other plus with fizzy drinks is that many come in returnable bottles which are re-used in most Third World countries.

Many Westerners consume larger quantities of fizzy drinks when travelling in the Third World because they dare not risk the water. If you take steriliser tablets for the water, this can overcome the problem – and will certainly be better for the environment, as well as your teeth!

The fast-food culture, which is steadily taking a grip the world over, has spread so rapidly that it has triggered the beginnings of a counter-revolution, in the form of a Slow Food Movement. Members, who would presumably not be seen dead inside a McDonald's, Burger King or Kentucky Fried Chicken outlet, wear a gold or silver snail on their lapels. The movement has not been enough, though, to halt the industry's progress. In Moscow, McDonald's first restaurant rapidly became the city's top attraction, pulling in 27,000 people a day – compared with just 9,000 visiting Lenin's embalmed remains.

A McDonald's is unlikely to spoil the streetscape of much of modern Russian architecture, but in other parts of the world the profusion of fast food outlets has produced the commercial equivalent of a plastic grin even in the historic hearts of some of the world's most beautiful cities.

Even so, we may be seeing the first signs of a greening trend. Some of the big catering and food companies are now commissioning environmental reviews – among them Gardner Merchant and Grand Metropolitan (which, following a recent shopping spree, owns such high-street names as Wimpy, Berni, Pizzaland and Burger King).

We are also seeing a much improved attitude towards the

once-maligned vegetarian. Despite the best efforts of the burger industry, there is now at least a vegetarian option in many restaurants. A small number of tour operators also now cater for vegetarians. Indeed, there is even a dating agency, Vegetarian Matchmakers, catering exclusively for lonely vegetarians!

WHAT YOU CAN DO

- Find out about local foods and specialities, wherever you are. They will almost certainly have been farmed or caught locally, and will be a part of the tradition of the place you are visiting.

- Try to make sure that the dishes you do eat do not include an endangered species – ask what you are eating if you are not sure.

- Seek out slow food.

- If you find yourself in the fast-food lane, keep an eye out for any environmental changes that fast-food companies are making. Write to them – and their competitors – if you have any ideas that you think they should implement.

- If you want food in a hurry, choose shops and restaurants that go in for as little packaging as possible – and ask what they plan on the recycling front.

- Drink draught beer, rather than canned; it saves on packaging.

- Steer clear of resource-greedy gimmicks, like the Japanese cans which instantly heat or cool your drinks when you open them.

- Try the vegetarian option.

- Don't smoke. Non-smokers are making some headway in their demand for clean air in restaurants, hotels, guesthouses and pubs. A useful book to track down is *Eat, Drink and Sleep Smoke-Free* (Headway Books), although this only covers UK restaurants and hotels to date.

- If you are a wine-drinker, seek out organic vineyards. In some places, you will also find organic cider-makers and fruit-juice producers.

- Buy direct from organic or other green producers if you can – it is usually a better deal for you and for them.

At loggerheads with the locals

 Some countries that went out of their way to attract foreign tourists are waking up with a painful hangover. 'We made a big mistake advertising the Algarve as the cheapest holiday spot in Europe,' said the head of Portugal's Tourist Board. 'We now want a different type of tourist, one who has greater buying power and is better behaved.'

Whenever relatively large groups of people travelled in the past, for example during the Crusades, the Mongol invasions or the colonisation of the Americas, they almost always left havoc and devastation in their wake. Entire cities were put to the sword, tribal peoples wiped out.

Obviously, we should keep a sense of proportion when considering the damage caused by tourists, even the worst incidents caused by 'lager louts'. But the European press is not far wrong when it talks in terms of the 'New Barbarians'. They steal artefacts from village churches, gouge out mosaics from walls and floors, cut noses off statues and carve their initials into ancient walls. Alcohol is often part of the problem and British tourists have been among the worst in this respect. In 1989 Spanish hoteliers singled out the customers of one particular operator as being particularly troublesome, so bad that they were considering banning them.

This new barbarism has led some tourist destinations to consider desperate measures. The tourism boom in Barbados, which attracts 400,000 holidaymakers each year, has brought a marked increase in violent crime and drug trafficking, and now the island has reintroduced the cat-o'-nine-tails, abolished by the British authorities on the island in 1881.

Barbarism is not always imported, however. In some countries the traditional abuse of animals has been a major cause of concern for environmentalists and animal lovers alike, and, in some cases, tourist protests are bringing about changes. In Spain, for example, the tradition of animal abuse during fiestas (page 249) is now being challenged. In one town, live goats were thrown to their deaths from a belltower. Now at least a tarpaulin is held out to catch the falling animals. Traditionalists may complain that these attempts to stamp out cruelty represent cultural imperialism – and certainly we should respect the best of the cultural traditions of the countries we visit – but it does not mean we have to support exploitative industries, like sex tourism in Thailand (page 202), simply because they have traditional roots. In this Global Village of ours, the likelihood is that the grossest forms of environmental destruction and animal abuse will be outlawed – and we must hope that the grossest forms of human abuse, among them sex tourism based on the abuse of young children, will also be consigned to the dustbin of history.

History, sadly, suggests that however much we try to respect the local culture, even reasonably well-behaved tourists can have a fatal impact on some communities. Remember what happened to the remote island of St Kilda, off the coast of Scotland? Tourists who flocked to the island at the end of the last century introduced money into a barter-based economy, while teachers and priests brought news of the attractions of the outside world. As the young people drained away to the mainland, the community lost its will to survive. The last inhabitant left in 1930.

The example of St Kilda demonstrates the problems with a remote community coming into contact with the outside world. Some communities have other problems to contend with, too. When the early missionaries arrived in Africa, Asia or Latin America, they saw exotic ceremonies and pageants – and promptly labelled tribal people as devil worshippers. Now these same ceremonies have often become little more than a curiosity, imported into tourist complexes for an evening's entertainment.

In Bali, lengthy religious dances and ceremonies have been shortened to suit tourist tastes and schedules. Tourism officials say that rushed, low-budget tourists contribute much of the damage – and little of the profit. 'It's the fast food of tourism,' said one Italian MP. 'The very contemplation of art becomes a rapid, superficial consumption.'

Ethnic arts, torn from their context, have become collectors' pieces – and as the art is commercialised to meet the new demand, old skills become undervalued and are lost.

When local people are showered with money, sweets, biros or other Western trinkets, it can be like feeding time at the zoo. Little children and adults alike clamber around a tourist mini-bus or grab on to tourists' clothes in their eagerness to be the recipient of these 'gifts from god'. To be able to hand out small sums and know that it is the equivalent to a month's or even a year's wage can make us feel like gods. But this sort of behaviour can be very damaging, because communities become reliant on donations, turning away from their traditional activities. In many cases, too, this dependence causes them to become aggressive and demanding towards tourists, and lose their original friendliness and hospitality.

Apart from anything else, the sweets some people strew on either side of their path can cause tooth decay. In the Annapurna area of the Himalayas, a Western dentist found that along the tourist trail – where there was a tradition of giving sweets and soft drinks – 70 per cent of the locals had tooth decay. Elsewhere in the region the figure was just 17 per cent.

Many of the countries we visit may well need our help if they are to enjoy a more sustainable lifestyle. The real challenge is to make sure that what we give is a force for good, rather than producing a world of beggars.

WHAT YOU CAN DO

- Remember, wherever you go, whatever you do, the more you try to cram into your holiday, and the faster you try to get from one place to another, the greater your impact on the environment, local communities and their cultures. *Slow down*.

- Try to get beneath the skin of the culture of the country or region you are visiting. Read everything you can about the area before you go.

- Learn the language – at least enough to get by. Try to meet local people, on their terms, not yours.

- If you see other tourists causing offence to local people, see if you can persuade them to be more considerate. Sometimes a few well-chosen words can work wonders.

- Accept that other races and communities may behave in very different ways. This does not mean they are *inferior*.

- Try to view the world from the locals' perspective. As Marcel Proust once said, the best journey would not be to travel through a thousand different countries with the same pair of eyes – but to travel through the same country with a thousand different pairs of eyes.

- Remember, good manners are appreciated, whichever country you are in.

- Appreciate that some things we do without a thought, like taking photographs, may be deeply offensive in other cultures – or to other people. Ask before you shoot.

- Giving money and gifts is not always kind. Think carefully before you do so.

- Don't accept cruelty to animals. Write to the Royal Society for the Prevention of Cruelty to Animals or the government of the country concerned.

- Keep the noise level down.

- Don't leave litter, even if the locals do.

- When you are in a different country, track down local

conservationists and environmental groups and see whether there are ways you can help them in their work.

- Don't think only in terms of money. All environmental and community groups need more funds, of course, but many also want better international contacts and more information on what is going on in other parts of the world.

Sex tourism corrodes

 'If you can suck it, use it, eat it, feel it, taste it, abuse it, then it's available in this resort that truly never sleeps,' promised Sunmed's 'Go Places' brochure. Thailand Pattaya resort 'is not for prudes', the brochure explained. 'Five or so paces outside your accommodation and you will have received more lewd invites than you could imagine.'

Whether in Kenya, Thailand or the Philippines, sex tourism is probably the most corrosive form of holiday package on offer, with the price of the women included in packages sold in Japan, Germany and the Netherlands. Now even Melbourne has found itself targeted by Japanese sex tourists, who are attracted by the regular compulsory health checks for prostitutes there – and by the fact that Melbourne is cheaper than Sydney.

Faced with the appalling news that as many as 300,000 Thais may now be infected with AIDS, the Thai government has pulled in the welcome mat. 'Sex tourists are no longer welcome,' said one cabinet minister. 'We are telling them to go home and exploit their own women and children.'

Some companies have responded to the AIDS threat in a different way. The Club, which was recently launched by the same management team as Club 18–30, claims to be the first company to offer free condoms with every passenger ticket.

Men are obviously most to blame, but women are not entirely guiltless. It is interesting to note, for example, that the biggest group of Gambians in Sweden are an estimated 1,500 boys brought back for sex purposes by Swedish women of a certain age (page 235). Some subsequently left for pastures new – and some were thrown out.

The environmental costs of sex tourism are not hard to find. In Bangkok, there are so many brothels and massage bars that their prodigious demand for water is now seen as a major contributor to the city's huge thirst. So much water is now being pumped from the ground that some parts of the city – which is sinking at two inches a year – are in real danger of sinking beneath the waves. By the year 2000, some two million people will have to move to dry land. If the Greenhouse Effect raises sea levels further, Bangkok may join Sodom and Gomorrah in the index of cautionary tales.

WHAT YOU CAN DO

- However great the temptation, don't.

- If you come across evidence that children are involved in this business, report it to the authorities – and to appropriate campaigning organisations when you get back home.

Photography through a green lens

 *Take nothing but photographs, leave nothing but footprints* has become an environmental slogan. But even photography can damage the environment. The first camera aimed at the mass market was launched in 1888 by Eastman Kodak. 'You Press the Button,' users were told, 'We Do the Rest.' Today, our snaps provide evidence that we have been where we say we have been – and that we have had the sort of holiday that will turn

friends and neighbours green with envy.

Once the main film materials used in photography were paper, gelatin and a range of chemicals. Now even the most basic camera user will leave a trail of packaging materials and spent batteries. Vegetarians may be concerned to hear that gelatin, made from rendered animals, is still used in most films, although this could be considered a plus point, too, because it is an example of using a waste from one industry as a feedstock for another.

When we challenged one of the film companies about the sheer volume of packaging used for films, their response was: 'That's the way the supermarket chains like it. The larger the package, the harder it is to steal it!' There is also a need to protect the product. Kodak pointed out that though it is in its financial interest to minimise packaging, if film is to reach customers in perfect condition it must be protected from heat, light, moisture and physical damage. Kodak is working to reduce the amount of packaging and noted that 'We use as much recycled material in the packaging as possible'.

Like other industries the big film companies are under pressure to clean up their act. Both Kodak and Fuji devote about a fifth of their total investment budget to environmental projects. Most camera companies use CFCs, mainly in their refrigeration systems, and Kodak managed to cut back its emissions by over 40 per cent between 1989 and 1990.

Ironically, however, Kodak is one of the companies responsible for the worst new camera product. This is the single-use camera, with names like *Fling*, *Fun Saver 35*, *Fun Saver Weekend 35*, *Fun Saver Panoramic 35* and, most misleadingly, Vivitar's *Eco 35*. Though the *Eco 35*'s packaging does contain recycled material, the camera is still disposable. Kodak, Fuji and Konica all say they have programmes to recycle the cameras – the whole camera is handed over to the film developers who develop the photographs and then return the camera itself to the manufacturer for recycling. But don't count on it. Some developing companies do not participate in the scheme. It is better not to use this type of camera and bring your non-disposable camera if you need it.

WHAT YOU CAN DO

- When buying a camera, write to the manufacturer and ask for a copy of their environmental policies.

- Learn how to use your camera before you go on holiday. Avoid wasting time and materials.

- Look out for the least packaged films – avoid display packs, when you can.

- Take all packaging and spent batteries home – and insist on low mercury batteries.

- Ask your developer if he participates in recycling programmes. If he doesn't, try to switch to one who does.

- Remember, even today some people believe that cameras steal their souls. Your photo opportunity may be someone else's nightmare. Too often, our cameras distance us from people. Talk to them instead.

Shopping for souvenirs

Pity the world's toiling customs officers. As though they did not have a hard enough time searching for over-the-limit alcohol or contraband drugs, they have to search your luggage for endangered species – or products made from them.

Sadly, the evidence suggests that some tourists are trying to cover at least part of the cost of their holidays by smuggling animals back into their home countries. One man coming from Ibiza was caught with 500 five-centimetre-long brown lizards in his luggage and the resulting fine was paltry. Although he turned out not to be an ordinary tourist, it is clear that the fines currently imposed for such eco-crimes are not high enough to be an effective deterrent. They should be raised.

But you don't have to smuggle home large quantities of live animals to fall foul of the law. At one time, as many as eight passengers on every plane returning to the UK from St Lucia in the Caribbean were found to be carrying souvenirs made from turtles. Turtle products are also for sale in airport shops in the Seychelles and Bali, and appear on restaurant menus, despite the fact that they are an endangered species and in some countries to kill and sell them is illegal.

Just because an item is for sale in a country does not mean it is legal. In the Madagascan capital, Antananarivo, crocodile skin products line many shop windows even though it is against the law to export them. In the Far East there is a lively illegal trade in products made from ivory and rhino horn and the forests are being stripped of their butterflies to satisfy the insatiable curio market.

European countries like Greece are selling products made from leopard skins and other cats including the lynx, ocelot, panther or jaguar. In 1990 *Holiday Which?* reporters found 21 out of 25 furriers, in Rhodes, Greece, were selling coats made from protected animals. Thankfully, according to the Consumers' Association, stricter controls have since been introduced and fewer feline species are now illegally traded in Europe.

Even where it is legal to trade, the sheer volume can cause concern. The depletion in numbers of one species may have repercussions on other separate species. For example, taking coral from reefs removes the potential feeding and spawning grounds for myriad marine species. And even the collecting of shellfish for their shells can leave big holes in marine ecosystems.

There has been an enormous increase in the marine curio trade over the last decade, with coral a favourite souvenir. Coral reefs all along the East African coast and all over the Caribbean have been damaged by trophy hunting. In 1991 customs officials seized 17 tonnes of coral imported from the Philippines for the aquarium trade.

Illegal trade in ivory, birds, reptile skins and rare monkeys is now a £100-billion-a-year industry. Ivory is used for jewellery, ornaments, cutlery handles and many other accessories like hair or shaving brushes. Birds like parrots and budgerigars are sometimes sold as pets, but more often they are sold to private collectors. The trade in their feathers has been particularly important historically. The RSPB was founded by women concerned at the trade in ostrich feathers to decorate women's hats. Reptile skins are used for a whole range of leather products from handbags, wallets and shoes to belts and suitcases, whereas monkeys are more likely to be sold for pets or to zoos.

Living animals offered for sale are generally only the tip of an iceberg, in that for every one on sale many others will have died during capture from the wild – or during transport. The capture of a young chimpanzee from the wild, for example, usually means its mother must be killed.

Appalled by the extraordinary scale of the traffic in endangered species, the World Wide Fund for Nature (WWF) has urged tourists to boycott Thailand until the government there improves its control over trade in endangered species. At the other extreme, the USA has very stringent wildlife protection laws. They will go as far as prosecuting for contravention of a foreign law, so if someone enters the States with a product that has been bought illegally in the country of origin, they could still be prosecuted.

As far as ivory is concerned, the 1990 CITES (Convention on International Trade in Endangered Species) ban has helped slow the alarming drop in elephant populations in some parts of Africa. In Kenya, elephant populations are beginning to recover and Dr Richard Leakey, director of the country's Wildlife Service, wants the ban to continue. In Zimbabwe, however, the number of elephants increased from 52,000 in 1989 to some 70,000 in 1991 – and the government wants to sell the ivory from the elephants it is culling.

One source of confusion in relation to some wildlife products is that 'captive breeding' programmes are in operation for some species, among them some crocodiles and such plants as cacti, orchids and carnivorous plants. Unfortunately, the ordinary tourist is rarely in a position to be able to tell the difference between legal and illegal products. So, while we should support the right sort of breeding

KNOW YOUR CITES BLACKLIST

Before you buy anything made out of animal products, let alone an animal, make sure you know where you will stand under CITES – the Convention on International Trade in Endangered Species of Wild Flora and Fauna.

More than a hundred countries have signed CITES, the only widely recognised agreement to monitor wildlife trade. The Convention divides protected species into three categories of risk, each covered in its own Appendix, as follows:

APPENDIX I This covers species considered to be most at risk from trade. So if you are thinking of buying elephant ivory, rhinoceros horn or products made from some crocodile species, marine turtles and most of the big cats, remember that they are probably illegal – and you could be arrested when the customs officers open your cases.

APPENDIX II This covers species that are threatened and considered vulnerable, but where trade is allowed by CITES if a valid permit has been issued. You will find here black coral, all hard corals, many small cats, most parrots, monitor lizards, birdwing butterflies and orchids. (Some of these last four are also included in Appendix I.)

APPENDIX III This covers any species identified by any country that has signed CITES which are thought to be endangered or threatened in that country. Any trade in these species requires similar permits to those needed for trade in Appendix II.

As a general rule, avoid anything made from wildlife products. If you have any doubt about a purchase you want to make, check with customs before you go – or contact TRAFFIC (see page 363) or CITES (see page 368) for a copy of the CITES convention.

programmes, we should beware of being hoodwinked.

Perhaps we should insist that all tourists take an exam at the airport or harbour before being allowed to set off on their travels? Some of the basic things you should know about CITES can be found opposite. Some airports have mounted wildlife exhibitions in their departure lounges to raise public awareness and understanding of these issues.

This is one area where all of us can do our bit to ensure that the veil of ignorance is pulled back – and the wilful eco-criminals are pursued and punished.

WHAT YOU CAN DO

- Don't buy what you don't need – or won't use and appreciate after your visit. Many of the things we buy on holiday – ornaments, trinkets, T-shirts – have a limited interest once we get them home.

- Steer clear of tatty souvenir shops – you only encourage them.

- If you are in a country where bargaining is the norm in the markets or shops, bargain right back. Find out what is a fair price and haggle down to that. Remember: paying too much can be almost as harmful as paying too little.

- Do everything you can to make sure that you are not buying or bringing back anything made from an endangered species.

- Remember that even if an animal or plant is not yet an illegal export it could still be environmentally damaging to remove it.

- Do not buy ivory, even in countries like Zimbabwe and South Africa, where elephants are culled and there is a surplus. You will still be encouraging the ivory trade. The sustainable culling of elephants may be the way forward, but the trade needs to be better regulated before ivory can safely be bought.

- Marine creatures and corals should be left in the sea, rather than being propped up on your mantelpiece.

- Before you travel, contact one of the main campaigning organisations and ask for information on the key problems to watch out for in the country or areas you are visiting. If they can't help you immediately, suggest that this is an area where they should be helping us all with better information and ready advice.

- Once you are overseas, ask the shopkeepers and stallholders about who made the products you wish to buy and whether you can visit the craftspeople or factories. It may be possible and sometimes better to buy directly from them.

- Watch out for social and environmental exploitation – and report the worst excesses to the relevant campaigning groups. We are their eyes and ears.

- If you are buying gifts, look for products that are made from renewable materials by local people.

4
ACTIVITIES

The impact of your holiday on the environment depends not only on when and where you go, and how many people you go with, but on what you do when you get there. The following section focuses on some fifty activities that you – or people you know – may have enjoyed while on holiday.

Most of these activities, and their effects, are still evolving. Golf, for example, started out with shepherds knocking stones into rabbit-holes with their crooks. Apart from a few rabbits with headaches, the environment remained pretty much unaffected. Now, by contrast, people pay princes' ransoms to play on vast courses that are kept manicured with mowers and chemicals.

As our technology becomes ever-more sophisticated, so ordinary people can do what mythical heroes like Icarus or Jonah only dreamed of doing. In fact you can view many of these activities as very much like new species that are colonising habitats that once belonged to other species. So jet-boats roaring across the waves or Everglades collide with whales or manatees, while eagles find their territory invaded by hang-gliders.

Star ratings

While researching and writing up the activities in this section we were asked again and again how we rated a particular activity in environmental terms. It's difficult to make generalised statements – inevitably some environmentally-unfriendly activities will have less impact if they are undertaken in a conscientious way, while some highly rated activities will have a considerable impact if undertaken in an irresponsible way – but the following star-rating system should get us all thinking about what can be done to lessen our impact.

The ratings are based entirely on our views of the activities, and you may disagree with some of our assessments. Five stars represents the top rating, zero the bottom. Obviously a top rating does not indicate that there are no problems associated with the activity. Rather, it is an indication that this is an activity that green tourists and other environmentally aware holidaymakers can enjoy without any great sense of guilt!

survived the ordeal, although the history books are mute on the subject of what happened to them next.

That same June, the first *manned* balloon flight followed. Two Frenchmen soared over Paris, burning wool and straw to keep their vessel airborne. They covered over eight kilometres in 23 minutes. By December, two of their countrymen had flown a hydrogen-filled balloon 43 kilometres into the countryside from the Tuileries garden.

The problem was that hydrogen proved to be extremely expensive – and horribly inflammable. There were many accidents and disasters, including the devastating wreck of the *Hindenburg*. Helium proved a safer bet, but gas ballooning was too expensive for most people's pockets. The real boom in sport ballooning had to wait until the late 1950s, which saw the development of new lightweight materials and propane gas burners. These burners proved to be both safe and economical – and rather more pleasant than burning straw and wool!

Inevitably, balloonists are not only warming their balloons. They also contribute to global warming: hot-air balloons use around 30–60 kilos of propane gas per hour of flying time, which means that they generate around 90–180 kilos of carbon dioxide per hour. One suggestion for overcoming this problem is the solar balloon, although no one has cracked this one yet and propane would probably always be needed as a back-up fuel.

Though ballooning is safer than it was, there are obvious dangers still attached to the sport. Sudden down-draughts can slam the basket into the ground and there have also been a number of much-publicised accidents where balloon envelopes have torn or collapsed, with the unfortunate balloonists plunging hundreds of feet to their deaths. Less serious accidents have resulted when balloons have run into power lines or crossed the sights of gun-toting farmers determined to protect their cows.

Landing can also present problems, as balloonists are generally at the mercy of the elements. As they lose height, they may knock branches off trees or they may land in fields of crops. It is also possible to imagine the burner starting fires in dry environments, such as the south of France. Generally, though, balloonists are made welcome by farmers, since it is fairly common knowledge that most balloons carry a bottle of champagne or whisky as a peace offering.

Hot-air balloons are used increasingly for wildlife safaris in Africa, particularly in Kenya. Critics complain that some balloonists chase wild animal herds to ensure exciting video footage, while enthusiasts retort that the balloon expeditions help to deter poachers. Ecology-conscious balloonists, it hardly needs saying, aim to leave wildlife undisturbed.

Longer term, the main environmental issues here could be the use made of airborne balloons for advertising. For marketing executives, balloons are a dream come true: 1,000 square metres of mobile advertising space in areas of the country where advertising hoardings are simply out of the question.

For this reason – and because the sport has an increasingly high profile – ballooning is likely to take off in the coming years. In France, some predict that ballooning will become as common as sailing by the early years of the twenty-first century. 'We're lagging behind sailing by just a couple of decades,' said Jean Le Marchand, director of Paris-based balloon firm Espace Plus. But while balloonists enjoy the sights, smells and silent places of our planet, earthbound mortals may come to resent the commercialisation of our open and unsullied skies by their sponsors.

GUIDELINES

- When coming in to land, it hardly needs saying, try to avoid both trees and standing crops.

- Is your balloon too noisy? All balloons should be fitted with 'whisper burners'. Make sure yours is.

- If you are on safari, keep your distance from wildlife that you might otherwise spook – particularly pregnant and nursing female animals.

- And if you opt for a sponsored balloon, consider this. Sponsors like their balloons to look bright and new, so the rate of obsolescence is faster for sponsored craft. The balloons look shabby after two or three years and have to be replaced to maintain a spotless corporate image!

Gliding ★★★

Sometimes their shadows are the first sign you have that they are up there. Like eagles or vultures, gliders or sailplanes wing silently across the land, moving from one thermal – a rising current of warm air – to the next. Once airborne, most gliders need no fuel, so are silent and do not spew out exhaust fumes.

Apart from the occasional accident, the main environmental problem caused by gliders is noise from motor gliders. Fitted with small engines, these are used for training and to enable pilots to taxi and take off without the need for ground crew. But they can be an appalling nuisance if they spiral round and round near your home on a quiet summer's afternoon. It is like having someone mowing the lawn above your head!

The ruder car stickers boast that 'Glider pilots do it quietly' or 'Glider pilots stay up longer'. For both sexes, gliding remains a relatively cheap way of finding out what it is like to be a bird. But maybe hang-gliding or parascending would be a little lighter on the earth?

GUIDELINES

- There is probably little – at least in environmental terms – to choose between a launch by powered winch or by a vehicle, but being launched behind a tug aircraft is both more expensive and produces more polluting emissions.

- Fly unpowered gliders if you possibly can.

- If you do fly a powered glider, spread the pain around the countryside rather than beating up the same community hour after hour.

Hang-gliding ★★★★★
Microlighting ★★★

 Hang-gliders get closer to the world of Icarus than anyone else, and many have also plunged to earth. But the attractions of the sport are considerable and hang-glider pilots point out that more people drown while fishing than die in hang-gliding accidents. The technology has come a long way since the sixties, when Californian enthusiasts first built ramshackle machines out of bamboo and polythene sheeting and launched themselves out across the sand dunes.

The top speed of these machines has risen from about 30 kph to perhaps 95 kph. And some pilots have taken their machines to extraordinary heights. One British champion, Judy Leden, has soared to 5,486 metres over California, high enough to see the curvature of the earth.

Hang-gliders fly higher than most birds and so disturbance tends to be low. The main problems tend to be disturbance of wildfowl and waders – which mistake hang-gliders for vast birds of prey – and competition for space in higher thermals with the birds of prey. Because hang-gliders often end up sharing thermals with birds of prey, they may disturb them – or even come under attack. Judy Leden recalls flying wing-tip to wing-tip over the Himalayas with a massive vulture. And she has been attacked by wedge-tailed eagles in Australia. 'You're an absolute sitting duck,' she said. 'Wedge-tailed eagles just dive-bomb and attack you until they feel you're out of their territory. That might involve ten strikes, five of which will hit the glider.'

Hang-gliding can bring other problems, too. A hilltop spot used repeatedly for launches may be eroded – although sports like fell-walking tend to be much more damaging. In lowland areas some people opt for launch by winch or car tow.

Not surprisingly, some people have fitted small two-stroke engines to their hang-gliders, producing yet another rapidly growing sport. Sometimes called 'mopeds of the air', micro-lights look like pterodactyls and sound like chain-saws. They deliver about 10 kilometres to a litre of (unleaded) fuel when flying at 60 kph, and have been used by the Los Angeles police to patrol urban areas.

Increasingly, however, the use of such machines is restric-ted. In Britain, for example, you are not allowed to fly within 15 metres of the nearest building, or higher than 900 metres in certain air corridors used by other aircraft. The key concern, though, is with the noise impact. Britain's Council for National Parks has called for a complete ban on the use of microlights in National Parks, and at least one firm has been forced to abandon microlighting following complaints from local residents about the noise.

GUIDELINES

- If you are starting out, hire the equipment – don't buy it. Too many people try the sport for a while and end up with the equipment rotting in the garage.

- Hang-gliders can last fifteen years, so consider buying a second-hand glider if and when you buy.

- Make sure that your launch point is not an environmentally sensitive site. If the ground shows signs of erosion, shift to another site before the problem becomes serious.

- Avoid areas where you are likely to disturb birds and other wild animals, especially during their breeding season. The same goes for livestock.

- If you are using a microlight, fill up with unleaded fuel.

- Microlighters are often advised to use chemical glove warmers to keep their hands warm while in flight. Those sold in the UK contain iron, cellulose, salt, vermiculite and water. They produce heat for a number of hours and then have to be thrown away. Non-disposable ones have been developed, but they have to be boiled in a saucepan for 15 minutes – and then last for only 45 minutes. Consider flying only on warm days!

- When landing, steer clear of crops.

- Follow the appropriate codes of conduct. The British Hang Gliding Association issues a code of good practice, although it mainly concentrates on safety and good relations with landowners – to ensure continued access to launch points!

Kite-flying ★★★★★

 Some say the kite was invented in the fifth century BC by a Greek scientist, Archytas, but Asian peoples have used kites since time immemorial for festivals, kite-fighting and – flown at night – to protect houses from evil spirits.

Most people like to fly kites simply for pleasure. The effect can be spectacular. One of the authors remembers, as a child, flying a huge orange ex-air-sea-rescue box kite in Cyprus. As the evening breeze picked up, kites of all descriptions rose into the sky. The sense of community could be tremendous, until someone tangled with your line! In Asia, they tangle lines intentionally – and coat the lines with gum and glass to give their kites a fighting chance of sawing through the opposition's lines.

Kite-flying can be dangerous, however. Remember Benjamin Franklin dangling a metal key from a kite line in 1752 to demonstrate the electrical nature of lightning? His successful experiment also illuminated the risk of flying a kite in stormy weather – when the line is likely to be both wet and highly conductive.

Kites can also pose a hazard for low-flying aircraft: in London, the official legal ceiling for kites is 60 metres, about the height of Nelson and his column. If you want to go higher, you must apply for a special permit. Many people have gone higher: the world kite altitude record is over 3,650 metres with a single kite, or 9,500 metres with a train of kites.

The traditional range of kite types – three-stickers, the malay and box kites – has been enormously extended in recent years as new materials and flying techniques have been developed. The kites of cotton cloth and spruce spars have given way to graphite carbon fibre and other high-tech materials, including all-but-unbreakable Kevlar lines. Highly manoeuvrable, steerable stunt kites have been introduced, including the 'Revolution' which can spin on the spot. Some modern kites can move at over 120 kph, which can mean they end up in tatters very quickly indeed. Don't try to drive the kite equivalent of a Porsche before you have learned to ride the equivalent of a bike.

GUIDELINES

- You can often tell where people fly kites, because their brightly coloured wreckage litters the tree-tops. Keep away from trees and if your kite does get entangled, try to retrieve it without damaging the tree.

- Keep well away from power pylons and other overhead lines.

- Look for a kite that crashes well. It should be designed to absorb the shock of repeated hard landings.

- Pick your weather conditions carefully. The ideal wind speed tends to be 8–24 kph. If you send your kite aloft in higher winds it could end up in the next county – or country.

- Check out the materials used to make kites, particularly Asian ones where the spars could be made from endangered tropical hardwood.

- If you damage your kite, try to mend it, or failing that find a kite shop that will do repairs.

Parachuting, paragliding and skydiving ★★

Once, only people facing the imminent prospect of being burned alive in a disabled aircraft would have chosen to launch themselves into space attached to little more than a large round tablecloth. But the technology has changed dramatically, to the point where most people who use parachutes now do so for fun. In fact, sport parachuting has been one of the fastest-growing aerial sports of recent years.

You can risk life and limb in everything from *accuracy landings* (hit a 3cm disc when dropped from 900 metres) and *free fall gymnastics* (skydiving is the ultimate in high-board diving) to *formation skydiving* (link hands with eight or more skydivers to form different patterns), *parascending* (parachute upwards, towed by a vehicle over land or boat over water), *paragliding* (exploit the steerable chute to its limit) and – the latest internationally recognised variant – *paraski* (master accuracy landing by parachute with slalom skiing, simultaneously!)

The main environmental impacts stem from the fact that – unless you are being towed up by a car or boat – you need an aircraft to bear you into the heavens, which will eat an enormous amount of fuel and produce polluting emissions. If you use a Cessna 182, for example, which seats four parachutists, you will use around 54 litres of fuel an hour, and an Islander, suitable for up to nine people, uses 112 litres an hour.

GUIDELINES

- Follow the same guidelines suggested for hang-gliding (see above).

- Watch out for power lines, and – in the Alps – cable car wires.

- If you can, parachute over uncultivated land – and if you cause any damage make sure that farmers or other landowners are compensated.

- If you are worried about the greenhouse effect, try

hang-gliding instead of parachuting because it does not use any energy.

Powered aircraft-flying   ★

You can race in them, do aerobatics in them and look down at the rest of the world from them. But aircraft cannot, by any stretch of the imagination, be considered green – unless linked to some *extremely* worthy environmental cause! They are heavy on fuel, are often cleaned with chemicals that cause water pollution, and are a significant source of noise pollution.

Helicopters are worst of all. In North America, they have become increasingly intrusive – organisations like the Sierra Club have been fighting helicopter operators in the Grand Canyon for years, arguing that they shatter the area's peace and tranquillity. A vice-president of Grand Canyon Airlines retorted that people who don't like the noise should go elsewhere. 'One wouldn't pick Coney Island,' he said, 'to have a pristine beach experience.' But an estimated 100,000 tourist planes, helicopters and military aircraft fly in and over the Grand Canyon each year, and the plague is spreading, with the introduction of heli-exploring and heli-hiking. In Glacier National Park, tourist helicopters have been 'dive-bombing' grizzly bears.

Heli-operators point out that they provide a way for the disabled or elderly to get to places they wouldn't otherwise get to. They also argue that helicopters are less damaging than all the ironmongery associated with cable cars and lifts. They argue, too – even less convincingly – that helicopters and other aircraft help to provide wilderness experiences for people in a hurry. But doesn't turning our great pristine areas into Coney Islands (see page 266) rather defeat the object?

GUIDELINES

- If you fly, keep to the agreed flight lanes – and fly as high as you reasonably can.

- When servicing your aircraft, ensure that all lubricants, hydraulic liquids, solvents and other chemicals are safely disposed of. If you hire an aircraft, ask the hire firm what they are doing with all the wastes.

- For tranquillity's sake, don't descend to heli-tourism.

WATER SPORTS

Playing with water, be it fresh or salt, has always had a deep appeal. But the impact of our water sports on wildlife and wild places is usually more serious than that of most air sports. And as we go down to the sea in ever-greater numbers, often in power-boats or astride jet-skis, so our impact builds.

Angling *see* Fishing

Barging ★★★★

 The revolutionary impact of our canals is hinted at by experiments carried out by the early canal-builders. They worked out that a pack-horse could carry one-eighth of a tonne, or pull over two tonnes if harnessed to a stage wagon on a reasonable road. If the same horse pulled a rail wagon, it could move eight tonnes. But if it pulled a canal boat, it could move fifty tonnes. Stick an engine on the barge and it does even better, providing the canal is big enough.

The heyday of the canals coincided with the early years of the Industrial Revolution. Eventually, however, they were overtaken by faster and more flexible rail – and then road – transport. Many fell into disuse, from which some are only now being rescued by leisure uses. But enough freight still travels cleanly and quietly along Britain's canals each year to fill 200,000 20-tonne lorries.

Many of us are unaware (or forget) that the construction of the world's canals caused tremendous environmental damage and changed for ever many of the regions and communities they cut through. Their tremendous transforming power is difficult to discern today, partly because the earliest ones hug the landscape contours and were built from local materials, but also because many have had a couple of centuries to settle in. They are also increasingly popular. Well over 2 million boaters, anglers, walkers and cyclists use Britain's canals each year. British Waterways owns the most extensive system of long distance footpaths in the country, a total of 2,400 kilometres of walking – longer than the Pennine Way and Offa's Dyke put together.

Barging through the countryside along these long-forgotten byways of the Industrial Revolution can be one of the most enthralling introductions to the natural environment. It can also bring us face to face with the damage we inflict on that environment.

As you putter along the River Severn, for example, you see kingfishers, common sandpipers, swallows and martins, streaking along the river or swooping in the air above in pursuit of insects. 'But for every striking, blue-backed kingfisher,' reported one Severn narrowboater, 'there must be a hundred pieces of blue plastic caught in the twigs of the willows and other riverbank trees.' Blue plastic bags have generally been used for fertiliser, but he noted that there was even more white and black plastic – a problem that can be laid at the doorstep of the great British public.

There is a long way to go before the ravages of litter and sewage and farm pollution are a distant memory. In many parts of Europe and North America, however, cleaner waterways are attracting growing numbers of holidaymakers. You can sail a converted Dutch cement barge down the Canal du Midi in France, for example.

Of course, barges can disturb some of the rare and vulnerable aquatic plants and other wildlife which colonise disused canals. But the presence of vociferous bodies of anglers, canoeists and narrowboat users committed to enjoying and protecting these watery worlds is going to be an important factor in their recovery.

GUIDELINES

- Wherever possible, if you are in a powered craft keep to the centre of the channel to avoid disturbing wildlife and anglers.

- Keep your wash to a minimum by maintaining a steady speed, below the speed limit. Remember, a breaking wash created by even slow-powered boats can erode bank sides and disturb fish.

- Avoid off-side banks – a favourite spot for anglers.

- Make sure that the engine is fitted with an effective silencer.

- Have your engine checked and soak up excess oil using one of the absorbents now on sale. Greasy water is polluting. Make sure there is an oil drip tray under an inboard engine to keep oil out of the bilges.

- Dirty bilges can also pollute the canal or river with oil. Barging clubs recommend that you pick your time carefully for discharging sink waste or pumping out bilges. We need to get to the stage where all such wastes are stored and discharged to treatment plants at the end of the trip.

- Many canal tow-paths have become linear wildlife reserves. Never pick wildflowers or try to transplant them to your garden – they are unlikely to survive.

- In short, leave the waterway and verges as you would wish to find them.

Canoeing and kayaking   ★★★★★

 In some parts of Africa, you can still have yourself poled around wetlands in dugouts. In the South Seas, there are outrigger canoes, while elsewhere in the world canoes are made from papyrus or balsa-wood. Most canoeists, however, use craft developed either from the North American Indian birch-bark canoe or the Eskimo's skin-covered sea-going kayak.

Canoeists have devised innumerable ways of putting their craft to the test: spring racing, marathons, canoe sailing, canoe polo, canoe orienteering, slalom racing, wild water racing and canoe surfing. New materials, aluminium, fibreglass and polyethylene, have been used to make these craft more robust – and more manoeuvrable. But whereas birch-bark canoes were biodegradable, most modern plastic and metal canoes cannot easily be recycled.

Even so, canoes and kayaks are quiet, non-polluting and generally an excellent way of bringing people into intimate contact with wilderness areas, marine mammals and other wildlife. In North America, sea-kayaking expeditions take in everything from killer whales in the San Juan Islands to the dolphins, porpoises and whales of Baja California. The Eskimos would understand: they have always valued the kayak for its noiseless approach to prey such as seals and whales.

Canoeing is not uncontroversial, however. Indeed, some anglers got so fed up with passing canoeists on one British river that they strung electric cattle wire across the water at head height – luckily without causing injury. Canoeists point out that our rivers have been used as highways since time immemorial, but the fact that anglers have often paid large sums of money for fishing rights means that they are sometimes unwilling to countenance competing water uses. They also argue that canoeists can damage spawning beds.

There have been some excellent voluntary agreements that help minimise canoeing's impact on wildlife. The Welsh

Canoeing Association and the RSPB, for example, have agreed that canoeists will not paddle close to seabird breeding areas between February and the end of July.

Because they are in such intimate contact with wild places, canoeists may cause problems. But, properly managed, canoeing and kayaking will always be on any list of 'green holidays'.

GUIDELINES

- Travel on your own or in small groups.

- Find out about – and respect – local access agreements.

- Try to avoid damage to riverside or lakeside vegetation when launching or landing.

- Recognise that paddling through reed beds can damage the reeds and disturb nesting birds.

- Avoid disturbance to wildlife and damage to fish spawning beds. Check with anglers where these are.

- When you encounter anglers, wait until they indicate that you can pass. Then pass by quickly, quietly and as far away as you can from their fishing tackle.

- Watch out for blue-green algae pollution in reservoirs, lakes and other standing or slow-moving bodies of water. It is a health hazard and also a threat to some forms of wildlife.

- Be aware that a small number of people – particularly anglers, bathers, canoeists performing 'Eskimo rolls' and water skiers – have contracted the potentially fatal Weil's disease (see page 110). Avoid rolling in stagnant or slow-moving water, and wash or shower after canoeing.

Cruising ★★

'*Dustbin of the Sea*' raged the headline in one tabloid newspaper back in 1989 when Cunard's *QE2* luxury cruise liner was found to be dumping plastic bags full of waste overboard. Upset crewmen had secretly filmed scores of sacks being tossed into the Caribbean, often called the cruise capital of the world. Cunard retorted that it had just had a hold in the *QE2* converted for garbage disposal. The non-plastic waste, the company said, *should* have been ground into a biodegradable slurry and discharged to the sea.

Cruise ships do generate a great deal of rubbish – for a ship with around 2,300 passengers and crew the daily amount of waste generated on board is about 1,600 kg of dry waste, 1,150 kg of food waste and 3,450 kg of glass and tins. This is equivalent to three to four garbage trucks *every day*. And though most of this waste is now incinerated rather than thrown overboard, standards for air emissions from the incinerators are still well below those required for shore-based plants.

Once, cruise liners were the only way of crossing the Atlantic, and Cunard could claim that 'Getting there is half the fun'. During the 1960s and 1970s passenger aircraft cut into the travel market and the business went through a considerable slump, but more recently the sea cruise sector has been enjoying a period of considerable expansion. By the end of the 1980s it had grown into a $5-billion-a-year industry. The number of Americans walking up the gangplanks had risen by an astounding 600 per cent over the decade. By 1990, more than four million holidaymakers took cruises. Meanwhile, the world's shipyards were busy again, building bigger and better vessels to meet the demand.

Many of these liners are effectively floating hotels, indeed some are floating resorts. On the *Norway*, for example, one side of the ship's main international avenue of shops is decked out as Fifth Avenue, the other as the Champs Elysées. There are theme cruises, music cruises, ballroom dancing cruises, slimming cruises. And today you can also choose ecological, botanical or bird-watching cruises.

Some companies aim to maintain the quality image, while others are determined to make cruising a mass-market product. The *Fantasy*, the *Ecstasy* and the *Sensation* are recent names chosen for ships ordered by America's Carnival Cruise Lines. They sound more like products you might find in a sex shop.

Cruise liners have all the environmental problems associated with hotels, with a few extras of their own. Like hotels, their air conditioning systems contribute to both ozone depletion and global warming through their use of CFC coolants and energy. Even the much-vaunted *Wind Star* and *Club Med 1*, ultra-modern liners that rely on computer-controlled sails whenever there is enough wind, are air-conditioned with systems using CFCs.

Unlike hotels, however, these floating giants have also caused significant damage to corals in the Caribbean, Pacific and Indian Ocean. If they drop their anchors near or on top of coral reefs, they can cut a swathe the size of a tennis court each time – and the damaged corals may take fifty years or more to recover.

Less visible, perhaps, is the impact of cruise ships on the communities they visit. Some tropical islands are, quite literally, put on the map by virtue of the arrival of cruise ships. The floating resorts arrive and disgorge their panting cargo of tourists, who expect to lap up a taste of the exotic in a matter of hours. As the locals become increasingly dependent on the income from tourists, they often abandon their traditional occupations in favour of manufacturing crafts for tourist consumption. This is hardly the best way for different cultures to learn about each other – and the re-routing of a ship or line can bring economic devastation.

GUIDELINES

- The passenger, the cruise firms insist, is king. Or queen, presumably? Take them at their word. Challenge them on the environmental front.

- Ask what they have done to ensure that sewage and other wastes are properly handled.

- Ask how they ensure the CFCs used in air conditioning and refrigeration systems do not leak into the atmosphere. Are the recovered CFCs recycled?

- Look for cruises with an environmental theme and insist on well-trained, knowledgeable guides when visiting wilderness areas or other ecologically important sites.

- Consider travelling on a passenger-carrying cargo ship. You can even travel on Geest banana boats!

Diving and snorkelling ★★★★

 People have dived throughout history, in search of lost possessions, sponges, pearls or treasure. To start with, the technology was very simple. North American Indians hunting waterfowl, for example, stalked their prey while breathing through cut reeds. The modern version is snorkelling, which involves wearing a mask, snorkel (or breathing tube) and – often – flippers.

The development of scuba (Self-Contained Underwater Breathing Apparatus) gear freed divers from the need to have air pumped down from the surface. A leading pioneer in this field was Jacques Cousteau, who co-invented the Aqualung. Divers often speak of their sport in the same way that the early American pioneers talked of pushing back the frontiers. The thrill of stumbling on a new wreck, a time capsule from the past, is one draw – but there are many others.

Coral reefs are one of the most powerful attractions, especially now that long-haul charters have opened up distant lands. Although they cover only around one per cent of the ocean floor, coral reefs support around a quarter of all marine species. Off Little Cayman Island, for example, you can visit 'Sting Ray City'. Here divers feed fish to the circling wild sting rays, which one diver described as 'packs of starving frisbees'.

The problem is that these ecosystems are generally both old and fragile. The main reef off Belize, for example, has been growing for 6,000 years. A snorkeller or swimmer standing on a rock-like piece of coral may appear to be doing no harm, but even the slightest touch from fin, foot or hand can damage the protective membrane of some corals. Algae, which co-exist with corals but compete for space, may then outgrow the weakened coral polyps.

But there may be other, less visible problems. Even sun-tan oil may leave its mark. In Hawaii, for example, the spectacular Molikini Crater, near Maui, is visited by as many as a thousand snorkellers and divers every day. The sheer volume of visitors not only affects the fish population, but is also said to leave a bath-tub ring of sun-tan oil around the crater wall.

Divers can play an active role in underwater conservation, however. In Britain, for example, the Marine Conservation Society was founded by divers; an early project involved a survey of basking sharks. And British divers worked with the RSPCA to bring in young seals for treatment during the North Sea seal plague. The Marine Conservation Society has also produced a voluntary code to cut tourist damage to reefs. And Reefwatch, based at the Tropical Marine Research Unit, York University, is an underwater project which encourages divers or expeditions visiting coral reefs to collect and feed back information which will enable reefs to be more effectively protected and managed.

Some countries too have imposed their own restrictions. Belize bans the use of spear guns, and the Barrier Reef is divided into zones with different restrictions on what you can do in each zone, ranging from just swimming to hunting with spear guns.

The pressure on the underwater world can only grow. Already the gathering of giant clams from Indo-Pacific reefs is so popular that they are almost extinct in many countries. At least twelve million Queen Conch shells are taken from the Caribbean each year, both as food and for curios. Television coverage of diving expeditions can only make diving more popular – and sound behaviour by divers more important.

Longer term, one solution may be to create artificial reefs. Even oil rigs provide shelter for fish and other wildlife, so there is now talk of sinking some of them and allowing them to become reefs. The *Rainbow Warrior*, sunk by French secret agents in Auckland harbour, was refloated, towed out to sea and sunk where it would form an artificial reef – and a suitable destination for future divers.

GUIDELINES

- If you are planning to learn to dive, join an organisation that promotes underwater conservation.

- The Marine Conservation Society suggests that you adopt a rock or site. Go back regularly and monitor changes.

- Anchor your boat away from the coral reef and don't stand on the coral.

- If you are visiting coral reefs do not behave as though you were mountaineering underwater! If you travel out to the diving area by boat, be careful where you drop your anchor. It can cause extensive damage if dragged through coral so keep the rope or chain taut and play it out slowly.

- Don't collect coral, shells, reef animals or other underwater 'treasures'.

- Only use spearguns or knives under water for your own protection.

- Abide by local restrictions – make sure you know them.

Fishing   Zero to ★★★★

Instant fishing is now the name of the game in Korea. During their lunchtime break, workaholic South Koreans dash across the road for an hour's indoor fishing in one of the scores of centres that have mushroomed around the country. 'Instant fishing is an ideal break for the businessman who loves to fish, but can't spare the time,' said Lee Yong-Jin, who invented the sport.

Whether you are interested in coarse, game or sea fishing, be warned: fishing can become something of an addiction! There are four million anglers, mainly men, in Britain alone and in a recent survey, 94 per cent of British anglers said they would not allow their daughters to marry anglers!

Anglers and fisherfolk can play an important role as unpaid environmental policemen, keeping a close eye on the quality of our rivers, lakes and other waters. They can also be a powerful lobby, for good or ill, especially where they are seen as an important source of foreign exchange. In Ireland, for example, some of the tens of thousands of foreign anglers visiting Ireland's fisheries in the late 1980s saw extensive fish-kills caused by farmers dumping pig and cattle slurry into rivers, or allowing silage effluents to seep into the water. 'Irish farmers think of rivers primarily as drains,' said one pollution expert. Among the loudest voices in support of a clean-up has been the fishing lobby.

But many anglers and fishermen cause environmental impacts of their own. Some anglers are very careful about retrieving their tackle and clearing up when they leave, but abandoned hooks and line litter many waterways. A significant number of anglers also continue to use lead weights even though these were banned in 1986. Lead weights have doubtlessly helped to poison many thousands of waterfowl. The swans may be recovering on rivers like the Avon and Thames, but buried lead will remain a problem for years to come.

Insensitive anglers can disturb nesting birds or help scare away otters. Others, as in East Anglia, have thoughtlessly introduced exotic game fish species, like the zander, which put up a good fight. But these introduced fish have cut a swathe through local fish populations – and may need to be controlled with chemical poisons.

Even digging for bait can have an effect on local wildlife, as English Nature found in Northumberland's Bugle Bay. Extensive bait digging by sea anglers was linked to a decline in the populations of local seabirds that depend on the same organisms.

The popularity of the sport has meant that in many areas there are simply too many people after too few fish. Ernest Hemingway reported seeing six marlin passing in the space of a single afternoon, while he was fighting another he had already hooked. Today fishermen think themselves lucky if they hook a marlin once every two weeks – and more and more of them are taking game fishing holidays much further afield to Alaska, Montana, Christmas Island, Mauritius and Australia's Great Barrier Reef.

The pressure will be increased by high-tech anglers, who leave little to chance. No longer do they simply use horsehair, silkworm gut lines and bone hooks. Indeed, one Idaho company, Computrol, offers a computer-controlled sonar kit which helps the user to pinpoint target species of fish in their particular habitats. You select the sort of fish you want – bass, salmon or trout, for example – and tell the machine whether you are fishing on a lake, in a river or under ice. Using sound waves, the machine will check the depth and clarity of the water and the composition of the bottom, and will look for the sort of underwater nooks and crannies where your favoured fish is likely to be found.

Presumably, it is now only a matter of time before the machine will do your casting for you – and microwave your catch to perfection when it has been automatically played, gaffed and gutted.

GUIDELINES

- When choosing a spot from which to fish, avoid the outside of bends where deep drafted craft may need to turn.

- Never fish near overhead powerlines, particularly when using a carbon fibre rod. You could end up grilled, instead of your quarry.

- Learn how to put fish back so they don't die later on. If you intend to catch and release, don't take the fish out of the water. Put it in a keep net until you let it go.

- Don't use lead weights. Alternatives include tungsten putty and stainless steel pin-weights.

- Don't leave litter behind, including fishing line, flies and baited hooks.

- Act as warden. Encourage other anglers to respect the environment. Report pollution or suspicious fish deaths.

Sailing and yachting ★★★

 Sailing should be a relatively harmless pursuit, but as increasing numbers of people take part in boating, sailing and yachting, their impact on the environment is causing ever greater concern.

Consider the case of the female dogwhelk (see page 43) whose sex change turned out to be caused by the use of TBT (tributyl tin) anti-fouling paints by boat-owners to protect their hulls against barnacles and weed infestations. The sailing fraternity protested loudly when TBT was banned on all pleasure boats less than 25 metres in length in 1986, but the Royal Yachting Association (RYA) says its members have 'totally and utterly given up the use of TBT'. TBT is not available to the public, but there will still be people using up old stocks. The RYA and the Department of the Environment have produced guidelines called 'Don't Foul it Up' on the use of anti-fouling paint.

You may want to think about the material used to build your boat. For example, you will find widespread use of tropical hardwoods, such as teak, whose felling is contributing to the destruction of the world's tropical rainforests. The decks of yachts are often made of such hardwoods, which are extremely resistant to rot. Look out for sources of sustainably managed tropical hardwood, or for woods that have been rot-proofed using the 'Wood Epoxy Saturation Technique'. But check this last option carefully before you use it: the RYA told us that if treated wood is damaged, the epoxy resin can let in water – and the treated cedar may still rot. Teak still performs best, because it is so oily, so there will inevitably be strong demand for any sustainably grown teak that comes on to the market.

As with any other form of human activity, boating and sailing can reach traffic-jam proportions. The developing overload is particularly clear in such areas as the Norfolk Broads and in many parts of Holland. Many boats are parked in the marine or estuarine equivalent of car-parks. Marshes and mudflats that nurtured large concentrations of birds have become petrified forests of masts and there is mounting protest at the unsightly developments that go alongside many marina complexes, including poorly designed time-share apartments, washing facilities and waste tips.

Even worse, the spread of marinas along the world's coastlines has also helped cause widespread pollution. Most boats still have direct-flush lavatories pushing sewage into the sea, with the result that the water in some marinas is thick with human waste as well as oil.

'Coarse sailing is not mucking around in boats,' Michael Green joked in *The Art of Coarse Sailing*, 'but boating around in muck.' Today, unfortunately, coarse sailing is often the order of the day. With some 30,000 berths on the Solent, for example, the equivalent of a small town can be afloat on a sunny weekend. One yachting organisation we challenged on the sewage issue summed up the general mood: 'Once you are out to sea,' they said, 'it doesn't matter, after all. Everything is crapping in the sea.'

The problems are obviously greater where there is a high proportion of motorised boats. Though most marine engines can use unleaded fuel, they still contribute to oil pollution, particularly in inland waters. In Switzerland the police now insist that boat-owners use highly biodegradable fuels.

But marine oil pollution is still a massive problem. Explorer Thor Heyerdahl astounded scientists when he reported seeing large areas of congealed oil mid-ocean during his Atlantic crossing aboard his *Ra* raft. The oil was not detectable by people on larger ships, too far from the water to see what was going on.

The pollution of our seas and oceans will inevitably be a major issue in future. If you take to the water, be it fresh or salt, keep your eyes peeled for developing problems. You are in a much better position to spot such problems than most environmentalists or politicians!

GUIDELINES

- Follow the RYA Clean Code.

- Don't just batten down the hatches and ignore problems you see when sailing. Report them to the authorities, the RYA, the media or environmental groups.

- Don't use TBT paints, encourage anyone still using them to stop. They don't only affect inedible dogwhelks: oysters suffer too. Follow the guidelines 'Don't Foul it Up' when using anti-foul paint.

- Avoid spilling oil or fuel, particularly when you top up your outboard motor.

- Don't use a sea toilet when in a marina or enclosed area. Every yacht should be fitted with and use a holding tank, both inshore and off-land – the wastes can then be discharged and treated at port.

- Don't dispose of refuse at sea. Even biodegradable material, such as banana skins and orange peel, may end up on the beach long before it rots.

- Make sure you can store rubbish as well as your supplies.

- Remember, the plastic from four-packs or six-packs

can prove a lethal necklace for birds, fish and other wildlife.

- Refuse to berth at marinas that are a blot on the landscape.

- Find out where nature reserves are and respect them.

- Keep at least 600 metres from roosting or feeding flocks of birds, as undisturbed feeding and resting time is vital to their survival. Some species – among them teal, widgeon and goldeneye – are particularly vulnerable to disturbance.

- Use recognised landing sites. Watch out for eggs and nesting birds when walking ashore on isolated shingle banks and spits during the spring and summer months.

Surfing and windsurfing ★★★★★

 Captain James Cook was the first white man to report seeing surfers in Hawaii. The Kings of these islands rode the waves on *olos*, large planks of sugar-pine and coachwood. The sport was surrounded in mystery and ritual, to the extent that Calvinist missionaries considered it a form of paganism and had it banned.

The sport surfaced again early in the twentieth century, although the real breakthrough came in the sixties, when the chart-topping music of the Beach Boys encouraged us all to go *Surfin' USA*. As the surf culture swept around the world, the design of surfing equipment was revolutionised. The list of board designs is endless: *single fin*, *thruster*, *pin-tail*, *swallow tail*.

But while many surfers have become experts on the designs of their boards, there are changes afoot which they may not have noticed. Environmental pressures have forced many suppliers of the rigid foam used for soft boards to switch to a less ozone-depleting CFC to blow the foam. The better companies are looking for a completely 'ozone-friendly' substitute. In fact, most major manufacturers say they have made this change, but say they cannot vouch for the Taiwanese suppliers.

Fibreglass boards also contain ozone-depleting foam, but so far there are no plans to replace such foams because their use is said to be 'non-intensive' and enclosed. If you are buying a new board, ensure that it is CFC-free. Remember, too, that cyanide is used in the manufacture of some boards, which can be a problem if old boards are disposed of by burning.

Once you have your board, there's no need to fly to California, Mexico, Hawaii or Australia. There are good surfing areas in Jersey, Cornwall and Scotland, too. But watch out for pollution problems. Surfers in California are reporting that the pollution of the ocean by sewage, agricultural run-off and chemical industry effluents is causing both red welts on their skin and diarrhoea.

But surfers, too, can help wreck the environment. While the Trailblazers commune with Mother Nature, the commercial surf culture that often follows in their wake can despoil large tracts of the coastline. The sport's camp-followers leave the beach much as they would the site of an open-air rock concert, covered in litter and the dross of barbecues.

Once, surfing was confined to areas with surf, but no longer. During the sixties, an American dinghy sailor stuck a sail on his surfboard and dubbed it a 'windsurfer'. The new sport boomed. In skilled hands, a sailboard can reach 60 kph or more and you can windsurf almost anywhere there is water and wind, whether urban reservoir or Pacific Ocean.

Unlike activities such as whale watching, windsurfing does not automatically attract people who are committed environmentalists. In fact, windsurfing resorts are sometimes described as summer's equivalent of ski resorts, full of sporty young people who are keen to windsurf all day and party all night. They cause the same sorts of problems as surfers – and there are more of them.

In England's Lake District there has been a raging controversy about whether or not windsurfers, with their fluorescent sails and wetsuits, should be allowed to perform on unspoilt Wastwater. Overall, however, most people would probably prefer to see windsurfers on their doorstep than waterskiers or power-boat fanatics (see page 112).

GUIDELINES

- If you are buying a surfboard, find out what the manufacturer has done to replace ozone-depleting substances and if they haven't already made the switch, write to them to encourage them to do so.

- Don't burn your fibreglass board at the end of its life.

- Do your best to blend in with the scenery.

- Don't leave litter.

- Take care not to disturb wildlife. Many birds nest along dunes, lake margins and other areas where land and water meet.

Swimming and bathing ★★★★★
(in swimming pool ★★★)

The hunt for a suspected man-eating great white shark off Tuscany in 1989, following the disappearance of an Italian diver, led to a spate of newspaper stories about the hunt for a 'real-life Jaws'. Whatever the facts of the disappearance, swimmers would be well advised to spend less time worrying about great white sharks and more thinking about some less visible threats that hover in the water around them. In Britain, one such threat is coyly dubbed the 'Mersey goldfish'.

Nor are the bobbing human faeces simply a European problem. If you go swimming off Bondi Beach in Australia, for example, you are likely to come face to faeces with the same problem. The winner of a recent swimming marathon near Sydney reported: 'It was like a toilet block. There was brown muck in the sea and globules of grease. The taste of the water was really disgusting.'

Huge blooms of algae have made parts of the Adriatic unswimmable. On the East Coast of the United States, there was a big scare recently when 'infectious' wastes from hospitals – including blood vials, bandages and syringes – were washed up on beaches. Even the golden sands of Sweden's Riviera have sported red warning signs in recent years, after swimmers reported them littered with dead fish and the bodies of seals, gulls and other birds.

It is often difficult to make out fact from media hysteria. What is clear, though, is that swimming in polluted waters is now a major cause of stomach upsets, skin problems and nose and throat infections. Despite years of assurances to the contrary from the authorities, many viruses and bacteria seem to live on in seawater, sometimes for as long as 17 months.

Once, bathing in the sea was the highpoint of British bank holidays but now British beaches regularly emerge in surveys as among Europe's most polluted. By the end of the 1980s, only twenty-two British beaches had earned the right to fly the European Blue Flag, which denotes a clean, safe beach, and there is widespread scepticism about the adequacy of the scheme.

There is also a worrying increase in the incidence of potentially fatal Weil's disease, or leptospirosis, which can be caused by a bacterium found in rat's urine. 'We used to think it was just farmers and country people who got leptospirosis,' said the director of the Leptospira Reference Laboratory in Hereford, 'but with the increase in water sports we are finding it in bank managers and yuppies now.' Reported deaths are currently around the 100-a-year mark and, worryingly, have been increasing by 10–20 per cent a year as more people have taken to the water.

Nor, it seems, are we always safe in indoor pools. More than 60 per cent of swimming pools recently failed UK government standards on water purity. Many municipal pools have failed to upgrade their water filtration systems, designed to remove pollutants such as sweat and faeces. In large doses, these can cause vomiting and diarrhoea. The chairman of the government advisory body advised bathers to keep well away from any pool that smells strongly of chlorine.

The manufacture of chlorine is itself a major environmental concern. In Los Angeles, which must have one of the largest concentrations of swimming pools in the world, 27,000 people had to be evacuated when a toxic cloud escaped from a chemical factory making chlorine tablets for swimming pools.

Energy efficiency for heating pools is also an issue. Some public pools use double the amount of energy they would need if they upgraded their systems. If you have your own pool, see whether the efficiency of its heating system can be improved.

None of the above should stop you from swimming, of course. On the contrary, take to the water often – and do everything within your power to ensure that the rivers, lakes or seas we plunge into are not polluted and harbouring unsuspected risks to our health.

GUIDELINES

- If you are thinking about a beach holiday in Britain, check the state of your favourite beaches before you go in the latest edition of *The Good Beach Guide*, compiled by the Marine Conservation Society.

- Once there, check the quality of the water before you swim. One tell-tale sign of sea pollution can be a flock of seagulls circling low around a sewage outfall.

- If you do encounter pollution while swimming, don't just grin and bear it. Report it to the authorities – and follow up later to find out what has been done to tackle the problem.

- When swimming you are also exposing yourself to the sun's rays – don't overdo the sunbathing (see page 145).

- Join an organisation that campaigns for clean rivers and seas.

- If you have your own swimming pool, look into the possibility of using solar collectors and heat pumps to heat the water.

- Cut back on your use of chlorine. New systems are emerging that treat water without using chlorine; see if you can find a suitable non-chlorine treatment plant.

- Use an insulating cover to help cut heating costs, warm the pool by absorbing sunlight and cut the amount of leaves and other material needing to be filtered out of the water.

Waterskiing and waterbikes   Zero

 With noise becoming an increasing nuisance along many of the world's most beautiful coastlines, one man we can thank is Ralph Samuelson of Lake City, Minnesota. In 1922, he became the first recorded waterskier and, shortly thereafter, the first waterski jumper. Later on, he tried skiing behind a flying boat, a trick which has not yet been developed into a mass sport! Then, as less expensive and more powerful boats and new ski materials came on to the market in the 1950s, waterskiing really took off.

Most waterskiers claim they are misunderstood – indeed put upon – by local authorities and communities, who maintain that waterskiing is a public nuisance. Around Lake Windermere, in Britain's Lake District, waterskiers have been wearing T-shirts emblazoned with the message: 'Stop the 10 mph limit'. The planners have decided that enough is enough – and say three-quarters of local people support them. Waterskiing is noisy, despite the fact that the industry says the noise produced by new boats has been halved over the last ten years. The problem is that there are now more of them and their increased power means that they need a fair amount of space, which can spread their impact over a large area.

Pollution caused by waterskiing boats has been cut by more efficient engines and new fuel mixes, although much depends on the behaviour of individual boat owners. The cleanest fuel is probably propane. Though diesel engines cannot be converted to propane, most petrol engines can. Practically all marine engines can be run on unleaded fuel.

Waterskiing has an impact on wildlife too – on some Greek beaches, turtles have had flippers amputated by the propellers of speeding boats. More likely in this country is the disturbance of over-wintering and breeding birds on inland waters and estuaries. However, the limited number of sites where waterskiing is permitted – and the limited number of skiers who brave winter weather – help to contain this impact. If the sport becomes more popular during the winter months, we may well see more of a problem.

It is hard to accept the waterskier's argument that, on balance, waterskiing is good for the environment. Enthusiasts cannily point out that the turbulence created by both boat and skier oxygenates lakes, reservoirs and other inland waters. And industry sources assured us that waterskiing had kept lakes at the Cotswold Water Park clear of blue-green algae, but the Park denied that any of their lakes had ever suffered from blue-green algae.

For years, waterskiers have fretted about the expense involved in having both a driver and observer in the boat that pulled them, and various attempts have been made over the years to develop remote control boats. As early as 1935, a man attached piano wires to his boat's throttle and steering wheel, and set forth. He fell, got tangled in the wires and drowned. Now you can use a 'personal waterski machine', which can pull a skier at up to 56 kilometres per hour. It uses a water jet, rather than a propeller, which should make it safer for both the user and for wildlife.

Another alternative, much favoured in Germany, is cable-tow waterskiing. A contraption powered by an electric motor pulls skiers around a circuit. This approach causes less noise and pollution, but can look very ugly.

A relatively new – and fairly hideous – development in this area is the jet-ski (first developed in the early 1970s by

Kawasaki) or waterbike. Walk along the harbourfront of many a Riviera resort and you will find some of the yachts festooned with waterbikes, while the waters around are a-buzz with them. Many harbour authorities have banned jet-skis as a major noise nuisance – and a threat to other water traffic. More should do so.

GUIDELINES

- Try a sailboard instead of waterskis. It can be just as exhilarating, and is much quieter.

- If you are set on skiing, don't rev the engine – or keep it running when it's not needed.

- Check that the boat has an effective silencer and sound insulation on and around its engine.

- If the boat runs on petrol, make sure that unleaded fuel is used. If it runs on two-stroke fuel, insist on a rapidly biodegradable brand. If you own the boat, consider having it converted to run on propane.

- If you are waterskiing or jet-skiing at a centre or resort, ask whether it has an environmental policy and code of behaviour. If it doesn't, suggest that one be developed.

- Once you are on the water, keep away from the banks – when moving at speed, your wash can help cause erosion.

- If there are designated zones for waterskiing, keep to them.

- Help to police the sport. If you see other people taking liberties, report them.

- Resist the temptation of waterskiing in remote and undeveloped areas where the impact is likely to be greater and where you may be 'starting the rot'.

White-water rafting ★★★★★

 This is a very different kettle of fish from the sort of thing that Huckleberry Finn and his cronies got up to. The idea is that groups of eight or so people, together with a crewman, battle their way down a rushing river in a large rubber inflatable. Enthusiasts describe the experience as a very wild and wet roller coaster ride.

'White water' is generally found where a river races through a relatively small space, usually lined with rocks. Most sensible people would not risk life and limb by 'shooting' such rapids in a highly manoeuvrable canoe, let alone a raft. Undaunted, growing numbers have decided that this is the sport for them. White-water rafting really took off in the States and Canada in the late 1970s and then began to catch on in Europe from the mid-1980s. One of the original European rafting companies which used to take 200 people in a summer season now takes over 10,000.

You can go white-water rafting on some of the world's great rivers, like the Zambezi. A 16-kilometre stretch of river starting at the base of the awesome Victoria Falls includes twenty rapids. Those taking part are asked to sign a disclaimer for insurance purposes. Reassuringly, the instructor also warns: 'If you get washed overboard, watch out for crocodiles.'

Ironically, some of the best rafting experiences are to be found on rivers controlled by power stations to generate hydropower. When they open their dam sluices, there is good rafting – but when the sluices are closed, the river slows to a trickle! Where there are no dams, rafting often takes place in the headwaters of a river.

The spray and mist caused by white water often creates ideal conditions for unusual plant communities, which could be damaged either during launching or landing. To tackle this problem, some operators have suggested building artificial courses. This may prove to be a real solution, although a visit to one such course suggests that poorly designed courses could permanently blight otherwise attractive areas.

GUIDELINES

- Check with the rafting outfit whether they have a free run on the river, and watch out for other water users, particularly anglers – you may disturb the fish or interfere with fishing lines.

- Avoid damage to riverside plants when launching and landing. Watch your feet – and the raft.

- Don't drop litter – even cigarette butts – in the water.

Windsurfing *see* Surfing and Windsurfing

LAND SPORTS

However much they may wish to spend every free hour in the air or water, most holidaymakers spend most of their time on terra firma – and this is where most of the problems they cause are inevitably found. Even the greenest forms of transport, like the cycle (see page 126), can become a major problem when – in the form of all-terrain bikes – they are used in National Parks and other fragile areas.

So, whether we are lolling on the beach getting a tan, lowering ourselves into a pothole or scaling one of the world's tallest peaks, there are issues that we should all consider when planning our leisure time and holidays.

Camping ★★★★

Camping is one of the best ways of staying cheaply just about anywhere. Young people in particular find it an exciting way to see the world. Like snails, some campers carry their homes and anything else they need on their backs, while others – including some of the same people grown up – travel in such style that they need anything from a large family car to a motor convoy to ferry them and their equipment to and fro. This increasingly involves a 'complete hook-up', with all services on tap, including electricity, hot water and flush toilets, refrigerators, TVs and, in some cases, even air conditioning.

People have camped since time immemorial, but leisure camping is barely a hundred years old – with the great explosion in family camping dating from the 1950s. Some people camp for its own sake, but most pitch their tent in or alongside areas where they can go fishing, walking, hunting, canoeing or swimming.

Along the Mediterranean coast the size of camp sites is growing at an astounding pace; you can now find restaurants, nightclubs, hairdressers and almost every type of amusement ready to hand. The coastlines of France and Italy in particular threaten to become one vast linear holiday camp during the summer months. Even in Britain there are concerns about the sheer numbers of people wanting to camp. The Forestry Commission has been forced to cut back on the number of people allowed to pitch their tents in the New Forest, which is now visited by 10 million tourists a year.

The Grand Canyon is one of the most popular camping destinations. The authorities now enforce a very strict code of practice whereby people have to book, in advance, into set camping sites over the course of their stay and abide by rules once there. Even the river rafters in their small rubber dinghies have to 'take out everything they take in', including human waste collected in a portapot – peeing in the river is strictly forbidden.

But don't let that put you off camping. Done in the right way, it will always be one of the greenest and healthiest ways of getting in touch with the natural world.

GUIDELINES

- When pitching your tent, try to find an area that is naturally suitable, rather than reshaping the environment to fit.

- If you are camping in a meadow or similar site, move the tent frequently, so you do not kill the grass. Tie ropes around trees, rather than using nails.

- Ideally, take your own stove with you. Fires can be great fun, but they can be dangerous in forest areas.

- Insulate stove sites, or you will leave a ring of killed vegetation.

- If you plan to light a fire, look upwards as well as around when choosing a site. Sparks can set overhanging trees ablaze – and in hot, dry areas the flames can spread through the forest faster than you can run. Sometimes forest fires have overtaken speeding cars, with fatal results for their passengers.

- Preferably, use a fire pit – and fill it in when you leave.

- Take great care not to pollute streams or other water with wastes or detergents. It is better to dispose of dirty water on the ground than into streams. Strain greasy water through dry grass or bracken.

- Leave the camp-site as you found it – or cleaner. Ideally, take your rubbish home. If this is not possible, burn or bury it.

Caravanning ★

 To put it mildly, caravan sites are not universally popular. They seem to wink at us from every corner of the landscape, like clusters of shiny beetles threatening a much-loved plant. Even on their own, caravans and mobile homes can raise the blood pressure – and on the roads, they are mobile road-blocks.

Some 600,000 people now go caravanning each year in Britain, many of them retired, and there are an estimated 8–10,000 sites. And caravanners are active. A quarter of the members of the Caravan Club go touring more than seven times a year in the UK. In Europe as a whole there are said to be 30 million people who use 'mobile recreational facilities' – and maybe another 50 million in America. Many of them like to pack in every convenience imaginable, from TVs and hairdryers to refrigerators and barbecues.

The UK Caravan Club stoutly defends its members by saying that many clubs have turned worked-out quarries, rubbish tips and even disused railway stations into caravan sites. It also points out that caravans do not sterilise the land they stand on, as buildings would. But there will be a huge market for the inventor who comes up with a chameleon paint, designed to adapt to background colours and help caravans disappear into the landscape!

GUIDELINES

- Towing a caravan behind your car uses around 20 per cent more fuel. It may be better to keep your caravan in one place and – ideally – travel back and forth by train.

- Choose a well-screened site, with good plumbing, to cut down on the need for chemical loos.

- See if you can encourage the landowner to plant more trees, or let you plant some. If you succeed, make sure that the saplings are native species and in character with the local environment.

- The positioning of caravan sites makes a great deal of difference to their intrusiveness. Make sure you use a site that is not highly visible for miles around.

- Keep quiet when returning at night so that you do not disturb the locals.

- Read the guidelines for camping (page 117).

Caving and potholing ★★★

In 1940, four young French boys followed a dog into the underworld – and stumbled across the Lascaux Caves. In what was promptly dubbed 'The Sistine Chapel of the Périgord', the walls of the original caves were covered in beautiful frescoes of bison, bulls, horses, deer, ibex and other animals. People flocked from far and wide to see this gallery of prehistoric art. Unfortunately, in spite of such precautions as weak lighting and air conditioning, visitor pressure produced two forms of damage: the so-called 'green disease' (excess growth of moss and algae) and 'white disease' (less visible, but more serious and resulting from a deposit of white calcite), both caused by the carbon dioxide in visitors' breath.

In fact so much carbon dioxide was produced by visitors that by the end of a day it wasn't even possible to light a match in the caves! The eventual solution was to build a facsimile of the caves in an open-cast quarry some 20 metres from the originals.

Few cavers and potholers ever set eyes on such treasures, let alone discover them. But they do see natural treasures, including stalactites and stalagmites built up over centuries from dripping water rich in calcite. Like children knocking down icicles, some early cavers took pleasure in shooting down stalactites. In fact, tough though they may seem, these formations can be surprisingly fragile: if you wipe a drip off a stalactite, the oil from your finger can slow or halt its further growth!

You won't find bears in most caves today, but you may find other cave-dwellers, bats among them. Remember, roosting and hibernating bats can be disturbed by noise, bright lights, smoking, or the heat and fumes from carbide lamps. Bats are extremely sensitive to changes in temperature; indeed, they can sense the warmth of a human from several metres away. If they do wake up, they waste valuable fat reserves, which may mean they fail to make it through the winter.

There has been a rapid growth in caving and potholing (generally involving vertical caves or shafts) over the last thirty years. The best caving areas are usually found in regions of mountain limestone, which can be readily eroded by underground streams. Some cavers also apply their skills to disused mines and fortifications.

The basic motto for cavers and potholers, as for any other leisure activity, must be to leave caves as you would hope to find them. Whatever you leave down there is likely to be around for a very long time.

GUIDELINES

- Take care not to disturb cave life. Bats in particular are both endangered and protected by law.

- Don't smoke.

- Never leave litter or spent carbide in caves. Spent batteries or carbide can poison cave wildlife, including crustaceans you may not have even noticed.

- Better still, use rechargeable batteries for lamps and lights.

- Observe any taped routes – they are there to safeguard the cave as well as for your safety.

- Play an active part in keeping caves clean and undamaged, and go to the loo before you go underground.

- If you spot problems, report them.

Climbing and mountaineering ★★★

The bigger a climbing resort is, the more climbers it needs to keep its local economy humming. The competition to attract more climbers – and the money they bring – was illustrated recently when a Swiss village council applied for planning permission to increase the height of its local Alp by two metres! The mountain, sadly, just fails to push its peak through the magical 4,000-metre altitude reached by more famous mountains in the surrounding Valais region, including the Matterhorn, in Zermatt, and when the president of Ross Boden village council announced his plans to spend £50,000 on an artificial crag atop the mountain, the news not surprisingly caused an uproar.

Today, there are few mountains that have not been climbed – and most have been climbed from every conceivable angle. Now climbers are going further and further afield in search of new pastures, with small teams heading off for places like Antarctica, Western China and Eastern Russia. At least one climber – if that is the word – has parachuted on to Himalayan peaks and skied down.

As a result of the droves of people now making their way even into the most remote mountain fastnesses, litter has become a major headache. Sir Edmund Hillary, who first conquered Everest, has called for a five-year moratorium on climbing the mountain – to give it a chance to recover.

'Everest is the highest junkyard in the world,' agreed mountaineer Chris Bonington. 'It is littered with discarded tins, tents, food and empty oxygen tanks. There is so much up there that a full-scale expedition will be needed to remove it. What is happening in the Himalayas is a microcosm of what is happening in the rest of the world.'

The problem is likely to get worse, as new equipment opens up the peaks to ever-growing numbers of people. The use of liquid oxygen, for example, can keep a climber going for up to eight times longer than a climber using compressed oxygen.

Closer to home, there has been considerable controversy about the way some climbers are using battery-driven power drills and expansion bolts to open up dangerous climbs – as at Dumbarton Rock. Climbing magazines have attacked the use of bolts in the heart of a Site of Special Scientific Interest as an act of vandalism. If the bolters prevail, the pressure on such sites can only increase.

Upland environments may see fewer people than do lowland footpaths, but they are generally much more vulnerable. Plants that have fought to survive and reproduce in thin soils and a hostile climate may find it impossible to recover from a single stomping by a climber's boot. Equally, climbers, in what is sometimes called 'gardening', may remove rare alpine plants from possible finger- or foot-holds.

Lower down, the problems are even worse. In Nepal, for example, some 3,000 climbing expeditions and 100,000 trekkers each year accelerate the deforestation of the hills they come so far to enjoy (see page 210).

Less exotically, climbers working their way up sea cliffs can cause significant damage to seabird breeding colonies. Eggs may be dislodged from nests and adult birds scared off. In their absence, incubating eggs may cool too far to survive – or may be picked off by predatory gulls.

To be fair, most climbers and mountaineers get into the sport because of a passion for the natural environment – or they acquire it as they go. The British Mountaineering Council and English Nature (formerly the Nature Conservancy Council) have drawn up a code of conduct called *Tread Lightly*, which takes as its text the old catchphrase: 'Take nothing but photographs, leave nothing but footprints'. The problem is that as more climbers take to the hills, there are often too many footprints for comfort.

GUIDELINES

- Find out about any restrictions placed on climbing for the protection of birds, animals and plants – and abide by them.

- Don't drop litter. Ideally, leave most packaging at home and carry out all rubbish. If you must bury wastes, make sure you crush cans and other containers – and bury them as deep as you can.

- Wear the lightest suitable boots – and tread carefully, particularly in descent.

- Walk on worn parts of the path – and try not to cut new zig-zags. In sensitive areas, walk in file if you are with a group, rather than in line abreast.

- Keep 'gardening' to a minimum.

- Do not paint or scratch route names into rock – or leave other signs of your passage.

- When climbing in winter, keep to well-frozen routes. Avoid climbing at the beginning of a general thaw.

Combat games   Zero

 If you have encountered wild-looking people wearing paint-splattered camouflage uniforms and goggles in your local bluebell wood, the chances are that you already know about what has been described as Britain's fastest-growing sport.

We can thank the Mounties for the rapid spread of 'paintgun' or 'paintball' combat games. What started out as a training exercise for the Royal Canadian Mounted Police was rapidly commercialised in the United States and spread to Britain in the late 1980s. The explosive growth of the UK industry is indicated by a single statistic: in the summer of 1988 there were forty-four combat games sites, whereas just two years later there were nearly four hundred.

Scores of companies have been set up with names like 'Combat Zone', 'Skirmish' and 'The Survival Game'. These in turn have persuaded much bigger companies that wargaming is a good way to build up the team spirit among sales people and other employees.

The basic idea is simple: using guns powered by carbon dioxide, combat gamers fire Malteser-sized paintballs at each other. The combatants are divided into two opposing teams of up to fifty people each. The object is to capture the other team's flag and then get back to your base.

Unfortunately, combat gamers tend to like ancient woodlands, on uneven terrain, which give them plenty of lush cover. These are the woods most valued by conservationists – indeed, the Forestry Commission has banned combat games on all of its land, arguing that they destroy vegetation and disturb wildlife and other people.

It's not simply a question of paint being splashed about – most of the ammunition is made of gelatine and biodegradable dyes. The real problem is that scores of heavily booted feet crashing around have turned damp areas into quagmires, while in the excitement of the moment combatants are very likely to break branches and even pull up complete saplings by their roots. The base camps, subjected to repeated games, are often surrounded by fairly extensive areas of bare earth.

English Nature is increasingly worried. It says that already combat games have caused 'serious ecological damage'. It also notes that combat games do not need planning permission, so long as permanent buildings are not put up and the games are not played on more than twenty-eight days each year.

If you are considering taking part in combat games, or if your company or organisation is thinking of sending a group of staff off to hunt each other through the last remnants of Britain's primeval forest, here are some points to remember.

GUIDELINES

- Pick a reputable company or centre.

- Ask the company you choose whether it has a conservation policy.

- If you see signs of soil erosion, insist that the company or centre rotates the areas where combat games are held.

- Beware of disturbing wildlife, particularly in sensitive seasons, when animals and birds are breeding or raising their young. Remember: ground-nesting birds are particularly vulnerable.

- Don't cut or pull down trees, bracken or other vegetation.

- Tie ropes around trees, rather than hammering nails or bolts into them.

- If you have reason to suspect damage is being caused, contact a local conservation body and ask their advice.

Cycling ★★★★★

Ask environmentalists to name their favourite form of transport, other than walking, and most will pick cycling. Bikes are about as environment-friendly as you can get: you can travel 1,600 kilometres on a thimbleful of oil! There has been an explosion of interest in bikes, partly because they are green – but also because they are often faster than cars in our congested cities. They can also be great fun. In just six years, the number of bikes in the USA soared from around 200,000 to 10 million. In Europe, too, the bike is back on children's Christmas wish-list.

Deceptively simple, modern bikes are often built by robots using the latest high-tech materials. They are lighter and faster than traditional designs and, as a result, more and more people are taking their lives in their hands and cycling to work. However, cycling conditions in Britain are the poorest in Europe, with the exception of Belgium, according to the European Cyclists' Federation. 'Riding a cycle in Britain is less fun than anywhere else,' the Federation concluded, 'with cyclists getting the least respect from other road users.' Cyclists who are not knocked off their machines are likely to be asphyxiated by traffic fumes. The Dutch and the Danes could teach the rest of the world a thing or two about planning for the bike. In Holland, around 40 per cent of people cycle to work on extensive networks of cycle-only routes.

At a time when we should be giving cyclists a following wind, at least one London borough says it will not spend any more money on cyclists, for fear of encouraging more of them on to roads where they are likely to be killed or injured by cars and other vehicles. By contrast, Sustrans (short for 'Sustainable Transport') has with the help of volunteers completed over a hundred miles of cycleways around Britain, in some cases converting old railways.

Cycling holidays look set to be a boom area in the 1990s. A number of small, flexible companies have sprung up to offer holidays from the Channel Islands to China. The basic idea is to enjoy the countryside without having to jostle with cars and juggernauts. Families cycling in countries like France find that even eight-year-olds can cycle 50 or 60 kilometres a day. And the French are set up for it: more than 2,000 SNCF trains run every day carrying cycles free of charge on the *vélo en bagage* service.

But in some areas environmentalists are beginning to feel that you can have too much of a good thing. The development of the mountain bike, also known as the ATB (all-terrain bike), has led to unexpected environmental problems. Invented in the mid-1970s for biking fanatics who wanted a machine to scale rugged Mount Tamalpais, north of San Francisco, the mountain bike has been a shot in the arm for the cycle business – the US industry expected them to account for over 40 per cent of its 1991 sales.

However, the controversy about the off-road use of ABTs is rocking US conservation groups like the Sierra Club. So great is the number of mountain bikers, some of whom disrupt other people's enjoyment of the natural environment, that in many parks near San Francisco rangers have been forced to close trails, set up speed traps and use radar guns to curb fast and reckless riding! Other National Parks in the States have gone as far as restricting cyclists to the same routes as cars. And apart from being a disturbance to walkers, bikers in large numbers, particularly down-hill riders, are seriously eroding pathways. Even the greenest form of transport can clearly cause problems in the wrong – or too many – hands.

GUIDELINES

- Follow the safety code – and wear a helmet.

- If you cycle at night, use a dynamo or rechargeable batteries to power your lights – not disposable batteries. If you are stuck with disposables, buy a mercury-free brand.

- If you like off-road cycling, find an area designed for the purpose. And respect other people's right to peace, quiet and safety.

- Keep away from ecologically sensitive areas, like peat bogs and other wetlands. Remember, too, that on steep slopes your tyre-marks can speed soil erosion.

- If you are going cycle camping, see if you can carry your equipment on your bikes – rather than having a vehicle follow you around.

- Ask your cycle association or tour company whether it has a conservation code or environmental policy. If it doesn't, suggest it puts one together – and ask to see it when it is ready.

Golf Zero

 Golf, it has been said, is a new religion. In Britain you can even take a three-year college course on golf, playing five times a week at the government's expense. And now golfers are at it in Antarctica, where players drive luminous balls around a course dotted with seal holes and snow tunnels. Environmentalists, on the other hand, view golf as an international contagion.

More than a million trees have been cut down in the Dominican Republic alone to make way for golfers, for example. In Ireland, a nine-hole course being built in County Kerry threatens breeding sites of the protected natterjack toad, yet changes in the use of land from farming to leisure need no formal approval.

Golf course construction has become one of the hottest growth industries in Thailand, where golf club memberships are now traded like oil futures. One course west of Bangkok imported $300,000-worth of Bermuda grass from the USA and installed a $1.6 million computerised sprinkler to keep it happy. The USA, it has been estimated, would have to build a new course a day for ten years to keep up even with current demand for membership.

If all the golf courses planned for Majorca are built, their water consumption will be equivalent to that of 300,000 people – the total population of the Majorcan capital, Palma. It has been calculated that an average Majorcan eighteen-hole golf course uses between 1,500 and 2,000 cubic metres of water per day during the summer – which is the same daily consumption as a village of 8,000 inhabitants.

Japan has over 1,700 golf courses with at least 300 more under construction and another 900 at the planning stage. With golf club memberships often costing millions of dollars in Japan, the Japanese resort to playing in multi-storied driving ranges and are now busily buying up golf courses around the world. They have even managed to overcome the Chinese reservations about golf being a capitalist sport and have constructed a golf course outside Shanghai – about 85 per cent of its members are Japanese.

So great is the demand that a $42 million public golf course was opened in Tokyo recently, built entirely on 18 million tonnes of garbage. The eighteen-hole course is dotted with over seventy vents, which release potentially explosive methane into the atmosphere. Smoking, not surprisingly, is not permitted!

Television viewers of the sport have become accustomed to seeing dark green courses manicured to the point where the grass looks like the baize on a billiards table. This effect is achieved by dint of considerable applications of fertiliser, herbicides and other chemicals. The natural wildflower swards, gorse and skylarks that helped golfers commune with nature could soon be a thing of the past.

There have already been several massive spills of golf course chemicals in Japan, killing fish in nearby streams or rivers. Nearly 2 tonnes of chemicals are used each year on the average eighteen-hole course in Japan. In Osaka, fish in a showpiece lake – called 'The Sea of Life' – at the International Garden and Greenery Expo embarrassingly succumbed to pesticides from a one-hole course on the same site. And in Britain, 95 per cent of courses were found to have over-fertilised their turf at least sixfold, while phosphate concentrations – often caused by fertilisers – went off the end of the measuring scale at a third of the courses sampled. The result can be algal blooms in nearby streams, suffocating fish and other wildlife.

The herbicides are used to turn rough into smooth. Once, these uncultivated areas provided shelter for wildlife – indeed, of the top fifty UK courses around half contain areas of significant conservation value. But because of the demand for the game, the aim of many of today's course designers seems to be to get golfers round the course and into the bar as fast as they can. They drain wetlands (often describing them as useless bogs) and widen the fairways, cutting into and killing off the natural vegetation, removing anything likely to get in the way of a ball. Throughput is the name of the game – and faster golf generally means less wildlife and more pollution.

There are some indications that 'organic golf' might catch on, however. One forty-five-hole course in Canada which used to spray 100 gallons of the herbicide Killex on its courses every year now lets weeds grow in the rough and has switched to organic fertilisers. At one course in Japan, meanwhile, golfers queuing for their next shot have been asked to weed the fairway by hand!

There is also increasing concern amongst conservationists that golf courses are being used as an excuse for inappropriate development in the countryside. Following the construction of a golf course, planners often receive requests for permission for a golf club building, car-parking facilities, golf time-share houses and more. If planning permission is given for these additions, it may then only be a small step to allowing other forms of development in the newly 'urbanised' area.

There are already 1,700 golf clubs in the UK, and 300 public courses, but the tide of new greens is unlikely to abate. Land-owners see the development of courses as a lucrative sideline for land where EEC grants are encouraging them to look for alternative uses to food production. With over 1,400 change-of-use applications already lodged with UK councils, opposition from organisations like CPRE and the Countryside Commission, as well as many members of the non-golf-playing public, is mounting.

The Golf war has begun.

GUIDELINES

- If you are thinking of taking up golf, think again.

- If you are already hooked, ensure that your club has a conservation plan – and sticks to it. Think about wildlife habitat creation.

- Golf courses could operate as an unofficial chain of nature reserves! In Britain, talk to the Golf Course Wildlife Trust.

- Suggest that your club bans golfers from collecting their balls from the rough, where they invariably swipe at their balls along with the heather or other plants, as well as trampling them under foot. The 'lost' balls could then be collected by the club and sold back to members at a knockdown price.

- Encourage the groundsmen to go organic – and to cut back on their mowing of areas suited to wildlife.

- Many golf courses are full of non-indigenous plants and shrubs that do not fit in with the surrounding countryside – encourage your club to blend into the local landscape.

- If you are planning to build a golf club, invest in an attractive, unobtrusive design.

Hunting ★

Whether or not you agree with Oscar Wilde's description of fox hunting as 'The unspeakable in full pursuit of the uneatable,' there is no getting away from the intense controversy that now surrounds many forms of hunting. The National Trust was rocked when its members voted on the issue of whether stag hunting should be allowed on its lands in the Somerset Quantocks. And the British Field Sports Society even had to hire an offshoot of Saatchi & Saatchi, the advertising agency, to counter the PR success of hunt saboteurs. Whichever side of the fence you come down on, one fact is indisputable: man has evolved as a predator, and the hunting instinct is still to a large degree engrained in us. 'We like to kill,' said one Louisiana hunter. 'I can no more explain this predatory instinct to the satisfaction of Friends of Animals than anyone else can. But I won't throw up a smokescreen of rationalisations when confronted with this unnerving but unavoidable fact.' Even animal rights campaigners may be fulfilling the urge as they 'hunt' the hunters and try to recruit new members.

However, while this instinct is natural, it can often become distorted. One of the worst examples was the late and un-lamented Romanian dictator, Nicolae Ceausescu. He frequently satisfied his bloodlust in special Carpathian hunting preserves, each with its own staff, helicopter pad, electric perimeter fences and guard posts. While his wife fished in a concrete pond filled to the gills with trout, game watchers skilfully lured and manoeuvred bears, deer and other animals so that the dictator, a bad shot, could not possibly miss.

Unfortunately, even though the Ceausescus have gone, hunting is developing as a major tourist attraction in post-socialist Eastern Europe . Hunters are attracted by the relative abundance of game, the cheaper prices for hunting and, it has to be said, by the lack of a vociferous anti-hunting lobby.

Few pastimes can equal the controversy caused by fox-hunting; what the anti-fox-hunting lobby in Britain does not concede is the role that the sport has to play in conservation of the countryside. The hunt can help preserve hedgerows and traditional gates, as well as control the fox or deer populations so they do not need to be culled by other, possibly crueller, methods. In addition to the cruelty issues, the sport has now become so popular in some areas that it suffers from the problem of overcrowding and the need to limit numbers. Hordes of hunters chasing across the fields are churning up some pastures and turning them into quagmires.

Other hunters, in search of more exotic prey, are heading for Texas. Would-be big game hunters can go on safari without any of the bother and discomfort of going to Africa. Zoos, circuses and fed-up pet owners have been selling lions and other 'big game' animals for 'canned hunts', in which the hunters and hunted are put together in conditions that leave the outcome in no doubt. The hunters can then return home with 'trophies' to hang on their wall and impress their friends.

Traditional hunters insist, however, that they should be thanked for the fact that there are now twenty-five times as many elk and forty times as many pronghorn antelope in the United States as there were in 1910. White-tailed deer have increased by almost 12 million since the turn of the century – and even the bison, almost extinct in 1900, number some 6,000 today. There is a certain amount of truth in their arguments: sport hunters, for example, were in the forefront of the campaign for setting aside areas like Yellowstone as National Parks. The US Pittman–Robertson Act, which taxes hunting licences and guns, has raised nearly two billion dollars since 1937 for wildlife research and habitat protection. Hunters are often big direct spenders in this area. Ducks Unlimited has bought 3.5 million acres of wetland and raises $50 million a year to preserve waterfowl habitat.

In Poland, meanwhile, the bison has been re-introduced. The last European bison living in the wild was shot in 1921 by a forester-turned-poacher. But, thanks to captive breeding of European bison in zoos, herds have also been built up in Russia, Romania and Czechoslovakia. As their numbers build, so the wild populations will take a certain amount of culling – and it will make a great deal of sense to charge hunters thousands of dollars for carrying out the task, as long as the money is ploughed back into conservation measures.

In areas where traditional hunting has been cramped by new housing, roads, railway lines or saboteurs, mock hunting – with the hounds following scents laid in advance – is taking off. This has the benefit of helping to keep the saddlers, tailors and horse breeders in business.

Like it or not, the chances are that hunting will always be with us, whether for the pot or for the luxury safari market (see page 160). The key question is whether it can be carried out in a humane and sustainable way; and for this we need a significant change in the attitudes of the hunting fraternity.

GUIDELINES

- Do not even consider going hunting unless you belong to at least one organisation seriously committed to the conservation of your prey or the countryside.

- Make absolutely sure that your quarry is not endangered, either nationally or locally.

- Kill humanely – and do not kill more animals or birds than you need for your own use.

- Respect – and make sure others respect – hunting restrictions designed to ensure that prey populations are not overtaxed.

- Make sure that any hunt-followers behave sensibly. In many fox-hunting areas, the followers cause as much damage as they drive their vehicles cross-country as do the much-vilified drivers of all-terrain vehicles (see opposite).

Ice-skating ★★★

 Several thousand years ago, some bright spark had the notion of strapping pieces of wood or bone to his feet and then – after a bit of practice – wobbling away across a frozen lake. Later, shaped wooden and iron runners were developed, turning skates into a useful means of winter locomotion along the Dutch canals or Scandinavian fjords.

In the so-called 'Little Ice Age' in Europe, particularly in the 1640s and 1650s, there were periods of intense cold. Many took to the frozen rivers on foot and skate – and there were even 'ice fairs' on the frozen Thames.

Up to that point, the freezing had been a natural process, but things were about to change. The first artificial ice rink, or *Glaciarium* as it was called, was built in London in 1876. Some early rinks were little more than extensions of ice-making plants devoted to freezing meat. Later, as the number of rinks grew, there evolved a whole range of ice sports, including figure skating, speed skating, ice hockey and ice dancing.

The main environmental issue with artificial rinks is the use of energy and a refrigerant to freeze the ice. One rink told us that they spend nearly £100,000 a year on energy in their ice plant. Ammonia or R22 (a CFC which is less ozone depleting than the CFCs it has replaced) are generally used as the refrigerant. One Finnish company has come up with one possible solution: an ice rink made of plastic coated plywood, which it hopes will open up the prospect of year-round, energy-efficient skating. The fly in the ointment here is that plywood generally comes from the rainforest.

GUIDELINES

- When skating in the open, give any wildlife time to get out of your way. Waterfowl are particularly vulnerable in freezing conditions.

- Check that any ice rink you use is doing its best to cut down on energy. Possibilities here include not heating the skating halls, and building rinks with glass walls to cut down on the need for artificial lighting.

- And do check that plywood!

Off-road driving and biking   Zero

They call it 'The Invasion' in the States. Holidaymakers used to expect oases of tranquillity along Missouri's Black River, whether they were fishing, canoeing or just floating around in an inner tube. But all too often these days their solitude is shattered by hordes of pickup trucks hauling trailers loaded with all-terrain vehicles, or ATVs. And where the USA goes today the rest of the world goes tomorrow.

Environmentalists in California have also been outraged by the damage caused by ATVs. 'They have ample room to play,' said Bob Hattoy of the Sierra Club, 'but they feel they have the cowboy's right to ride the range wherever they want, whenever they want and how far they want.'

Cross-country motorcycling, or 'moto cross' racing, can be just as damaging. If confined to small sites, sometimes known as 'wheel parks' or 'trail parks', the main problems are soil erosion and noise. But the infamous 'Hare and Hounds' race in the United States, between Barsto and Las Vegas, can involve as many as 2,500 riders streaking through the fragile desert ecosystem. Apart from the direct damage caused to cacti, shrubs and trees, the desert soil is compacted – which can make it much harder for seeds to germinate when the rains eventually come.

In Britain, where there is often a great deal of rain, the problems are different – but could become equally serious. Often the old 'green lanes', or unpaved trading routes that criss-cross unspoiled parts of the country, are used for off-road driving and biking. Used by sheep-drovers and traders for thousands of years before the motor vehicle erupted on to the scene, green lanes were until very recently the preserve of people on foot and horseback. Now the Ramblers' Association is calling for an outright ban on the growing number of off-road vehicles that are going 'greenlaning', arguing that they are turning green lanes into quagmires.

The 'expensive, purpose-built two- and four-wheel machines', the Ramblers say, are 'ripping up sensitive landscapes and inflicting noise, pollution, disturbance and danger on legitimate users of the countryside.' As in so many other areas of our lives, a handful of people might get away with something that becomes a complete nightmare if it is allowed to take hold.

GUIDELINES

- Avoid motorised 'greenlaning' like the plague. Many of these ancient routes are extremely valuable wildlife habitats.

- Protest if you see other people churning up these relics of the distant past.

- Unless you have special consent, you are not allowed by law to ride or drive on a footpath or bridleway, across an open moorland or through a forest, but some greenlanes may not be protected.

- If you are determined to go off-road, do it through organised clubs affiliated to either the Auto-Cycle Union or the RAC Motor Sports Association, and get a copy of the guidelines produced by the Motoring Organisations Land Access and Rights Association (MOLARA), which are backed by the Sports Council and the Royal Society for Nature Conservation (RSNC).

- Use only designated vehicular rights of way – and keep to the defined track.

- Travel at a quiet and unobtrusive pace. Be courteous to walkers and take great care when passing horses.

- Even if you are riding off the road, make sure your bike or vehicle meets the legal standards on exhausts and silencers.

- Remember, too, that there is no public right to drive on common land, moorland, sand dunes or beaches.

Riding and pony trekking ★★★★

 If you want to experience the delights of the open countryside without having to walk, nothing really rivals the horse. Few sensations are as glorious as galloping across alpine meadows or catching the scent of trampled water-mint as your horse picks its way along a stream.

Once, the horse was the main form of long-distance transport. Today horse-riding is usually a leisure pursuit and the countryside is no longer designed for horses. There is only a one in fifty chance of being able to ride sixteen kilometres without coming across some form of obstacle, such as a barbed wire fence. Consequently, too many horses are often ridden in too small a space – or across sensitive sites – resulting in significant environmental damage.

In Epping Forest, Essex, for example, riders sometimes churn the footpaths into bogs. The forest conservators have mixed feelings: 'They have a love-hate relationship with the horse,' explained the forest superintendent. 'They love it for the vitality it brings to the forest, but they hate the beast for the damage it can cause.' At the moment there is no ideal solution – riding on roads in the age of the car is dangerous with over 3,000 road accidents involving horses every year in Britain alone.

One good idea, however, is a toll bridlepath scheme which has recently been set up in some parts of the country. Riders are charged £2 a week to use bridlepaths that have been opened up and kept clear. Roughly 70 per cent of the revenue goes to the farmer for keeping the tracks open, while the remaining 30 per cent goes to provide maps, signs and written instructions.

Some public bridleways originated from Britain's old 'green lanes' and pack-horse routes, used formerly by strings of ten or more pack-horses carrying everything from salt and lime to pig-iron, lead and bales of cloth. There are plans afoot to re-open the Pennine Bridleway, indicating that the tourist potential of these routes is at last being recognised.

GUIDELINES

- Poorly managed horses can trample sensitive vegetation, disturb nesting birds and turn paths into a morass. Make sure you know about any seasonal restrictions, designed to protect sensitive areas in wet weather.

- Too many horses are bought by people who forget that they have to be looked after 365 days a year. This is hard work – and it can be costly.

- Try a riding school before buying a horse, to make sure you really are up to the challenge.

- When out riding, remember that courtesy is a two-way street. Riders expect drivers to show restraint when passing, but then often forget that they can upset walkers.

- Find out where the old pack-horse routes ran and see whether you can still use them.

Shooting ★

Man's love affair with the gun goes back a long way, but the impact on nature hit new heights as the West was won in what is now the United States. Even a painter and natural-ist like Audubon, a patron saint of modern conservationists, cut a bloody swathe across the country with his guns. And thanks to Buffalo Bill and his ilk the uncountable buffalo were blasted from the Great Plains.

One of the most striking examples of wilful destruction involves the passenger pigeon, a different species from the modern-day pigeon. Once numbered in their billions, these birds literally darkened the skies for days on end as their endless flocks passed overhead. As settlers pressed west-wards, the birds were shot in their millions and shipped by rail to the cities. Many were shot for sport. The last passenger pigeon in the world died in 1914, but the bird left an impor-tant legacy. The disgust of some Americans in the wake of this bloodbath helped fuel the early growth of the conservation movement.

Many conservation groups are split on the subject of shoot-ing, though most wish that the shooting of living creatures could be brought to an end. In France, for example, some 50 million animals and birds are shot annually – indeed, French hunters are so aggressive that they also kill around thirty hunters or innocent passers-by each year! There are places in

France, Italy, Malta and Cyprus where migrating birds have to run a massed gauntlet of hundreds of thousands of guns. The total death toll may be around 900 million birds a year.

As bird numbers fall in many areas, so that only migrating birds are left to fire on, the hunters blame the farmers, while the farmers blame the hunters. The fact is that both are to blame. Not surprisingly, however, most politicians fear to get in the way of the gun and hunting lobbies. When the European Commission limited the legal hunting season for waterfowl, 100,000 French hunters took to the streets.

But there are other reasons why some conservationists are unwilling to call for a total ban. For one thing, a fair proportion of conservationists are themselves members of the hunting, shooting and fishing fraternity. For another, there are some areas where shooting actually promotes conservation through the income it generates and through helping to preserve the bird's habitat.

One example of this can be found in Britain's grouse moors, where upland moor that is preserved for grouse, rather than being turned over to sheep or commercial forestry, is also preserved for birds like the golden plover, merlin, hen harrier and golden eagle. It is a pity, though, that gamekeepers continue to shoot the wrong birds when trying to clear the moors of predators. They have shot, for example, short-eared owls, which feed on voles, not grouse. However, given that two of the most endangered habitats in Britain are heather moors and estuaries, both areas where game birds are shot, it is hardly surprising that the RSPB and other conservation groups have somewhat grudgingly decided to work with wildfowlers.

One of the key issues, if you accept that birds can be shot, is how they are shot. An incompetent shot can wound more birds than he kills, and even an experienced shot may have difficulty in identifying a bird down the barrel of a gun. This is not surprising when you consider that even trained birdwatchers may need a pair of binoculars to decide which bird is which.

And then there is the issue of lead shot. Pellets that miss their targets are scattered all over the countryside, where they are often swallowed by birds – particularly waterfowl seeking grit for their gizzards. One study found that six in every ten pochard had lead shot in their gizzards and millions of ducks, swans and other fowl die each year from lead poisoning. European conservation groups are calling for a ban on the use of lead shot by sportsmen. Denmark and the United States have already committed themselves to phasing it out from 1992 to 1993 but most of the European Community's six and a half million hunters continue to carpet the landscape with their lethal lead. Some shoots are also prone to carpeting the landscape with spent cartridges, which can only be considered as litter.

No one disputes that the shooting business has made real progress in some areas. The development of clay pigeon shooting, where the targets are made from pitch, tar and chalk, was a marked improvement on the situation where captive birds were released from cages – a practice banned in Britain seventy years ago.

GUIDELINES

- Try clay pigeon shooting rather than shooting live game, but make sure the club you join is doing everything it can to avoid becoming a noise nuisance.

- Consider switching to a lead-free, noise-free 'ray-gun'. A new firm, Laser Sport, has developed an electronic gun that can be shot at a specially wired flying plastic target. Hits are registered on an electronic scoreboard.

- If you use a shotgun or an air rifle, insist on lead-free ammunition. Make sure that your shotgun is suitable for steel shot.

- Know your prey. Make sure you know which birds or animals are protected or endangered.

- Use well-trained gun dogs, to make sure that wounded birds are found.

- Don't shoot at birds that are out of range – you are likely to only wound them.

- Pick up your spent cartridges. Even though one manufacturer, Winchester, offers cartridges with biodegradable wads, the cases are still plastic.

- Join a conservation group that is working to develop wildlife habitats and to make shooting sustainable. Find out about the local issues and see if you can tackle them.

- Turn your back on shoot-anything-that-moves holidays. One tour company offered shooting trips in Mauritius for amateurs where you could shoot everything from deer to monkeys.

- If you come across this sort of thing, let one of the leading conservation groups know what is going on.

Skiing ★★

 Until fairly recently, skiing was simply a way of getting from A to B. The big shift came after the Second World War, with the leisure revolution and the introduction of totally new ski designs and materials – particularly for downhill skiing. Today, from Aspen in Colorado to Zermatt in Switzerland, millions of fun-seekers scour the slopes in search of ideal skiing conditions.

The statistics are mind-numbing. In Austria alone, if you laid all of the country's ski-runs end to end they would stretch right around the world. Fifty million people visit the Alps each year, two-thirds of them on winter skiing holidays. The Alpine ski industry caters for over 10 million skiers with 40,000 ski-runs and 14,000 ski-lifts.

Entire regional economies are now propped up by skis, though in recent years they have been hard hit by a shortage of snow. Following their third successive year of poor snow, some French resorts sought disaster zone status in 1990. Whether or not the greenhouse effect was to blame, many resorts had to lay on summertime pursuits like hiking, canoeing and swimming in the depths of what should have been winter.

To cover their bets, Zermatt and a growing number of other resorts have invested heavily in artificial snow machines. These electrically powered sprays shoot compressed air and considerable quantities of water through a nozzle when temperatures are below freezing point. Environmentalists worry about the effect of the chemicals contained in the water and about taking all that water out of lakes and other water resources, particularly when rain is already in short supply.

They also argue that the artificial extension of the period of snow cover could cause problems. Apart from upsetting the lifestyle of local marmots, more skiers will be wearing down the snow and skiing on muddy patches. As the spring encroaches, the snow recedes up the mountains and the lower slopes are revealed, preparing for the summer flowering. Whilst skiers are allowed on the slopes, there is a great temptation to ski right down to the town rather than to descend via the ski-lift – trampling or crushing sensitive vegetation on the way.

In the Rocky Mountains, some resorts are using genetic engineering to make artificial snow. Many environmentalists oppose the use of Snowmax, a tapioca-like protein usually found in bugs in the soil but now genetically engineered and mass produced. The protein, which speeds ice-crystal formation, is then added to the water supplied to the snow-making machines. This helps convert more of the spray into useful, powdery snow. The protein is said to break down within a month of being sprayed.

Whatever one's feelings about genetic engineering, a much more damaging activity is generally the construction of the resorts themselves, often involving extensive bulldozing, blasting rocks and reshaping of the slopes. One of the longest running conservation battles in the UK centres on Lurcher's Gully, in the Cairngorms, where a ski resort has been trying to expand on to areas zoned for wildlife.

In the Alps, meanwhile, hundreds of thousands of trees have been cleared to give skiers a clear run. As a result, the natural avalanche protection provided by the forests has had to be replaced by unsightly concrete, metal or wood avalanche barriers. Experts say that two-thirds of the several thousand avalanches that thump into the inhabited part of the Austrian Alps result from deforestation. In just three weeks in 1987, landslips in the Italian and Swiss Alps killed sixty people, made 7,000 homeless and damaged fifty villages and holiday centres.

As the pressures build, several hundred animal, insect and plant species are threatened with extinction. Indeed, the Alpine environment is now on the critical list. Some conservation groups are calling for a ban on artificial snow, much stricter control on all-terrain vehicles and off-piste skiing, and a tax on ski-lifts.

And some individuals are prepared to go even further. In 1991, for example, a radical activist from America's deep green Earth First! was sentenced to six years in prison for blowing up power lines and ski resort property in Arizona. He explained that he was trying to wake people up to the death of wilderness at the hands of developers.

At last there are signs that others are waking up to the problem. Prince Sadruddin Aga Khan, for example, has launched Alp Action, to find business sponsors for Alpine conservation projects. The London-based Conservation Foundation distributed Alp Action leaflets to UK ski and alpine walking tour operators. Skiers are being asked to donate one per cent of the cost of their holidays to fund such projects as tree-planting and encouraging the return of brown bears to the Austrian mountains.

Future archaeologists will find more than the odd pair of skis when they start digging among the ruins of our civilisation. The Japanese, among the world's keenest skiers, are going indoors and opting for all-year skiing in complexes like refrigerated multi-storey car-parks. The irony is that the emissions produced when the energy used is generated could worsen the greenhouse effect, while the CFCs bleeding from their refrigeration and air-conditioning equipment waft up into the heavens and open up new ozone holes.

GUIDELINES

- Check whether tour operators and resorts have active conservation programmes.

- Donate at least one per cent of the cost of your holiday to tree-planting and other conservation projects.

- Steer clear of areas heavily dependent on artificial snow.

- Don't ski when the snow is patchy. Skiing over rocks ruins your skis, and skiing over muddy areas can churn up the mountainside, contribute to erosion and threaten plant life.

- Think about the gentler pleasures of cross-country skiing, or *langlauf*, instead of rocketing down the pistes.

- Good skiers in particular are tempted by the greater thrills of going off-piste but you should avoid this if you can. Off-piste skiers can frighten wildlife and damage saplings, contributing to deforestation, as well as precipitating avalanches.

- Don't be seduced into heli-skiing, where skiers are helicoptered to virgin slopes and picked up at the bottom of their run. It is fuel-hungry and intrusive.

Sunbathing ★★★★

 Every year, millions of people flock to the sun to build up that ultimate status symbol: a suntan. Some 40 million sun-worshippers go to Spain alone. But the evidence suggests that sunbathing can be a life-and-death business. In the UK, where skin cancer has become the second-commonest form of cancer, the Health Education Authority recently ran ads headlined: 'Are you dying to get a suntan?'

A spot check of Australians discovered that 20 per cent had some form of skin cancer. And the scientists tell us that for every one per cent of ozone depletion, the world can expect a 1–2 per cent rise in skin cancer rates. The Australians have a word for what is happening as a result: *heliophobia*, or fear of the sun. With the Antarctic ozone hole sometimes reaching up as far as Melbourne, and with skin cancer one of the commonest cancers in Australia, some people are even putting on suntan cream to go shopping.

If you wear a sunscreen or tanning lotion, buy one that has not been tested on animals. There have been some appalling stories of laboratory animals grilled alive in silver foil to test sunscreen products. Remember, too, that such products may not give complete protection. Doctors are seeing numbers of young women suffering from what is described as 'skin fragility syndrome'. This is particularly common among people who use a sun-bed three or four times a week.

One new idea is a credit-card sized sun meter, called Tanscan, made of ultraviolet-sensitive spots covered with silver latex. Sunbathers scratch off the covering to reveal a yellow dot, which gradually turns red when exposed to the sun. You can even apply your sun lotion to the dot, to show when it is losing its effectiveness. The worry, of course, is that all these flexible friends are going to end up on the sand, along with all the other litter so many sunbathers leave behind them.

GUIDELINES

- Fight to save the ozone layer. Join campaigning groups dedicated to protecting the planet's atmosphere.

- Sunbathe, don't sunbake, say the doctors. You really don't have to go red to go brown.

- Don't smear yourself with suntan oil and then dive into the water. A little oil goes a long, long way on water. If enough people wearing enough oil swim in enclosed, calm waters, they can produce an oil slick.

- Littering beaches is a real problem – don't assume

there will be someone coming along behind to pick up your debris.

- You could go to the beach equipped with a bag and gloves and pick up other people's litter. (One of the authors thinks this can be quite fun, because of the satisfaction of seeing the transformation that has been achieved. The other has done it on a number of occasions, but considers it intensely irritating – because the task is so great and some people dump litter even as the clean-up proceeds.)

Tennis ★★★

 *Anyone for tennis?* is now a worldwide cry. The game is played in over 140 countries by more than 50 million people.

Most people play on hard courts nowadays, which in some parts of the world must almost rival car-parks in terms of their appetite for land. Indoor tennis has also been a big growth area – before 1980, for example, there were only sixty-seven indoor courts in the UK, but by the end of 1990, that figure had exploded to nearly 500.

Grass courts need regular watering and fairly considerable volumes of fertiliser, fungicides and herbicides to maintain a smooth, weed-free surface.

Even with hard courts, chemicals are needed to keep the weeds at bay. Probably the least damaging chemical used is ammonium sulphamate, which breaks down to the less toxic ammonium sulphate over a period of two months. Alternatively, for annual weeds many people prefer to use a flame weeder. Hand-weeding would obviously be more energy-efficient!

Tennis racquet strings used to be made from sheep gut, not cat gut, as many people supposed. Now they are made of nylon, partly because sheep gut became too expensive. The racquets themselves are more likely to be made from carbon fibre, fibreglass, Kevlar and aluminium than wood. If a racquet goes wrong in the factory, we were told, it can often be reground and turned into a new racquet. Once it has been coated with resin, however, it becomes impractical to recycle it because the resin would need to be removed.

As far as tennis balls are concerned, the world uses prodigious numbers each year. The leading UK manufacturer, Slazenger, annually sells around three million balls in the UK – and exports an even greater number. The balls are made of Malaysian rubber, covered with a nylon wool cloth. Slazenger says it is impossible to work out exactly how long balls should last, but at Wimbledon the players get new balls after every nine games! Even the manufacturers admit that there is absolutely no need to throw them away so often. If you look after them, and avoid the use of extremely thin gauge strings which can cut into the cloth, you should be able to hang on to your balls for much longer.

In 1991 Wimbledon focused attention on one environmentally suspect tennis product. Shock absorbers for tennis elbow were found to contain very high quantities of mercury, which is very toxic. Friends of the Earth say that the amount of mercury in this sports aid is enough to pollute five Olympic-sized swimming pools. With a planned production of 100,000 units worldwide, this would amount to three tonnes of mercury ending up in the environment. At the time of writing, the Dutch government had said they would stop further sales, while the UK government was pondering what to do.

GUIDELINES

- If you have a grass court, cut back on your use of chemicals.

- If you have an unwanted aluminium racquet, it could be recyclable. If no one else can use it, take it when you next go to the civic amenity site and leave it with the metal scrap.

- Don't buy shock absorbers for tennis elbow, unless you can be sure they do not contain mercury.

- Store your tennis balls in their box or container in dry conditions to make them last longer.

Walking, hiking, rambling, trekking ★★★★★

 Walking is Britain's favourite leisure pursuit, although you would hardly guess it from the way people behave when they get out into the country. Even when visiting National Parks most people do not venture more than 400 metres from their cars, as though attached by an invisible umbilical cord to their vehicles. It's probably just as well: much of the countryside isn't what it was.

Farmers plough their fields to the very edge, uprooting hedgerows and doing their best to disguise footpaths. One recent survey found that almost a fifth of footpaths, bridleways and byways in England and Wales are unusable. Even in the wilds of the North York Moors National Park, ramblers have complained that they were (accidentally, presumably) sprayed with herbicide by aircraft. The chemicals were designed to kill bracken, which can damage grouse habitats.

About sixty years ago, ramblers staged their first mass trespass, designed to open up large tracts of the countryside to walkers, and the issue is still live and kicking. But even walking, it now turns out, can damage the environment if enough people do it – or do it in the wrong way. Just as walking boots raise blisters on sensitive feet, too many boots can wreck a sensitive landscape.

The Ramblers' Association, which campaigns for moorland to be opened up to walkers, has been working hard to persuade landowners that ramblers do not wear out the moors – and that they do not disturb birds like the red grouse and golden plover. The ramblers are also campaigning to keep ordinary landscapes open. They say that if public rights of way are 'illegally ploughed up or blocked by farmers . . . walkers are doing a favour to the general community if they trample down the crops . . . thus re-opening footpaths'.

Even they admit, however, that the sheer pressure of walkers is wearing holes in some parts of the landscape, especially in sandy or peaty areas. Vegetation on and around the path is killed underfoot as people pass, opening up the soil to erosion and exposing tree roots. Once the process starts, a path will tend to gully. Walkers then prefer to walk alongside the original path, opening out the eroded area.

As more and more people want to walk at least a short distance from their homes or cars, these problems, particularly in heavily promoted areas, can only get worse. Visitor pressure is helping to drive the demand for new roads in wilderness areas. America's national forests alone already contain enough roads to circle the globe fourteen times. One solution will be to find routes that are less vulnerable and to repair and strengthen existing footpaths. In Britain and America, for example, we are seeing the opening up of old railway lines and canal and river towpaths for walking, cycling and riding.

Another solution is to place restrictions on some of the most frequented spots. Take Arizona's Grand Canyon, visited by five million people every year. The National Park Service now limits the number of hikers who can use the trails at any one time. When you unfurl your map, it is likely to warn: 'LOOK! THINK! Pack up your trash, including toilet paper, cigarette butts, orange peel and egg shells! PLAN AHEAD! Do not interact with wildlife!'

If you can escape the overly beaten track, the world still holds some great walking, from the John Muir Trail in California to the 3,416 kilometre Appalachian Trail, from England's Pennine Way to Kilimanjaro in Tanzania, from the Tour du Mont Blanc to the Cordillera Huayhuash Trek in Peru. The problem is that today's pioneers eventually encourage others who bring with them not only soil erosion, but also many of the problems that blight the places they came from, the litter, graffiti and erosion of traditional values.

In the Himalayas, for example, poorly planned trekking has helped to accelerate tree felling and soil erosion. Fewer than one in ten climbers carry their own fuel, with most climbers using more than 100 kilograms of firewood over a fifteen-day trek. Each climber consumes, directly or indirectly, between five and ten times as much wood per day as the average Nepali. One hectare of cleared forest loses up to 75 tonnes of soil a year. At this rate, the day will yet come when you won't have to walk uphill when you get to the Himalayas.

Of course we have focused on some of the problems with hiking – but, as usual, a lot depends on who is doing the walking, how many people and where. Don't be put off. Walking is fun, healthy and generally less of a problem for the countryside than almost any other recreational pursuit!

GUIDELINES

- Follow the country code. As a minimum:
  - Guard against all risks of fire
  - Fasten all gates
  - Keep to paths when crossing farmland
  - Avoid damaging fences, hedges and walls
  - Leave no litter
  - Safeguard water supplies
  - Protect wildlife, plants and trees
  - Respect the life of the countryside

- Remove unnecessary packaging from food and other products before you leave home. Make provision for bringing the rubbish you do produce back with you.

- Keep noise to a minimum.

- Keep to marked paths, where they exist. Try to walk on the worn parts of paths or on stony ground. Avoid cutting corners on zig-zag descents.

- Contribute cash for environmental upkeep. In the Lake District, for example, people are used to seeing collection boxes for mountain rescue. Now these have been joined by boxes for footpath repairs.

- If possible, use public transport, cycle or walk to get to National Parks or other walking spots – traffic jams can be a problem, even on minor roads, during peak holiday periods.

- Keep dogs under full control.

- Choose trekking companies and lodges that use kerosene, rather than wood. Don't use firewood for heating, when putting on an extra sweater would do the trick.

- Stay on trails and camp in designated sites, especially at high altitudes where the environment is often extremely fragile.

- Don't pick wild flowers or crowd wild animals.

- Find out about local conservation issues and see what you can do to help.

- Join the British Trust for Conservation Volunteers in their repair work of footpaths in walking areas.

WILDLIFE

Whether you want to see the marine iguanas of the Galapagos Islands or the gray whales of Baja California, the range of wildlife holidays on offer has exploded in recent years. Unfortunately, in some areas the sheer pressure of visitors is beginning to have a very detrimental effect on the animals that they come so far to see.

At the same time, however, our appetite for conservation is being whetted as we see interesting fauna and flora in the wild. Fascinating success stories range from the Mountain Gorilla Project of Rwanda (page 156) to the reintroduced bison of Poland (page 133). Wildlife conservation is an area with which we must be prepared to experiment – and to learn from the successes, often hard-earned, of other countries. In some cases, as in Poland (page 133) or Zimbabwe (page 224), controlled hunting may be an essential ingredient in effective wildlife conservation.

Birdwatching ★★★★★

Most people think of birdwatchers as that relatively small group of fanatics who descend in their scores – or even hundreds – when a rare bird is spotted. They are often called 'twitchers', a tag they picked up in the 1950s when they would arrive at a favoured spot twitching with excitement and, in the winter, shivering with cold.

Although not completely disowned by the mainstream bird conservation groups, the twitchers are not exactly encouraged. Some of them are so keen to build up their scorecard of species spotted that the welfare of the birds themselves can be overlooked. One twitching party in Florida organised a drive across a marsh to flush out a rare bird, a black rail. After the main group had stomped through without forcing it out into the open, a more alert member of the party found the bird mangled and dying, trodden into the mud by a heavy boot.

Fanatical twitchers are in a minority, and birdwatching, if suitably organised and sensitively undertaken, can provide an excellent way of funding conservation. Britain's Wildfowl Trust, set up in 1946 by the late Sir Peter Scott, provides tremendous entertainment for large numbers of people at Slimbridge and a number of other sites around the country. At the same time, it also carries out first-class research on bird ecology and conservation. While some American tour operators shamelessly justify the use of helicopters in National Parks on the basis that they (occasionally) fly disabled people, Slimbridge is genuinely concerned about the disabled, to the point of offering 'birdwatching for the blind'. By using Braille notices, a cassette commentary and tactile exhibits, blind or partially sighted visitors are encouraged to build up a sense of the size, shape and texture not only of the birds but also of their nests and eggs.

As birdwatching holidays make the value of birds in the bush ever clearer, we are beginning to see real changes in people's attitudes. Trinidad and Tobago recently celebrated their amazingly rich wildlife – including 400 species of birds – with a month-long Natural History Festival.

Birdwatchers, in fact, are probably better provided for than any other type of wildlife enthusiast. For a start, we have seen live birdwatching on TV. In addition, some conservation groups and a wide range of operators offer birdwatching holidays around the world. Many are accompanied by leading ornithologists, who act as guides. Whether you are interested in the birds of East Anglia or East Africa, the Camargue or Zimbabwe, your main problem may well be in choosing between the profusion of holidays on offer.

As more and more people go birdwatching, the potential for friction with hunters also inevitably grows. In the Pyrenees, for example (page 245), birdwatchers have sometimes come to blows with hunters. Such direct action may prove to be as necessary today as that taken by some ladies in Victorian England. They did their bit to protect exotic birds by abusing – or, in some cases, even attacking – women who wore hats or dresses decorated with the feathers of rare birds.

GUIDELINES

- Abide by the bird protection laws that are now embodied in the Wildlife and Countryside Act. They are the result of hard campaigning by previous generations of birdwatchers.

- Join a bird conservation group. It is important to lobby for the proper conservation of existing protected sites – and the protection of new sites.

- Take part in local or national counts and surveys organised by bird conservation groups and send records to your county bird recorder.

- Avoid mass descents on areas where a rare bird has been spotted – remember that the welfare of birds must always come first.

- If you find a rare bird, tell the RSPB or another respected bird conservation organisation but otherwise it is almost always best to keep the record secret in order to avoid disturbance by other birdwatchers and attacks by egg-collectors.

- Do not visit breeding sites of rare birds unless you know they are adequately protected – and check with the bird protection organisations before going.

- Keep disturbance of birds, nests and habitats to an absolute minimum.

- Never take or disturb eggs, whatever species they belong to.

- Either leave dogs at home – or make sure they are under control whenever you are near birds.

- Keep to these guidelines even when you are abroad, whatever the local laws. Remember that bird-watchers can be important ambassadors for bird protection.

Gorilla watching ★★★★★

One of the best examples of how tourism can help to conserve threatened wildlife can be found in the heart of Africa.

By the end of the 1970s the mountain gorilla was close to extinction. The animals live only on the forested slopes of the Virunga volcanoes, straddling the borders of Zaire, Uganda and Rwanda. For decades, poachers – among them the Twa pygmies – hunted the gorillas, selling their heads, hands and feet to tourists and collectors. Baby gorillas, whose capture often involved the slaughter of fiercely protective adults, were sold to zoos.

American conservationist – and, ultimately, martyr for the cause – Dian Fossey spent twenty years with the great apes and eventually concluded that *gorilla gorilla berengei* was fated to become a 'species discovered and extinct in the same century'. Her book, *Gorillas in the Mist*, was published in 1983 and later filmed. To build on her efforts, the Mountain Gorilla Project (now called the International Gorilla Conservation Programme, see page 359) was set up in Rwanda's Parc National des Volcans. The central idea of the project was to make the gorillas worth more alive than dead to Rwandans. Fossey had shown how wild gorillas could be habituated to having close contact with friendly people for research purposes – and the technique was adapted to acclimatise the animals to tourists.

Although the Mountain Gorilla Project has been criticised by some conservationists, who argue that wild animals are being tamed for the benefit of tourists, it is generally seen to be a model for the protection of endangered wildlife and it can be an excellent way for us to learn about ecology and conservation at the same time.

Several groups of gorillas can now be visited by small groups of a maximum of six tourists, for just one hour a day. Even those who, by some remote chance, fail to see gorillas agree that the walk through forests of bamboo and giant heather is a magical experience. To protect the animals, visits are cut short if visitors do not behave and children are restricted to just one group. The research results are reassuring: gorilla numbers have begun to increase slightly and tourist visits appear to be having no significant effect on the stability, health or reproduction rates of the gorillas.

The money the tourists inject has also helped to build up one of the finest wildlife conservation centres in Africa. At any one time, half a dozen patrols are out looking for poachers and traps. The Rwandan government, eager for foreign exchange, has been doing its best to support the project.

Gorilla tourism received a considerable boost when the film of *Gorillas in the Mist* was released. The director of the Mountain Gorilla Project admits 'We're still dealing with a very shaky situation,' but he says 'I think it's fairly safe to say now that the mountain gorilla is going to accompany us into the twenty-first century.'

The main problem has been that demand has far exceeded supply, and with the latest threat to the gorillas – guerillas – this problem could intensify. War has come to the Parc

National des Volcans, with a group fighting the government occupying part of the park. At the time of writing only one group of gorillas can be seen in Rwanda, although tourists can still visit the other two gorilla centres, based in Zaire and Uganda.

GUIDELINES

- If you want to visit these gentle giants, make sure you travel with a reputable firm.

- When you are out with a group, keep with the ranger at all times and heed his or her advice. Remember not to point at the animals, nor to look them direct in the eye. You must never be higher than the gorillas. And if the animals become upset or seem agitated, leave.

- Don't try to touch the gorillas. There is a big concern that they may catch diseases from contact with humans.

- Donations can be made to the International Gorilla Conservation Programme (see page 359) even if you are not visiting the animals.

National Parks ★★★★★

A few years ago, almost no one had heard of the Kakadu National Park in the Northern Territories of Australia. Then the film *Crocodile Dundee* became a worldwide box office hit. Almost overnight, Kakadu became a top tourist destination.

It has happened many times before, although rarely so dramatically. National Parks were an American invention, starting out with Yellowstone Park in 1872, and have since spread around the world. More than 3,000 such areas have been created in over 120 countries, covering more than four million square kilometres – roughly similar to the size of India and Pakistan combined.

New Parks are still being created, one of the latest (and least attractive to anyone who does not own a lead suit) covering an area with a 30-kilometre radius around the devastated Soviet nuclear power plant at Chernobyl. The authorities have banned all human activities, including farming, in the area most affected by radioactive fall-out. Here the idea is partly to stop visitors being irradiated – and partly to study the evolution of irradiated plants and animals.

The benefits of Park status are perhaps clearest in California, where satellite photographs show commercial logging continuing right up to the boundaries of Yosemite, which protects many of the state's increasingly rare great redwood trees.

In Rwanda, the only place you will now find wild gorillas is in the Parc National des Volcans – and even there they are under intense pressure from poachers (page 156). Tourist revenues may help to protect the gorillas, but tourists and wildlife do not always mix happily. In Yellowstone Park, for example, bears are drawn to tourist areas by open garbage tips and campsite food caches. As a result tourists have been killed or mauled by bears (page 271). Some parks now post notices advising tourists how to avoid bear attacks. The main recommendation is to avoid attracting the bears' attention. This could prove quite tricky, given that they are apparently interested in a wide variety of smells – including the odours from cooking, cosmetics, toothpaste, sexual intercourse and even menstruation!

There has been considerable controversy – particularly in the US – over whether National Parks are for people or for animals. Most people are attracted to the Parks because they are 'wilderness areas' – and animals are an essential part of that wilderness experience. But as visitor numbers climb, and people treat the experience as a day out rather than preparing themselves properly and taking the appropriate precautions, so it becomes increasingly necessary to control some of the more dangerous animals to ensure the safety of the visitors. If someone is mauled by a bear there is inevitably an outcry, yet wilderness areas, by their very nature, are not tame. Many people feel that limiting this risk by killing or restricting the wildlife seriously detracts from the conservation value of the Parks.

Despite the obvious benefits of National Parks, some conservationists argue that they are undesirable precisely because they attract more people to wilderness areas – people who in turn bring new roads, hotels, restaurants, souvenir shops and rubbish tips in their wake. Visitors may also bring in exotic plants as seeds on their vehicles, clothes or tents. In Tenerife, more than a dozen such species have invaded the Teide National Park. The danger is that some of the invaders will out-compete plants that have been there for centuries, possibly even destroying a food-source for key insects or animals.

Around the world, National Park authorities continually have to balance the needs of the wildlife and other natural resources that are being protected and those of the visitors who provide the Parks with much of their income. Some of America's Parks are so popular that you now have to book a visit to them more than a month before you travel.

Other Parks remain remote, although the world is beginning to close in. One of the world's most imaginative Park projects is the Purnululu National Park, in the remote Bungle Bungle area of Western Australia (page 196). By contrast, most of Britain's so-called National Parks have been hopelessly compromised since the outset. While the statistics look quite impressive – with some 10 per cent of the country designated National Park – people are allowed to live in all of them, some are actively quarried, and others are used as gunnery ranges. As visitor pressure continues to build, the concern must be that these areas will either become glorified theme parks or will need much more vigorous protection.

As such areas approach overload, we will need to take Prince Charles' advice and insist on the principle of the 'long walk-in'. If some of the more vulnerable areas are made less accessible, most of the 'candyfloss and beer brigade' will settle for less exotic sites. And our National Parks will need more money. It is revealing that the total government grant for all of the UK Parks is less than the subsidy for the Royal Opera House!

GUIDELINES

- Don't use the car where you can go by train, bus or cycle – or, even better, walk.

- Visit the Park information centre before deciding where to go and what to do. In Britain there is often a mix between natural features and historic monuments, whereas most US Parks focus on nature alone.

- Stick to the roads if you are driving and slow right down when passing wild animals.

- If you are taking a picnic, make sure you remove most of the packaging before you enter the Park, and take your litter home with you.

- Buy local products, such as water and cheeses, to support the local economy.

Safaris ★★★

If you mention 'green tourism' most people assume you are talking about what have become known as eco-safaris – small groups of people travelling into the very heart of nature. Certainly, with the help of films like *Out of Africa*, safari operators in areas like Kenya's Masai Mara National Reserve have enjoyed boom times in recent years. But critics argue that some of the parks are already suffering from visitor overload.

Those who go on safari today are very different from those who went on big game safaris in Hemingway's time. Then safaris took as long as was needed to satisfy the hunters' bloodlust and yield sufficient trophies, and they cost a small fortune as a result. Today people have less time, and they don't go to kill elephants or tigers but to see 'nature, red in tooth and claw' – almost at the drop of a bush-hat. To find the best photo-opportunities, visitors tour the reserves in minibuses, known as 'combies', and are often driven from one attraction to the next at breakneck speed. The vehicles leave deep ruts which last for years and speed soil erosion. Some parks, in fact, are being turned into dust-bowls by the growing herds of minibuses.

There have been many cases when scores of minibuses have congregated around a single animal and ecologists are already reporting clear signs of stress in the animals, caused by visitor pressure, speeding vehicles and night driving. One distressed cheetah, surrounded by tourist minibuses, was even seen to kill her own cubs.

'Put any more vehicles in there,' said one tour operator of the Masai Mara, 'and you will turn it into a zoo.' Now the pressure is building further with the use of hot-air balloons, which can spook the more timid animals. Some wildlife experts fear that the more nervous animals may leave the Masai Mara for good. The number of cheetah in the Amboseli park, for example, dropped from fifteen to five in little more than a year. If the tourism authorities don't recognise that they must limit the number of tourists, they risk seeing the reserves turned into a cross between an adventure playground for off-road vehicles and a series of traffic islands on which remnant groups of psychotic animals perch.

Another key challenge will be to make the parks and game reserves seem worth protecting to local people. 'Just how does one convince the poor rural blacks living up against a game reserve fence that the area is actually for them, too?' asked one South African wildlife expert recently. 'Especially a man whose family hasn't seen meat for weeks, yet who knows there's millions of tons of the stuff being photographed by rich tourists on the other side of the fence?'

One of the most interesting experiments in this direction has been the Campfire approach, pioneered by Zimbabwe's Ministry of Environment and Tourism. The idea is to use market forces to enable rural communities to manage – and benefit directly from – wildlife.

Large wild animals, in particular, have always been a threat to local villagers – killing people and trampling crops. The Campfire approach encourages local people to take an active role in wildlife management and practise controlled hunting.

Its success was strikingly shown when the Mahenye community voluntarily abandoned its villages on the island of Ngwachumeni, near Gonarezhou National Park, to allow migrating animals the freedom of the area. Zimbabwe, it is clear, has a lot to teach the rest of Africa.

Poachers remain a massive problem in many of the game reserves of Africa, however, hunting down the rapidly shrinking herds of elephant and rhinoceros for their tusks and horns. The problem erupted into the world's headlines when poachers killed George Adamson, who had done so much to protect Africa's lions and other wild animals.

Inevitably, there has been huge controversy as international conservation organisations have tried to halt sales of ivory and other poached products, with even greater controversy following the shooting of poachers in some areas. Obviously, killing poachers will not solve the problem in the long term. The only sustainable way to protect wildlife is to make sure that governments commit themselves to wildlife conservation – and that local people have a stake in the survival of wild animals and wild places. Organised in the right way, safaris can help provide some of the income needed to persuade local people to protect their natural heritage.

GUIDELINES

- If you are going on a safari, give yourself the time to travel by foot. Bush-walking may mean that you see fewer animals than if you roared around in a vehicle, but the experience will be one you remember for the rest of your life.

- Take a camera, not a gun.

- Follow the camping guidelines on page 117.

- If you find that an area you are visiting is being damaged, or if you see signs of stress in the animals you come across, don't keep it to yourself. Ask the tour operator to make a report – and check what local conservation organisations are doing to deal with the problem.

- Pick a conservation group that is doing effective work and, if you can, give at least 5 per cent of the value of your holiday to help it ensure that the sights you have seen are still there for your children.

Whale watching ★★★★★

Imagine the excitement that seized Captain Charles Melville Scammon and his whaling crew when they stumbled on the secret breeding ground of the California gray whale, in Baja California. But their arrival spelled disaster for the whales. Within a few years the whales that gathered each year in what soon became known as Scammon's Lagoon had been slaughtered.

Paradoxically, Scammon's Lagoon and nearby San Ignacio Lagoon are now part of a Mexican National Park, the Biosfera El Vizcaino, which has become a Mecca for whale watchers. By 1990, the gray whale population had bounced back to nearly 20,000 and Baja California was attracting some 250,000 visitors a year.

The whale-watching business developed even earlier in the United States. As the whaling industry went into its death throes around North America in the 1960s, the unexpected happened: whales started reappearing in the inshore waters they had been forced to abandon. Soon people were taking to their boats with binoculars and cameras to see the whales at close quarters. They found them remarkably friendly, were deeply moved by the experience – and the whale-watching industry was born.

The industry now earns more than $100 million in the States and has spread to other parts of the world, including Patagonia, Iceland and Norway. 'If we can't sell them dead,' say the ex-whalers who now act as whale-watching guides in Norway, 'we'll sell them alive.' In addition to California's grays and the sperm whales of northern Norway, you can now choose between Hawaii's humpbacks, Vancouver's killer whales, Sardinia's sperm whales and a number of places where dolphins come close inshore.

We must hope that the countries that are still actively whaling – among them Japan, Denmark's Faroe Islands and now Norway again – will recognise that their whales could well be worth more alive than dead. But there is still a fair amount of public opposition to overcome in Scandinavia, for example, with many people convinced that whales damage the region's fishing industries by competing for fish. Encouragingly, both Japan and Iceland have recently launched whale watching tours.

Those who have seen whales like humpbacks at close quarters have found the experience profoundly moving. 'The sight of a creature which is the size, and perhaps ten times the weight, of a London bus leaping clean out of the ocean and doing a mid-air twirl can make you feel that perhaps the world is a more wonderful place than you had ever dared hope,' said writer Mark Ottaway after a trip to the North Atlantic.

Unfortunately, even this burgeoning new eco-tourism industry is now beginning to cause problems. There is strong evidence in California and off Cape Cod that the sheer number of tour boats may be upsetting the whale populations. According to the US National Maritime Fisheries Service, the boats often sail much too close to the whales. The whales are forced to split up – which is particularly worrying among breeding whales, given that a whale calf will not survive if separated from its parents for any time. The bigger tour ships used off Canada have also been unsettling humpback whales, which have responded by 'lobtailing' and other signals of annoyance or distress. While most whales would probably prefer to be harassed by tourists than harpooned, if this is to be a sustainable activity we must work out ways of balancing the interest of the visitors with the interests of the whales.

A new craze in California of shark watching could also cause problems – fear of sharks is encouraged so as to sensationalise the spectacle. If sharks continue to be seen as frightening it will be difficult to encourage their conservation, even when they are endangered. At the same time, if such entertainment can be used to communicate conservation messages, it could do a great deal to promote the future health of our seas and oceans.

GUIDELINES

- Check that whoever organises your whale watching is helping to conserve the whales, either by contributing to the relevant conservation organisations or by supporting scientific research.

- Help to conserve the whales' friendly behaviour. If your boat moves too close, complain. Today's welcoming whales could become tomorrow's marine misfits.

ATTRACTIONS

The Roman Emperors organised savage games to keep their people from thinking about more serious matters. Today, more than ever, there are any number of attractions to divert us from the big environmental issues. But, whether we are going to a bullfight or to Disneyland, we should consider the environmental balance-sheet. There are a thousand and one ways in which each of us can promote the conservation of our natural and cultural heritage.

Aquaria and sea worlds ★★★

Snap-happy visitors have caused havoc to fish in some of Japan's hundred or so enormous aquaria. When flash bulbs pop, startled tuna take off at high speed in the opposite direction and crash into the glass walls of their tanks. In one exhibit's first six months, half of the original 1,500 fish died in this way.

Japan is not alone in this field. Cities all over America are pouring millions of dollars into state-of-the-art, high-technology aquaria, the like of which we have yet to see in Europe. Florida probably has the greatest concentration of artificial oceans, but other states have also woken up to the fact that a new aquarium can be a licence to print money.

Visit Baltimore and you will find the once depressed waterfront dominated by the new National Aquarium, which cost over $20 million to build. Opened in 1981, it became Maryland's leading tourist attraction, pumping tens of millions of dollars into the state economy and creating thousands of new jobs.

The picture is the same on the West Coast. From Sea World in San Diego north to Seattle's Underwater Dome, the coastline is dotted with aquaria. Walk to the end of Monterey's Cannery Row, immortalised by writer John Steinbeck, and you will find that the canneries that once processed hundreds of thousands of sardines have been replaced by the Monterey Bay Aquarium. The brain-child of a group of marine biologists, which included two daughters of David Packard, co-founder of the computer company Hewlett-Packard, the $40 million aquarium reproduces the Monterey Bay ecosystem for an ever-growing public. Visitors learn much about the marine world, but Julie Packard harboured no illusions about their main purposes for squeezing through the turnstiles. 'People who come here ain't doing it primarily to learn,' she said. 'They're here to have fun.'

There is no doubting the ingenuity of the new breed of aqua-engineers. Consider Epcot, a few miles down the road from Sea World in Florida. Walt Disney's original concept for Epcot (subtitled 'Experimental Community of the Future') was a model city where scientists could test out future technologies and life-styles. It has been heavily watered down, but do visit the Living Seas Pavilion, billed as the 'world's sixth ocean'. Sponsored by United Technologies, the Pavilion cost more than $60 million to build and was Disney's first venture based on living creatures. It is claimed to be the world's largest man-made saltwater environment, holding 5.7 million gallons of seawater and more than 200 species of fish and mammals, including sharks, dolphins and sealions. The seawater is man-made, with 1,000 tonnes of chemicals in each filling of water. The water treatment facility is huge, big enough to service a town of 600,000 people.

Environmentalists, however, have expressed concern about the rash of aquaria and the sensationalist approach some of them take in order to attract visitors. They have called for a better balance between making money on the one hand and education and conservation on the other.

Environmental groups like Greenpeace and animal welfare groups like the RSPCA are also concerned about the welfare of marine mammals in captivity. Despite the protestations of the managing director of Windsor Safari Park that there is 'no scientific evidence to suggest that there is any reason why killer whales and dolphins need to be in water deeper than 10 metres', such groups are right to campaign for improved facilities.

Many aquaria are now steadily improving the conditions in which animals are kept and providing the public with much better information about the animals they come to see and conservation issues relating to them.

The best of the world's aquaria offer an important window into a new world – with new limits and new opportunities – as well as new responsibilities. 'We are faced with a sobering and humbling choice,' as the director of the Seattle Aquarium put it. 'We can pursue our present course of blind exploitation and commit evolutionary suicide, possibly even complete genocide – the murder of the Earth – or we can assume our full responsibility as the keepers of the ocean and preserve our existence and that of all life on the planet.'

GUIDELINES

- Shun aquaria if you think the animals are being exploited or mistreated.

- Seek out the best aquaria – those committed to education and conservation. Some carry out important ecological research and help maintain populations of rare and endangered species.

- Always check that aquaria are doing enough for

conservation in the wild. Sea World, for example, runs a Beached Animal Programme, which has come to the aid of many animals, from spinner dolphins to pygmy sperm whales.

- Ask aquaria to promote the conservation message. Seattle Aquarium, for example, encourages visitors to help clean up and protect nearby Puget Sound.

Bullfighting   Zero

 For years now, bullfighting has sparked heated controversy. Supporters argue that the sport is not simply watching a man go into the ring with a bull and kill it. Spectators want to see skill, grace and daring, so that a *corrida* is less about the struggle between man and bull than about the struggle of the matador with himself. How close will he let the bull come? But, whether the matador comes on foot or horseback, it is almost always the bull that gets it in the neck. And, despite practice in slaughterhouses on captive cattle, few matadors can kill cleanly with a single sword thrust to the heart.

Fans say that much has been done to clean up the sport, particularly in protecting the picadors' horses from being gored and disembowelled. But the RSPCA says the horses, generally animals whose working life is over, are kept in poor conditions, and significant numbers are still gored so severely that they can only be slaughtered.

No self-respecting green tourist enjoys seeing animals suffer, even if they are bred for it. Interestingly, tourists in the erstwhile Soviet Union were also recently denied the opportunity of seeing bullfights. When an attempt was made to introduce bullfighting in 1990, then President Gorbachev banned it. The Justice Ministry denounced the spectacle as decadent and medieval.

The *corrida* celebrates the spirit of the Spanish-speaking world. Culturally, the world would be the poorer if the *corrida* were to be abandoned. But this remains a cruel sport – and one that can only encourage further cruelty to animals.

GUIDELINES

- Don't go if you have any choice in the matter. Most local people in bullfighting countries leave the *corridas* to the tourists.

- Don't buy bullfighting souvenirs.

- Write to the relevant tourist office and voice your opinion.

Circuses   Zero

The ultimate threat was used against Lord Delfont, owner of the Blackpool Tower Circus, which finally closed in 1989 after ninety-four years. Lady Delfont, who agreed with the RSPCA's claim that 'The Circus is No Place for Animals', had threatened to divorce her husband unless he shut the circus down.

The main issue with circuses is the health and welfare of the animals. Although some circuses are better than others, no circus can ever provide an acceptable way of life for animals genetically programmed to live in the wild. As the RSPCA puts it, 'The need has never been greater to protect and conserve the world's wild creatures. How can we recognise this need and still permit circuses to subject animals to close confinement, constant travel and a totally alien way of life in the name of entertainment?' Worse, unlike animals in zoos, there is little chance that animals in circuses will contribute to conservation, education or research.

An animal psychologist commissioned by the RSPCA to look at circus animals in the UK shocked the animal lobby by concluding that many of the animals actually enjoyed the training and performances. She concluded that the acts were no less dignified than showjumping, dog racing or cat shows. As a result, the RSPCA softened its earlier implacable opposition to circuses and began to work more closely with some operators to improve the lot of their animals.

A key issue was whether captive-born or wild-caught animals were being used. But even captive-born animals deprived of natural stimulation develop strange behaviour like rocking, weaving, throwing the head back or chewing their own bodies. Deprived children often develop similar symptoms.

Relatively intelligent animals like chimpanzees are even more at risk when kept in the monotonous confinement of the travelling beast-wagons. Once they have been in a circus, many animals continue to show the same neuroses even when moved to better surroundings.

Circuses that include animal acts are relics of a bygone age which permitted such obscenities as bear-baiting and cock-fighting. Circus-owners may say it is better to dress up a bear in a woman's clothes than to set dogs on it, but many circuses not only impose a totally unnatural way of life on animals but also degrade and humiliate them. These animal acts, particularly with wild animals like lions, tigers or elephants, are beginning to look antiquated, too, reflecting man's desire to show dominance over nature. It is interesting that many children when asked what they enjoyed most at the circus recall the trapeze artists or the clowns.

The picture is much worse elsewhere in the world. Compared to the RSPCA, anti-circus groups in other countries are either non-existent or dreadfully underfunded. The Soviet Society for the Protection of Animals operates from a tiny flat in north-east Moscow. It faces the mighty resources of Soyuzgostsirk, the state organisation that runs the Soviet Union's seventy permanent and thirty-two travelling circuses – which use 7,000 animals belonging to 140 species. Two Soviet journalists who investigated the circus world in the USSR uncovered horrific examples of cruelty to animals – and concluded that animals are much better off in the wild, where poachers are sometimes punished, than in circuses, where the animals are unprotected.

Circus operators in some countries have been accused by environmental groups such as WWF of importing gorillas and other animals as contraband just before the countries joined the Convention on the International Trade in Endangered Species (CITES). And many foreign circuses would also be vulnerable under the Trade Descriptions Act. In Italy, for example, Circus Medrano advertises *I terribile squali*, or terrifying sharks. You are unlikely to be too terrified by the single listless shark housed in a cramped tank, absolutely motionless except for its gills. Even Madame Tussaud's could teach Medrano a trick or two.

Various attempts have been made to develop animal-free circuses. One example, Archaos, is a bizarre mix of gunpowder, chainsaws and rock music. The President of the Circus Society commented: 'They're not a circus, they're a loony theatre.' He added, with some amusement, that Gerry Cottle tried an animal-free circus in the early 1980s 'and he lost thousands – it was one of the weirdest shows I've ever seen'. But then the President of the Circus Society would say that, wouldn't he?

GUIDELINES

- If your children ask you to take them to a circus that features animal acts, tell them the facts and see if they are still enthusiastic. Most children are extremely sensitive to animal cruelty.

- If you must go to a circus, either choose one that is animal-free or one that devotes a great deal of attention to the welfare of its animals.

- Never go to – or stay at – a circus that you discover to be using endangered species. If you find one, report it.

- Watch out for signs of ill-treatment or illness in any performing animals you do see.

Galleries and museums ★★★★★

 It seems that too many rare and beautiful things in too small a space can cause a physical reaction – involving dizziness and even a loss of balance. The existence of Stendhal Syndrome, as it has been named, was confirmed in recent years after a study of tourists in a psychiatric ward in Florence.

At the same time too many people in too small a space can damage unique and priceless works of art. It's not simply a question of lunatics throwing acid at a painting by Rembrandt or chipping a toe off a statue by Michelangelo. Scientists have long known that the breath of ordinary visitors was damaging the priceless paintings, whether in Rome's Sistine Chapel or the Lascaux Caves of the Dordogne (see page 120). But now they have found that wet clothes worn by visitors also emit sulphides, chemicals which corrode precious silverware, blacken paintings and destroy valuable photographs. They also note that the main source of air pollution in most galleries and museums is what they call 'bio-effluents' – and the rest of the world knows as the humble fart.

Getting conditions like temperature and light right inside a museum obviously takes a good deal of money, something that even some of the best-stocked museums and other collections are remarkably short of. As a result, it seems inevitable that we will need to pay more to see and enjoy the treasures of the past.

Until recently, most museums – designed as homes for the Muses, or seats of learning – were dead, boring worlds, full of stuffed creatures staring out of vast glass cases with dull glass eyes. The implicit message was that the only animal worth having was one that was stuffed and mounted. But now the museum industry is beginning to haul itself into the modern world. In the UK, for example, the Natural History Museum has opened an Ecology Gallery which uses a 20-metre video wall to illuminate the interdependence of everything living on this earth.

We are also seeing the spread of open-air museums. Some,

like the Weald and Downland Open Air Museum in Sussex, are devoted to historic buildings and traditional crafts such as spinning and horseshoe making. You can even taste the past: the museum has a working mill and sells stoneground flour.

Other 'museums', like the one in Grizedale Forest, Cumbria, offer extraordinary sculptures made by artists like Andy Goldsworthy from natural materials such as wood, grass, twigs and rocks. Over sixty artworks are spread out along a 14-kilometre trail, in such a way that you can never see two at the same time – and have to hunt around for many.

Most startling of all, if you happen to be passing without knowing what to expect, is an open air 'gallery' near Albuquerque in New Mexico. Built on the high desert plain, the Lightning Field is composed of four hundred gleaming steel rods set in a rectangular grid over a mile-long area. It attracts both single and multiple lightning strikes, particularly during the stormy evenings of August and September. An extraordinary illustration of the ways in which art can illuminate nature.

More traditional museums or galleries can play a vital role in preserving records of our heritage, educating us about the places we visit and the pressures on them. They can also demonstrate the diversity and value of other cultures or societies. By enhancing our understanding of the past, they help us prepare to protect the future.

GUIDELINES

- Support the conservation of our heritage by contributing to the upkeep of museums, if you can.

- If possible, visit museums and galleries during off-peak seasons and periods.

- Abide by museum rules, like not touching the exhibits, because the rules are usually set to protect what you have come to see.

- Suggest to the staff of any museums you visit that they feature environmental themes. If they have done so, and effectively, compliment them.

- Encourage galleries to consider exhibitions of wildlife or environmental art – and to donate a proportion of their takings to the cause of conservation.

- Take off wet outdoor clothing and leave it in the cloakroom!

- Support initiatives which, like the Grizedale Forest or Lightning Field projects, are designed to ignite people's interest in the natural environment.

Holiday camps and theme worlds ★★★★

 Holiday camps represent one of the British tourism industry's most eccentric but enduring products. They certainly have a major image problem. The American travel writer Paul Theroux spoke for many when he described Butlin's as a combination of 'the security and equality of a prison with the vulgarity of an amusement park'. But there are those for whom the ideal holiday is Hi-de-Hi good cheer and entertainment laid on, from donkey rides and beauty contests to bingo and sing-alongs.

Although much of the industry seems to be stuck in a 1950s time-warp, some companies are trying hard to give their camps a facelift. Butlins, for example, commissioned new red coats from designer Zandra Rhodes and has concentrated much of its new investment in four huge centres, each able to accommodate around 7,000 people. Increasingly, too, the industry talks in terms of 'centres' and 'worlds', rather than 'camps'.

A few years ago, a Dutch company – Center Parcs – introduced its much more imaginative holiday village concept to the UK market, each built around a 'Subtropical Swimming Paradise', with whirlpools and waterslides, housed in a vast dome. The idea began in Holland in 1967 and spread to Belgium and France.

Given that Center Parcs aims to put its developments into

the heart of unspoiled nature, it is scarcely surprising that conservationists have become concerned about possible environmental impacts. There have been major disputes over the siting of theme parks, particularly about the increased traffic they encourage and the problem of the buildings looking out of character with their natural surroundings. But if such schemes are properly planned and managed they should be able to operate cheek-by-jowl with nature reserves.

And though they use a fair amount of energy, particularly in the Swimming Paradises, the energy balance is likely to be better than it looks, because the holidaymakers are concentrated in one complex. They do not need to fly abroad or use their cars to get to the 'beach'.

Meanwhile, the Disneyland theme park concept is spreading to Europe, with a major Disney resort near Paris and the Millenium Centre opening in Italy's Po Valley. The sheer size of these projects is ensuring that they raise the hackles of environmentalists.

But if such theme parks can be used – rather like the sugar coating on a pill – to get across otherwise unpalatable environmental messages, perhaps we should welcome them. At the same time, the benefits of concentrating tourists in one area and often closer to home can help outweigh the admitted problems. There is also no doubt that a green version of 'imagineering' or 'edutainment', two terms coined by the Disney people, could have a very positive educational impact.

A hint of what the future may hold can be seen in the Arizona desert, where a mini-world called Biosphere II has been constructed. Although the public are not allowed into Biosphere II itself, the complex – built around six environments, including a rainforest and a 10-metre deep 'ocean' – has inevitably attracted a great deal of interest and visitors. The plan is for scientists to live in the complex for two years, and have no physical contact with the outside world. Whether they succeed or fail, we will learn more about the earth and work out ways of creating new urban habitats for ourselves.

Indeed, it may only be a matter of decades before the planet is orbited by the ultimate in upmarket leisure worlds that really live up to their name, although the environmental costs likely to be involved in putting these new Edens into orbit beggar the imagination. Our bets are on the Japanese getting there first, as the Land of the Rising Sun increasingly sets its sights on fun (see page 201).

GUIDELINES

- If you are booking a holiday at a holiday camp, Center Parc or other centre, check whether it has an environmental policy.

- Choose one where you can walk or cycle to most of the places you are likely to want to go.

- Ask if people arriving by train are catered for with a service to pick them up from the station.

- Ask whether a proportion of the company's profits are ploughed back into conservation measures.

- See if any educational facilities are getting across the right sorts of messages. If they are, congratulate the staff. If not, think how they could do better.

- Also ask what they are doing to improve the energy efficiency of their buildings.

Monuments and sites ★★★★★

 Would you mind if a developer tore down the Parthenon or the Pyramids? Of course you would, yet both these ancient Wonders of the World – and many others – are being destroyed by rock-eating fumes and by the sheer pressure of people crawling over them. Indeed, if there is one thing that the Parthenon, Stonehenge, the Lascaux Caves, the Sphinx and the Nazca Lines in the Peruvian desert have in common it is that none of them was designed to cope with the pressure of hundreds of thousands of tourists.

A number of these treasures took hundreds – or even thousands – of years to build and seem colossal achievements even in today's world, yet they could be wrecked in a matter of decades. Stonehenge, for example, was developed over a period of 2,000 years and even today the means of its construction remains a mystery. Yet the scale of the achievement is overshadowed by the sheer volume of traffic and tourists streaming around and through the site. The sacred site has been stripped of its dignity and surrounded by the usual clutter of refreshments stands, gift shops and posters – and barbed wire. A synthetic 'Foambridge' was proposed as an alternative attraction, but the idea was rejected by English Heritage.

In Peru, some of the images among the world-famous Lines of Nazca, 'drawn' on the desert floor by Indians up to 2,400 years ago, are around eight kilometres long. The Lines survived for so long because they were remote from people and protected by the rarefied climatic conditions. Now, however, air pollution has started to cause dramatic changes in the frequency of rain, and many visitors drive unchecked across the plains, erasing the images with their churning tyres.

Even Egypt's ageless Pyramids are now threatened. Nearby factories and old vehicles spew out huge volumes of noxious air pollutants, which become particularly corrosive when dissolved by rain. Vibration from the traffic produces cracks in even the toughest monuments. And the sheer pressure of people walking over the ancient site would be enough to reduce blocks of stone to dust.

But perhaps the greatest threat to the Pyramids is the destruction caused by salt deposit erosion, which in turn is caused by the rising water table in many parts of the Nile Delta. An estimated 80 per cent of Cairo's incoming water leaks from crumbling pipes, and its sewerage system, built nearly eighty years ago to cope with a population of half a million, now chokes on the wastes produced by 13 million people.

The Aswan Dam – built to produce energy – is also suspected of helping to raise the water table. As the groundwater rises, it dissolves mineral salts from the soil and bedrock. In hot climates, ancient buildings act like sponges, sucking the salty water from the ground. When the water evaporates, it leaves the salts behind, where they crystallise and cause a slow explosion process inside bricks and stone. Nearly a fifth of the wall paintings in the tomb of Nefertari, in Egypt's Valley of the Queens, have been destroyed by salt deposits. Now even the Sphinx's head is in danger of falling off.

By the late 1980s, several million people came to look at – and breathe on – Egypt's treasures. Just a few people breathing inside a tomb for an hour can raise the humidity significantly, providing a wonderful environment for the bacteria, algae and fungi that grow on paintings. 'Three thousand people a day visit King Tut's tomb,' said the man who is responsible for the antiquities of the Giza Plateau. 'They sweat. I can't prevent that, but it is destroying the tomb.' The Egyptian government, which increasingly sees its 10,000 ancient sites as a non-renewable resource, fears for their future – but cannot cope with the scale of the impending disaster on its own.

In Hawaii the authorities are tackling a different kind of problem, and have come up with a clever wheeze to preserve their treasures. They spread the rumour that if people continued to chip the lava from a sacred site they would be cursed by the volcano god. Some bits of rock were subsequently returned!

In Paris, too, over 100 people a minute enter Notre Dame during opening hours. It's bad enough that the fumes from their coaches damage the outside of the cathedral, but on an average summer day the visitors themselves present the cathedral with 292 kilograms of vapour, 225,000 litres of carbon gas and leave behind an indelible residue of grease. In addition to the environmental issues, visitors pay little attention to the fact that the building is a place of worship, talking through the services and treating it with as much (or as little) respect as they would a museum.

St Paul's Cathedral in London is also suffering from the volume of tourists, though the curators of Notre Dame are said to envy St Paul's the one hundred steps to the door, which deter some visitors. The crowds that do make it are apparently wearing down the historic floor by importing grit and salt on the ridged soles of their trainers. The

National Trust has recognised this problem too and is considering issuing over-shoes to trainer wearers, in addition to the slippers it already gives to high-heel wearers.

Even the British government is worried about the growing impact of tourism on the country's heritage of historic monuments and beauty spots. Although ministers accept that the tourist industry brings immeasurable pleasure to visitors and much-needed income to the areas visited, they fear there may be a backlash against tourists. 'Some rural beauty spots attract visitors like bees to a honeypot,' said the employment minister. 'This can cause overcrowding, traffic congestion and erosion of footpaths.' But it is clear that the government wants more growth in tourism. 'I don't believe there is any absolute limit on the number of tourists that can be absorbed into Britain,' the minister concluded. 'I am sure there is tremendous scope before even the honeypots become full.'

Tell that to the people stuck in the honeypots.

GUIDELINES

- Accept that some fairly unpopular decisions may need to be taken in this area. Maybe the best thing for the Sphinx, for example, would be to bury it again. In many cases numbers of visitors will have to be restricted by introducing a cost or raising prices.

- Ultimately, many ancient monuments and beauty spots may have to be closed to the public for their own good. Visits to others will have to be rationed.

- If you plan to visit such a site, avoid peak periods.

- Respect the rights of those who live around – and use – such monuments.

- Fight plans to commercialise ancient or sacred sites.

- Never take any part of any monument away with you, whether you picked it up yourself or were offered it by hawkers.

- Find out about and support groups that help

countries such as Egypt to organise travelling exhibitions in order to raise funds for conservation work.

Smokestack tourism ★★★★★

As the tourism honeypots disappear beneath swarms of visitors, government ministers have been suggesting that people visit power stations instead of palaces, sewage works and coal mines instead of beaches. Not a bad idea.

Many of us visited factories as school-children – often those that made sweets or chocolate. Most of us are fascinated to see other people at work, as long as we have a guide who can bring the subject alive. You can visit ropemakers in Hawes, North Yorkshire; a silk mill at Crayford, Kent; or a pencil maker in Keswick, Cumbria. Food factories, though, are a bit more of a problem. In these days of food tampering, with major brand names being held to ransom by poisoners, the food industry is less keen to allow the public into the factory proper. So companies are building separate visitor centres, like Cadbury World, to cater for the demand in industrial tourism.

Less popular, so far, are areas where visitors can see the uglier sides of our industrial world. But we are already seeing guided tours to the evacuated areas around the Chernobyl nuclear reactor in the Soviet Union.

In fact some communities in other countries already earn so much money from local environmental dereliction that they are going to great lengths to keep their problems on the map. Take Queenstown, in the south-west of Tasmania. Pollution from a local copper smelter killed most of the vegetation around the town. Then a bush fire and heavy rains followed, leaving the area looking exactly like a lunar landscape. The area began to draw in tourists, curious to see the phenomenon, and the local community reaped the benefits. Unfortunately for them, many years after the smelter was closed down, the vegetation began to recover in places.

Worried that they might lose their tourism income, local people tried to kill the vegetation again with weedkillers.

In most places, however, smokestack tourism helps to provide money for environmental regeneration. In Britain, where the Industrial Revolution began, smokestack tourism is becoming a growth industry in its own right. You can visit quarries, coal-mines, whisky distilleries, potteries, car factories and even nuclear power plants.

Even less romantically, you can now visit some of the sewage treatment plants that help clean up our environment. Britain has built up an unenviable reputation as the worst polluter of the North Sea: find out why. Go and talk to the people of whom the old sewermen would say: 'It may be crap to you people, but it's just bread and butter to them.'

Alternatively, try Sellafield. In 1986 Britain's nuclear inspectors warned British Nuclear Fuels that they would shut the nuclear fuel reprocessing plant unless the company made a whole series of changes to its machinery, safety measures and management. With the company's reputation at an all-time low, British Nuclear Fuels – which had previously been extremely secretive – took the advice of the advertising industry and opened its doors to the public. The result: a local tourism boom in Cumbria and a growth in the number of people who felt nuclear power has an important role to play.

Sellafield's visitor centre has been a very successful public relations exercise but, not surprisingly, the views of Friends of the Earth and Greenpeace are not given much of an airing in their information centre on nuclear energy. A visit to the Centre for Alternative Technology in Wales would perhaps be more informative about the range of sustainable energy options open to us.

GUIDELINES

- Ask your local tourist board or the national Tourist Boards for information on smokestack tourism opportunities.

- Be imaginative. Visit sites that illuminate the links

between our industrial past – and present – and the problems we face.

- If you visit an operating factory or site, ask what they are doing to protect the environment.

Zoos and rare breed centres ★★

Zoo keepers are not a happy breed. Not only has the Green Party threatened to shut down Britain's zoos in the unlikely event that they win power, but the European Commission has – so far unsuccessfully – proposed a law that could close 40 per cent of the zoos in Europe!

Ironically, probably the people who have done most to damage the future prospects of zoos are TV naturalists. By showing us animals in their natural habitats, they have opened our eyes to the fact that many zoos are little more than animal prisons. Once, London Zoo ranked among the top tourist attractions in London, alongside Buckingham Palace and Tower Bridge. No longer. Visitor numbers have plummeted from more than three million every year in their heyday in the 1950s to around one million today.

As the turnstiles have clicked less frequently, so zoo-keepers have found themselves forced to invest more to satisfy an increasingly sophisticated public and at the same time keep up with inflation. An elephant costs £6,000 a year to feed – and even an ant's diet costs £15.

Many people were delighted when they heard that London Zoo might close, but Britain's zoos remain dramatically better than many others around the world. In Moscow Zoo, for example, the reptiles – including the crocodiles – went off both food and sex because of the cold, cramped conditions in which they were kept. Conditions in zoos like Limassol Zoo in Cyprus and Limburgse Zoo in Belgium, which operate on a shoe-string budget, are even worse.

Some animals, such as polar bears, should never be kept in

zoos. No zoo can keep such an active and inquisitive species mentally healthy. It is thought that six out of every ten polar bears held in zoos are deranged, while bear cubs born in zoos are twice as likely to die as those born in the wild.

Apart from the conditions in which the animals are kept, critics like Zoo Check point to the link between zoos in some countries and the international trade in endangered species. If the animals are taken from the wild many will have been killed, by animal trappers or in transit, before any arrive at the zoo. Even transporting animals from one zoo to another can be stressful for animals and they do not always survive the journey. Now even China is coming under enormous pressure to stop lending giant pandas to foreign zoos.

The other side of the coin is that many zoos now breed their own animals – indeed, they defend their existence by pointing to successful campaigns to reintroduce zoo-bred animals like the Arabian oryx and the Hawaiian goose into the wild. Unfortunately, zoos are often more successful in breeding such animals than they are in teaching them to survive once released into the wild. So a few pioneering zoos are now offering Outward Bound-like courses for animals due for release.

Some zoos will survive, even so. The best zoos have often been developed by individuals with an extraordinary rapport with animals, among them Gerald Durrell at Jersey Zoo and John Aspinall – whose Kent zoo, Howlands, has tried to put animals before people. If you visit Arnhem Zoo in Holland, you will find a man-made rainforest ecosystem housed in a vast plastic bubble. The forest, which houses 1,600 species, has doubled the zoo's visitors to 1.6 million a year.

The foremost zoos are replacing turn-of-the-century cages with so-called 'immersion' exhibits, which show animals in simulated natural habitats. At the Bronx Zoo's Jungle World and Seattle Zoo's African Savannah you can see how animals have adapted to their natural surroundings – and learn how human incursions now threaten them.

Groups like the Sierra Club and Zoo Check lay down a number of guidelines for acceptable zoos. If zoos house species that are endangered or rare in the wild, for example, they should run captive breeding programmes and aim to reintroduce them into the wild. The animals must be kept in natural and social conditions which are as close as possible to nature.

Given that we are keeping these animals in an artificial environment, we may even need to provide artificial stimulation. This may mean bears being allowed to hunt for food, cheetahs being given exercise machines and chimps being allowed to watch TV! Perhaps most importantly, all zoos should become actively involved in preserving the natural habitats to which they may restore captive-bred animals.

In the future, many zoos will be primarily committed to conservation. Their educational and entertainment aims will also be important, but secondary. Some zoos may even be animal-free. One proposed 'insect' zoo would use the latest advances in video, holographic and computer technology to entertain and educate visitors. Viewers would 'drive' video cameras fitted with periscope lenses through microscopic underwater worlds, magnified to hundreds of times their normal size. 'Lions and vertebrates are boring compared with invertebrates,' enthused micro-zoo pioneer Bob Golding. 'Seeing slugs copulating or insect larvae feeding is absolutely riveting!'

GUIDELINES

- If you are planning to visit a zoo, call first and ask what they are doing in the fields of animal welfare, captive breeding and nature conservation.

- Only visit zoos that try to keep animals in conditions as close as possible to their natural habitats – and that invest heavily in environmental education.

- If you suspect that animals are being abused or misused, take photographs and send them to groups like Zoo Check or the RSPCA.

- Visit specialised zoos, like Cornwall's Monkey Sanctuary, founded in Looe nearly thirty years ago by Leonard Williams. Monkeys from the Sanctuary have been reintroduced to a Brazilian reserve.

- Look out for – and visit – city farms and other ventures that aim to introduce children to ordinary domestic and farm animals. Make a beeline for the growing number of Rare Breed Centres, which conserve the farm animals of the past and – maybe – future.

- Support good zoo projects in the developing world, which only keep animals from their region or country. They can become focal points for local nature conservation programmes and can keep animals in conditions much closer to those for which they are adapted. And local people can be helped to see the value of wild animals alive rather than dead.

- Join organisations, like Zoo Check and the RSPCA, that are committed to cleaning up the zoo industry.

5
DESTINATIONS

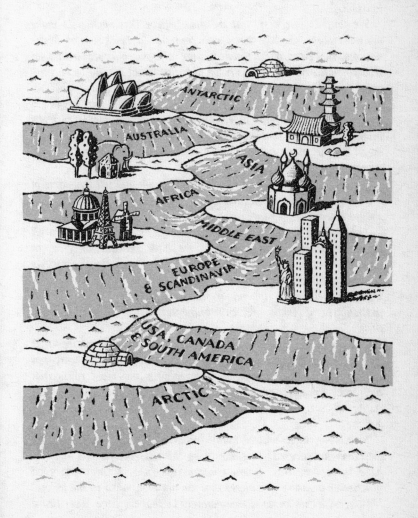

Whichever way you plan your holiday, once you have decided to go on holiday your choice of destination is probably the most important decision you will make.

At this point most people expect to be given a checklist of where to go and where not to go. They want to be told that Brighton is fine, for example, but Bombay is bad. That the Galapagos Islands are off-limits, but the Kalahari Desert is open for green tourism.

We will do our best, but we also believe that such lists make matters worse. So we have not compiled a black-list of destinations that are over-crowded, nor are we offering a list of recommended beauty spots. If we did, we would simply be encouraging holidaymakers to abandon today's black-spots, possibly knocking the bottom out of their economies – and ensuring that they have no hope of recovery. Meanwhile, hordes of well-intentioned green tourists would stream off to the empty green areas on the map, helping to turn them into tomorrow's black-spots.

Instead we look in turn at each world region and tell you some of the things you should be aware of – and some of the things you should beware of.

This section is not designed to be used as a guide book to all that's green worldwide. Rather, we have set out to give an impression of how tourism affects the environment in the various world regions to which most of us are keen to travel. Generally, we have focused on the major tourism attractions of each area, particularly if there are environmental issues associated with them.

In many cases, the interesting projects and other initiatives that we have spotlighted are very small. Typically, too, they are not well known. They may thus appear bigger and more influential than they are. Nevertheless, we feel that they are worth publicising as early examples of 'green' or sustainable tourism in action.

Inevitably, there will be many initiatives – and problems – that we have not covered. In some cases this was because we did not have the space. But if you come across cases of industry good practice or pioneering projects that are not mentioned in the following pages, let us know. It may simply be that we have never heard of them – and that is something we want to set right as soon as possible!

THE ARCTIC AND ANTARCTICA

Once, only the extraordinarily brave and the completely fool-hardy went to the Poles – and many died there. Today, however, growing numbers of tourists are following in the frozen footsteps of those early pioneers. As a result, the ultra-stressed environments of the North and South Poles are coming under even greater pressure.

Most visitors to the polar environments tend to eat, sleep and shop aboard ship, with the excursions – for obvious reasons – tending to be fairly brief. Visitors want photographs, not frostbite. But anyone who thinks of the Poles as worlds apart, untouched by pollution and other human ills, should know that the evidence now points in very much the other direction.

Pollution with your ice?

Scientists who have studied the Greenland ice cap, for example, have found that lead levels in ice cores rose from low levels in 1750 as the Industrial Revolution spread across Europe and North America. But the lead pollution found in the Greenland ice really took off when lead was added to petrol in America during the 1930s – and then soared as the number of cars around the world exploded in the 1950s and 1960s. Since lead-free petrol was introduced in the early 1970s, however, the ice cores show that lead levels have fallen to less than one seventh of their peak concentrations.

But that doesn't mean that the Arctic is unpolluted – far from it. When two balloonists soared above the North Pole recently they were stunned to find a yellow smog wreathing the horizons. Like the tourists, the smog drifts up from Europe, North America and the erstwhile Soviet Union. 'It used to be said that the North Pole was somewhere God goes to escape mankind,' noted balloonist Paul Lavalle, 'but he may have to change his destination in the light of what we've discovered. When you are in a balloon you have a 360° horizon. When we looked towards Europe, all we could see was sort of yellow fog.'

Magnetic attractions

As interest rises in seeking novel experiences, it is not surprising that the Poles are increasingly on the intrepid traveller's agenda.

In the wake of the oil industry, regions like Alaska attract people who are searching for a different form of natural wealth – in the form of the wilderness experience. On the other hand, some people go to the Arctic or Antarctica simply to be able to say they have been. If you are heading north from Europe, Spitsbergen – a group of islands in the Arctic Ocean – is probably the furthest you can go without funding a major expedition.

The Arctic holds many attractions, not least the extraordinary displays of the Aurora Borealis. And if you like to burn the candle at both ends, Spitsbergen offers 24-hour days from April to November. Most people, however, prefer a greater degree of comfort than they are likely to find inside the Arctic Circle. Iceland may be a better bet. If you stop off there on your way to the Arctic Circle, you will find you can swim out of doors all through the year. Some of Iceland's swimming pools are heated by water from natural hot springs and reservoirs.

But as the tourism industry begins to spread its tentacles into the remotest world regions, the environmental pressure is inevitably building. The number of people visiting Iceland has doubled in the last five years, and since most of these visitors want to arrive in July or August some areas are now suffering from overcrowding – among them Lake Myvatn and the area around Gulfoss, the famous waterfall.

If you do not like arriving and travelling around with the rest of the world, book off-peak – being in the Gulf Stream, Iceland is warmer than you might expect outside the peak tourism season.

The Antarctic 'Riviera'

Antarctica, at the other end of the globe, is hardly the ideal holiday spot. It is the world's remotest, highest, windiest and iciest continent. The Antarctic ice sheet covers over five million square miles – and is an average of a mile thick!

But that doesn't seem to stop people coming. Although tour operators are keen to point out that if you add up all the people who had visited the Poles since 1959 you would be lucky to reach 20,000, in recent years the numbers have been growing rapidly. Nearly 3,000 people went to Antarctica in 1990, and over 4,000 were expected for 1991. These numbers are expected to increase at least ten-fold before long.

Chilean aeroplanes began flying visitors to the Antarctic peninsula in the mid-1950s, with the first regular cruises arriving around a decade later. The cruises took off – and now tourists in America are paying tens of thousands of dollars for their tours. The ports of call are concentrated along the peninsula, which has been dubbed the 'Antarctic Riviera'!

Inevitably, some of the early attempts to take tourists into the heart of Antarctica ran into problems. The Australians, for example, were particularly keen on flying over the continent's frozen mountain ranges – until an Air New Zealand jumbo jet flew straight into Mount Erebus, killing all 256 people on board. Not surprisingly, the numbers booking such tours fell off steeply, but this hiccup has not taken the wind out of the tourism industry's sails.

The Australians have talked of building a huge runway in Antarctica, capable of taking Boeing 747s, alongside a five-storey building able to house 500 guests. The fact that such plans get a cool – not to say frosty – reception from environmentalists and many polar scientists will probably not stop them. Indeed, there is now an even more grandiose scheme on the stocks, called 'Project Oasis', to build a tourist city in Sydney and float it across to Antarctica.

Antarctic footprints

Even the relatively few visitors who have already set foot in the Poles have left an unmistakable mark on some parts of the world's least disturbed continent. Some visitors, clearly, are worse than others. One scientist reported seeing the crew of a Chinese ship playing football – with a live penguin as the 'ball'.

Less extreme – but more damaging long term – is the impact of visitors on the vulnerable Polar vegetation – grasses, mosses and lichens. A stray footprint on a mossbed is often visible a decade later. And, all too often, money can bend the rules. One cruise even offered helicopter flights over a penguin rookery, a flagrant breach of international law.

Photographers, particularly the sort of photographer who has to get spectacular shots in a rush, can be a real headache. Many are so eager to catch a good picture that they push right into the middle of colonies of sleeping seals or brooding penguins, which can lead to the penguins abandoning their eggs. Given the extremes of the polar environment, photographers may seem to be the least of the penguins' problems, but animals living in extreme conditions are often particularly vulnerable to disturbance. So if you want good photographs, make sure you take your zoom lens.

A licence to cruise

The Polar problem has been high on the list for many campaigning environmentalists. Following an international campaign, spearheaded by WWF and Greenpeace, the Antarctic Treaty nations have agreed that all tourist ships should obtain 'environmental impact certificates', and that the building of airstrips should be subject to much tighter control.

Nor are environmentalists resting on their laurels. The US Environmental Defense Fund is already calling for much stricter limits on the size and frequency of tours – and for civil and criminal penalties for operators who fail to comply with the rules. Most tour operators, it has to be said, are doing a good job and are following guidelines agreed with the polar scientists. But there is always the danger that some operators will 'push the envelope', seeing just how much they can get away with.

There is absolutely no reason why genuinely interested travellers should not book a holiday in Antarctica or the

Arctic. The more people who understand these extraordinary places – and support efforts to conserve them – the better. But if we choose to travel to such places we are under a special obligation to check that those who take us there – and those who guide us around – recognise their own responsibilities for leaving these ice-bound worlds as they found them.

AUSTRALIA

Tourism is a boom industry in Australia. Just fifteen years ago the country received fewer than 500,000 overseas tourists a year, many of whom came on business or to visit relatives. By 1985 this figure had more than doubled – and it doubled again, to over 2 million, by 1988. By the year 2000, Australia could be hosting as many as 6.5 million visitors a year, equivalent to one third of the country's estimated population at that time.

Only sheep beat tourists
Even today, Australia is a long way away from most places. It takes over twenty hours to fly from Britain to Melbourne, for example. Not surprisingly, much of the tourism activity in Australia is accounted for by domestic demand. Even so, international tourism is now the country's second largest export earner, after wool.

Like Antarctica, Australia is sparsely populated. This vast island continent, which covers 7.7 million square kilometres, still boasts enormous stretches of undisturbed natural environment. In Tasmania, the island state off the southern tip of Australia, there are still many places where no man – or woman – has ever trodden. There is a strong environmental movement in Tasmania – people have rallied together to support forest conservation and against the development of hydro-electric dams.

Although Australia has its own rainforests, many tourists

fail to stray far from the Eastern belt of cities, among them
Sydney, Melbourne and Brisbane, and the many east coast
resorts. And those who do emerge, perhaps visiting Ayers
Rock or Alice Springs, often fail to appreciate the sheer size
and diversity of this extraordinary continent.

Inevitably, there are seasonal peaks in tourism arrivals.
These, coupled with a relatively small host population, result
in a concentration of the social and environmental impacts.
Insensitive development has affected many of the most popular areas, with an estimated 30,000 kilometres of the New
South Wales and Queensland shoreline blighted by what
some dub 'architectural pollution'.

Green magnets

The first stop for around half of the country's international
visitors is Sydney. Partly as a result, Australia's most popular
tourist attraction is the Sydney Opera House. Apart from the
problems that any major city will face in hosting large
numbers of tourists, Sydney has had major problems with its
polluted beaches (see page 109). Some Australians, however,
are waking up to the fact that tourists can be attracted by
'green magnets'. Townsville in Queensland, for example, has
planted 200,000 trees, to attract more tourists.

If you want to see Australia's answer to Disneyland, walk
through the gaping mouth of Melbourne's Lunar Park. But
green tourists are more likely to enjoy Adelaide's Bicentenary
Conservatory which houses a young sprouting rainforest of
ferns, palms, shrubs and flowers under a glass curved roof.
Sponsored by BP Australia, the complex combines state-of-
the-art technology with state-of-the-earth greenery. The aim
is to help students and the general public to understand the
special environment of the world's rainforest regions.

But the relatively small number of green magnets
developed to date are having little impact on the flood-tide
of visitors. Now even the Australian Tourist Commission is
expressing concern about the effects of the rapid pace of
development. It has warned that tourist developments and

inadequate pollution laws are threatening the very coastal regions, rainforests, wilderness areas and even National Parks that tourists come to see.

And this problem is likely to be aggravated as tourists begin to travel to increasingly remote areas. Here the arid and semi-arid ecosystems are often extremely vulnerable to visitor pressure – and the disputes about Aboriginal land rights continue to rage.

Although the Australian government is alert to such problems, and indeed has brought together a working party to look at what ecologically sustainable tourism development might involve, there is little sense as yet that it has got its act together. So, to get a better feel for the problems the country faces, let's take a closer look at the environmental balance sheet for some of Australia's most noted attractions.

Into the Outback

Rainforests, deserts, savannah, temperate forests – Australia has them all. In the wake of *Crocodile Dundee*, the Kakadu National Park is perhaps the best-known wilderness area. And the film, which helped put Kakadu on the map, also helped turn the tide against a proposed mine that would have torn the heart out of Coronation Peak, a local mountain which plays a central role in Aboriginal myth.

The Aboriginal heritage goes back millennia, but the Aborigines were appallingly abused throughout Australia's colonial history. Even with abundant wildlife to hand, some white settlers sank as low as staging Aborigine hunts. Yet here, too, the tide is beginning to turn. Aboriginal art and culture have become fashionable – and people worldwide are waking up to the fact that indigenous peoples knew a great deal more about the environments they were thrown out of than the settlers could ever imagine. Today there are signs that Aboriginal perspectives are beginning to enrich Australia's appreciation of its natural inheritance. In some areas Aboriginal guides are employed to help visitors see the environment in new ways – and in some instances the

Aborigines themselves now own the land and organise the tours.

Two of Australia's most highly commended eco-tourism centres give visitors the opportunity to see Australia through Aboriginal eyes. Bungle Bungle and Seven Spirit Bay have both been developed in remote parts of Western Australia – and have both won awards for 'green tourism'. A few such swallows do not make a summer, but the approach developed by such early pioneers needs to be tried in other regions and other countries.

No one knows where the name Bungle Bungle came from, although some say it may have been a corruption of the name of the local Aborigine tribe, the Purnululu. The newly created 700,000 acre Purnululu National Park aims to protect an area which was once a tropical sea-bed. As you walk around, remember that it took some 370 million years for wind and water to carve the sandstone into those endless gorges and beehive-shaped domes.

The area has a wealth of wildlife, including over 140 species of birds, the largest of which is the blue-winged kookaburra. Tourists stay at one of two campsites, where the facilities are very basic. Water is pumped from a storage tank by solar power. Helicopter tours are offered but we would recommend that you think long and hard before you use such an energy-intensive form of transport. Remember, too, that the noise can disturb wildlife over a wide area.

At Seven Spirit Bay you can choose between the seven distinct habitats of the Cobourg Peninsula – the Ocean Wilds, the Shoreline, Waterworlds, the Paperbark Swamps, Rainforest Jungle, Arnhem Bush or Age-old Rocks. Trained naturalists will guide you on walking expeditions to see birds and animals either in the bush, along the coast or in the reefs.

From Berry Springs to Shark Bay

Slightly tamer but still an interesting alternative to urban zoos is Berry Springs. Located in the Northern Territory, 60 kilometres south of Darwin, Berry Springs is a wildlife park set up exclusively for indigenous or feral Australian animals. Kangaroos, wallabies, buffalo, banteng and dingos can all be seen in an open-plan, natural setting.

If you prefer to see animals in the wild, you could also try Shark Bay, in Western Australia. Here you can see dolphins coming inshore, actively seeking human company. When their visits started, in the 1960s, only the locals were in on the secret, but it was not long before the crowds poured in. Without proper supervision, the dolphins were mistreated, and the flow of traffic pouring in to see them caused increasing pollution problems. Now, however, the area is a reserve and research centre, and access to the dolphins is carefully managed.

In Queensland an excellent idea is being pioneered by the Gulf Local Authorities Development Association. It involves a community-based system which introduces tourists to wilderness areas, whilst protecting the environment. All the guides must live in the area they cover, and have an intimate knowledge of the bush, as well as acting as guardians of the local environment.

Ayers Rock

Australia has an extraordinary wealth of rock-art sites – an estimated 5,000 in Kakadu alone – but the best known of these is Ayers Rock in the heart of the Uluru National Park.

One of the country's top three tourist attractions, this outstanding red monolith has been handed back by the National Park Authorities to the Aborigines. To the Aborigines, Ayers Rock, or *Uluru*, as they call it, is equivalent to Westminster Cathedral and the Acropolis rolled into one – a place where, in what they call 'Dreamtime', past, present and future mix like great currents. The Aborigines have insisted that memorials erected on the rock to commemorate climbers who expired before they reached the summit are removed. They are keen, though, that people who visit the Rock have a real understanding of its history; on a 'star tour' evening you can learn from them about the stars and about the aboriginal myths.

Unsurprisingly, however, the hands and feet of several hundred thousand tourists each year are leaving their mark. The dune soils and plant life at the foot of the mountain have been damaged by too many tourists wanting a 'hands-on' experience. And the visitors have also accelerated the fading or smudging of Aboriginal paintings that had lasted through the centuries. If you go do make sure that those you travel with realise that Ayers Rock is a cultural monument, not a glorified climbing frame.

The Great Barrier Reef

If, on the other hand, you find yourself in Queensland, the chances are that you will visit the Great Barrier Reef, the largest living reef system on earth.

There are over 2,000 individual reefs making up the main barrier. One of the most diverse ecosystems in the world, the Barrier Reef is sometimes referred to as 'the tropical forest of the seas'. And, like the tropical rainforests, the interest lies in a thin layer of living material – in this case the coral organisms, which sit on top of limestone accumulated over millions of years by their ancestors.

Some of the islands that people stay on while visiting the Reef, among them Lizard Island (sixteen miles off the Cape York Peninsula and 170 miles north of Cairns), are upmarket and carefully managed. In fact, Lizard Island is the most northerly and most remote of the Barrier Reef resorts. With only twenty bungalows, it is also one of the most exclusive and pricey. Elsewhere, you pay less – and the chances are that the environment will be less well tended.

Doomsday headlines abounded when the Barrier Reef was found to be suffering from a plague of crown of thorns starfish. Before long they were reported to have chewed away about a third of the living coral on the north-eastern coast. There are various theories about how the problem started. Some say offshore oil drilling started the rot, others that populations of the starfish's main predator, the triton, were disrupted by over-fishing and removal by shell-hunters. Others blamed pesticides or soils washed off from sugar plantations. But the plague, which has recently died back a bit, illustrates the vulnerability of even the world's largest ecosystems. The Queensland aquarium in Townsville has done extensive research on the crown of thorns plague and they have a fascinating exhibition which illustrates the problem.

And, like it or not, tourists must share part of the blame. More than 500,000 international tourists visit the Barrier Reef every year, bringing a range of problems in their wake. A major campaign was launched recently against Australia's first floating resort, the Four Seasons Barrier Reef Resort, built right on top of the Reef to enable hundreds of tourists to get a bird's eye view. Even if the resort had an effective sewage treatment system, such vessels introduce large numbers of people into the very heart of vulnerable ecosystems. Environmentalists charged that it was dragging its anchor and destroying the coral. They and most Australians heaved a sigh of relief when the floating resort upped anchor. Later, it moored off Saigon.

The anchoring of boats is a serious threat to the Reef – 30 seconds of careless anchoring can kill 30,000 years of coral formation. The large hydrofoils are another nuisance: apart from the noise, their wash causes erosion. And 'reef-walking' – where people walk out along the corals – can be just as deadly to the reef organisms.

The Marine Park Authority has been straining every sinew to stop this damage, but some guides, keen to pander to the tourists' desire for a feet-on experience, turn a blind eye to damage and littering of the sea-bed. If you are visiting the Reef, watch your step!

Spread the message

Like it or not, the chances are that mass tourism will continue to boom in Australia. If you visit the Gold Coast holiday strip, for example, you will find that it has become a top-spot for the Japanese. As the Japanese economy went into overdrive, a wave of Japanese tourism spread around the world, but particularly to Australia. As a result many locals fear a Japanese 'takeover' – and some have even gone as far as organising gang attacks on rich Japanese.

But, despite its admitted problems, Australia has great green tourism potential. If you are visiting the country, get in contact with one – or more – of the leading environmental organisations (see page 344) while you are planning your trip and check whether there are projects or initiatives that you can help to support.

Although organisations involved in such projects will not want to be overwhelmed by visitors, they often appreciate people taking a lively interest in their activities. By finding out what they are up to and spreading the message, we can all add to the momentum of the green tourism lobby.

ASIA

'East, west, home's best,' ran the old proverb, but the East has always held a huge fascination for Westerners. Now, with the twenty-first century just over the horizon, the so-called 'Pacific Rim', stretching from Southern California through Japan to Australia, is primed for convulsive economic growth. And tourism is already booming in many parts of Asia – including India, Thailand, Malaysia, Hong Kong and even, as the dust settles, Vietnam.

Already, the East Asia and Pacific region accounts for just over one in ten of world tourism arrivals. The total number of tourists visiting the region exploded from just 5 million in 1970 to almost 47 million by 1990. Add in South Asia, which includes countries like India, Nepal and Sri Lanka, and the figure is over 50 million.

Sadly, but perhaps inevitably as the boom builds, the worst environmental excesses of the tourism industry's early days in other world regions are now being repeated in many of the region's favourite tourism destinations.

Vietnam, for example, may have attracted just 3 per cent of the tourists pulled in by Thailand in 1989, but the country is keen to put itself back on the map. Visit Saigon (officially Ho Chi Minh City) and you will find the airports and almost every tourist hotel lobby overflowing with wildlife products. Many of these are banned by international conservation laws, including ivory, tortoiseshell and products made from tigers, leopards and bears. Nor is Vietnam alone in this respect: Bangkok is the centre of the wildlife trade and scandals are being reported right around the region.

Japan: land of the rising yen

Only one in four Japanese takes as much as two days off a week, and most people rarely take all of the fifteen days of holiday they are due each year. Increasingly, however, we are seeing evidence that at least some Japanese, particularly the young, are turning from their well-publicised roles of workaholics into funaholics. They now rank as the leading group of international tourism arrivals for the East Asia and Pacific region. Typically, too, whether they go to Hong Kong or Honolulu, they still want their holiday experiences carefully packaged.

The green revolution has been particularly slow to catch on in the Land of the Rising Sun, and it has certainly not yet reached its tourism industry. The Japanese are exceptionally skilled at coming up with technological fixes for environmental problems, excelling in such areas as energy efficiency, but are less interested in environmental activism and green consumerism. Happily, however, as their country becomes ever-more closely integrated politically and commercially with the rest of the world, the Japanese are learning to see environmental issues in a different light.

If you are visiting Japan, there is no shortage of issues that you can raise with your hosts. Many of the country's disposable chop-sticks, for example, are made from wood from disappearing rainforests. Packaging, too, is a big problem in Japan. Elaborate gift wrapping has become part of their culture and, coupled with the Japanese custom of giving gifts to visitors, this is no small problem. In Tokyo, as a result, the environmental issue that most people are aware of is the lack of space to put their garbage.

Tokyo did find room for its version of Disneyland. Indeed, this has proved so popular that, unless there is a heavy typhoon, you can expect to queue for at least half an hour or more for each attraction. Part of the fun is to hear Mickey Mouse, Donald Duck and Country and Western singing in Japanese.

More traditionally Japanese is a small reserve being developed on Nakamura, the smallest of the country's main-land islands. An area of rice paddies and swamps is being set aside as a sanctuary for over sixty species of dragonfly, or *tombo*, as the Japanese call the glittering insect jewels. This project underscores one of the most striking facts about the traditional Japanese on holiday: they generally like their plea-sures highly controlled, neatly tended and – usually – modest in scale, as in their highly manicured gardens. But the young are proving to have rather different tastes, often heavily influenced by Western fashions and styles.

Unfortunately, though, you have to be a fairly wealthy Japanese to afford a reasonable holiday in Japan. So the number of Japanese tourists travelling abroad is growing very rapidly. Many end up in Thailand, for golf, sex – or both.

Thailand: AIDS could make sex economy droop

Anyone who watches developments in Thailand, now one of the top tourism destinations worldwide, will know that the country is primed to become the golf capital of Asia. It is investing in a huge number of golf courses, particularly on the island of Phuket. And, as in other parts of the world (page 128), the raging thirst of these golf greens threatens to trigger water shortages.

But Thailand is best known not for its golf clubs but for its sex clubs and brothels. Bangkok is notorious, and known, deservedly, as the 'sex capital of the world'.

The country's Visit Thailand Year was such a success that it was extended to cover 19 months. The result was that 5 million tourists visited the country in 1990 alone, creating real environmental problems. The government subsequently announced that in any future conflict between tourism and the environment, the environment would be given top priority.

Despite such problems, however, Thailand has exploited tourism very effectively as an economic development tool. Its success in attracting tourists owes as much to the promotional activities of the Tourism Authority of Thailand (TAT) as it does to the country's undoubted attractions. These include relative political stability, a year-round tropical climate, palm-fringed, white sand beaches, sea and mountains, a deeply entrenched Buddhist culture, a fascinating cuisine and, of course, the Thai people themselves.

But the sheer speed of growth has left the environment gasping. Bangkok's notorious traffic jams are estimated to cost around 10 per cent of the region's GNP – and pollution levels in the city are constantly in breach of international standards. Most of the country's fresh water is polluted and the pollution stretches well out into the Gulf of Siam.

Like many other Asian countries, Thailand is wrestling with the interlinked problems of population growth, pollution and forest loss. Tourism may bring money to help fund important environmental work, but as often as not it brings its own problems in its wake.

The wave of foreign visitors is inevitably having its effect. 'Some people are money-oriented as never before,' explained the director of the Chiang Mai tourism authority. 'Human dignity is in decay.' And there is now an even greater concern: although the government long insisted that the disease would not affect Thais, AIDS is making rapid headway in the country. There were just 100 reported cases in 1988, a figure which had ballooned to unofficial estimates in the region of 30,000 by 1990. They will go much higher.

Sex tourism in Thailand attracts tourists from the world

over, with the Japanese, Danes and Germans being the keenest participants. Even in the northern city of Chiang Mai, once called 'the Rose of the North', there are now some 20,000 male and female prostitutes, most of them still teenagers. Paradoxically, though, while the Thais tend to blame the AIDS epidemic on foreigners, the deep domestic roots of prostitution are highlighted by the fact that only one to two per cent of the country's prostitutes service foreign tourists.

When the King's third daughter spoke out against sex tourism, the growing criticism of the sex industry began to take effect. In 1989, for example, Thai women's groups crowded airports to protest against Danish sex tours – and the government protested against a British company for advertising sex tours.

Not all parts of the country are as easy-going as Bangkok in this respect, however, as some more enterprising travellers will have discovered. For example, one foreigner trekking through the northern mountains stopped and had a brief affair with a young tribal girl. He left after a few days, but in the tribe's eyes the girl was now married to the foreigner – and therefore had little chance of ever marrying within the village. A good trekking guide will ensure that his party does not unwittingly transgress local mores.

Meanwhile, Thais still have some way to go before they can be held up as a model of environmental propriety. The thousands of people who visit Khao Yai forest each weekend, for example, dump several tonnes of rubbish there – and no one seems to have much of an idea about how the forest can be cleaned up and kept clean.

An even worse horror was reported by the Earth Island Institute, which investigated the illegal – and rapidly growing – trade in dolphins in Thailand. Earth Island investigators visited the catching area, some 20 kilometres from the border with Cambodia. 'Here we found Irrawaddy and Indo-Pacific humpbacked dolphins in what can only be described as sewage pits,' they reported in 1991.

Earth Island was assured by the Thai government that action would be taken to tackle such abuses. Certainly, as you travel around the country you will see signs of an emerging and energetic local green movement. It embraces an unlikely mix of monks and businessmen, university professors and peasants. They will, however, need sustained support from outside the country if they are to succeed.

The World Wide Fund for Nature has long been active in the country. Among other things, it has launched a campaign to stop the illegal wildlife trade in Thailand. The country is still a world centre for the illegal trade in wildlife and related products, importing a million caiman skins each year from Latin America alone. So avoid such products like the plague.

Slowly, however, the green tourism pressures are building. The German Travel Agents' Association, for example, has now said it will only do business with Thai hotels that help to protect the environment. If the pressure can be developed, it could do a great deal to reinforce the position of environmentally minded Thais.

Malaysia and Singapore: clean, not green

When Malaysia encouraged the world to stop by in Visit Malaysia Year (1990), the spotlight was on the country's natural splendours, including its rainforests and culture. But the first thing that will strike you if you fly into Malaysia is the effort that is now being put into controlling the drug trade.

In the first eight months of 1989 forty-four drug traffickers were sentenced to death. As your plane slants in towards Kuala Lumpur, expect the chief steward to make an announcement about the death penalty in the same tone that he would use to advise you on how to put on your life-jacket.

Once on the ground, you have a wide range of options to choose from. Eco-tourists, for example, are encouraged to watch giant leatherback turtles lay their eggs on the sandy beaches or visit the endearing but endangered orang-utans in one of the two places in which it is still found. But the country still remains a hostile environment for most forms of wildlife. Many of them live in the rainforests which are being felled at an alarming rate.

The Malaysian government is much happier to talk about its clean-up campaign than it is to discuss what it plans to do to protect the region's ecology. The campaign aims to raise standards of cleanliness and tidiness – and most of the main tourist areas are indeed spotless. But you can still find places, like the beaches in Penang, where the environment needs a good scrub.

Across the Johore Strait is the city-state of Singapore, the cleanest, safest city in all of Asia, if not the world. As a British colony it used to conjure a strong and enduring whiff of sin, but it has been cleaned up with a vengeance. It is now against the law to eat on the subway (you risk a $250 fine), drop litter in the gutter or fail to flush a toilet – probably the only place in the world where spending a penny could cost you $125.

Singapore's unofficial slogan is 'Clean and Green' – but here the green stands for park lawns and money rather than ecology. At one stage, even the world-famous Raffles Hotel – named after Sir Stamford Raffles, who effectively invented modern Singapore – was going to be knocked down to make way for more steel and chrome. Following widespread protests, however, it was decided to keep the hotel and restore it to something approaching its original glory – although traditionalists are unlikely to be happy with the result.

If you are intending to check in at the Raffles, or other major hotels, check out the use of tropical hardwoods around the hotel. Architectural conservationists will point out that such hardwoods were a mainstay of the architecture and interior design of the period, but they come from Malaysia's hard-pressed forests. Remember, rainforest campaigners from the Malaysian version of the Friends of the Earth have ended up in jail for their efforts to protect the country's jungles. Even as you prop up the bar, you can do something to advance the environmental crusade that put others behind bars.

China and Hong Kong: welcome Rambo!

An *Economist* survey recently dubbed squeaky clean Singapore the 'World's Most Boring State', an accusation that cannot be levelled at Red China. As the students of Tiananmen Square were mown down live on the world's TV screens, the geriatric communist leader Deng Xiaoping – who gave the troops the order to fire – told his colleagues from his hospital bed: 'In China, one million people dead is only a small number'. Not surprisingly, the number of tourists visiting China went through the floor.

The year before Tiananmen, China earned some $2 billion dollars from tourism, income it was loath to see evaporate. Slashing prices to coax back tourists, it also pulled out the stops to entice just about anyone. It even aimed to pull in fans of Rambo – the musclebound one-man army who, until he discovered environmental issues, dedicated his fictional life to killing communists. A few miles outside Beijing, foreigners were soon being charged $100 to let rip with mortars and machine guns at a nearby hillside.

The most popular tourist destination in China is Shanghai, which is also the most western city in China. Beijing, on the other hand, is popular with backpackers who have taken the Trans-Siberian Railway from Bucharest – which at the time of writing cost just $45. If you are visiting Beijing, consider travelling around the city by bike as most of the locals do. Unfortunately, however, there are still enough cars there to cause smog and the air is often horribly polluted. If you go in the wrong season this will be made even worse by sand blown in from the Gobi Desert.

The most popular tourist attraction in Beijing is the Forbidden City, which is certainly spectacular. You will be joined there by hordes of Chinese tourists, who now flood in from Mongolia, the Steppes or other rural areas. Another favourite spot is the Mao Mausoleum, although it is at least conceivable that this will go the way of Lenin's Tomb in Moscow, where the most popular spot is no longer the last resting place of the great Bolshevik revolutionary but McDonald's.

China is still very much a place for Travellers or Trekkers. Generally, it is impossible to book by telephone – and if you are travelling, you will find that egalitarianism has resulted in there being no first class. Instead, you can often choose between second, third, fourth and fifth classes!

One popular excursion involves taking a boat down the Yangtse River. Again, the scenery is spectacular in places, but expect to find the river heavily polluted. The flotsam you will see also includes what are delicately referred to as 'floaters' – dead bodies. Cities on the river, Chungking (or Chongquing in Mandarin), for example, throw most of their waste into the river, although the authorities are waking up to the need to invest in sewage treatment technology. The key problem now is finding the money. But there are major development plans afoot which could affect the country's major rivers, including proposals for a number of massive dams.

Longer term, one suspects, the world's most populous country's success in persuading the rest of the world to over-look its past crimes will very much depend on the extent to which it succumbs to the democratic tide now sweeping around the planet. But it will also depend on China's willing-ness – and ability – to clean up some of its appalling environ-mental problems and to develop its natural resources in a sustainable way.

The day may yet come when China, home of the giant panda, will be on the eco-tourism trail, but that day still seems fairly remote. With Hong Kong – a more popular tourism destination – due to return to Chinese control before the end of the century, we can only hope that China's next Great Leap Forward takes it in a greener and more democratic direction. If that day comes, the billion-plus mainland Chinese will inevitably make a huge impact on the world economy and the world environment – particularly if even a fraction of them start taking their holidays abroad.

Taiwan: polluters shown welcome mat

Taiwan is nobody's favourite tourism resort. Cheap Taiwanese goods have flooded the world market, but there has been a huge local price to pay. Today, the island is one of the most polluted places on earth. 'When other countries were phasing out polluting industries in the 1960s, we welcomed them with open arms,' explained a National Taiwan University professor.

At least a third of the island's rivers and one eighth of its farmlands are contaminated. Asthma cases among Taiwanese children have quadrupled in recent years, while the incidence of cancer – the leading cause of death – has doubled in just a generation.

The country's Environmental Protection Agency was forced to launch what it called 'Operation Rambo', involving raids on factories suspected of midnight dumping. But many violators just pay the fines, even though they have been increased ten-fold, and keep on polluting. So if you are planning to visit Taiwan during the next few years, you may want to take a gas-mask!

India: destination of the nineties?

At the other extreme, if any one Asian country is likely to dominate tourism in the region over the next decade, it is probably India. The 1984 Bhopal disaster focused world attention on the environmental risks posed by industry, but India faces much graver problems – as its population soars. From 442 million people in 1960, India's population doubled to 853 million by 1990, and is expected to reach almost 1.5 billion by 2025. Even relatively large numbers of visitors disappear in such a sea of humanity.

Around 1.7 million visitors arrived in India in 1989, injecting well over a billion dollars into the country's economy. As a result, tourism is now India's largest net earner of foreign exchange. The tourists come in large numbers, tend to stay a long time (averaging twenty-nine days) and frequently return. The Ministry of Tourism forecasts that some 5 million tourists will visit India each year by the turn of the century.

The country's 450 National Parks are being aggressively promoted – and the government is working to encourage visitors to break out of the golden triangle of Delhi–Agra–Jaipur. They are being coaxed to travel south to the lush and as yet unspoiled coastline, east to the temples and north for trekking, river rafting and heli-skiing.

In the foothills of the Himalayas you can trek – or ride elephants – through nature reserves where wild elephant, tiger and leopard still roam. Tour operators are clearly targeting this region because it offers some of the wildest, most unpolluted and uncommercialised environments in the world. Without effective controls and proper planning these regions too could be destroyed as a result of their very popularity.

The Himalayas: on the critical list

The Indian Environment Minister has warned that many parts of the Himalayas are already being destroyed by deforestation, soil erosion and tourism. In addition, the greasy black fallout from Kuwait's burning oilfields, torched by Saddam Hussein during the Gulf War, blackened snows in the Himalayas, thousands of miles away. One party of Swiss tourists said their skis were caught in sticky oil-black snow as they descended the slopes at speed.

Gulf War aside, however, the plight of the Himalayan environment is largely a result of the region's exploding population. And to some extent it can also be laid at the feet of Western tourists, with their desire for warm fires and hot water at night – and ample funds to pay for the wood needed to light them. Each climber uses around 230 pounds of wood during a fifteen-day trek, with only 7 per cent of climbers carrying in their own fuel.

In Nepal it took just five years for the country to lose 15 per cent of its forests – and they are still disappearing at around 3 per cent a year. Meanwhile, tourism has been growing at over 15 per cent a year, bringing new pressures to bear on the fragile mountain ecosystem.

Sir Edmund Hillary, who conquered Mount Everest in 1953, has warned that the area is 'in danger of becoming a rubbish dump' (see page 122). Worried by the mounting problems, Nepal's Ministry of Tourism quadrupled the charges for climbing Everest early in 1992.

Here and there, however, tour operators and resort managers are doing their bit to slow the avalanche of environmental destruction. Many of the UK tour operators taking people to the Himalayas have supported guidelines being drawn up through Tourism Concern (see page 349). The guidelines give advice to tourists on how to minimise their environmental and cultural impact.

And it is even more important to win the support of local people. The Annapurna Conservation Area Project (ACAP: page 354) has been set up to manage 2,600 square kilometres of Nepal with the three aims of sustainability, education and participation. ACAP has set up forest management committees, which include members of local communities. Tree nurseries have been developed and over 100,000 tree seedlings have been planted on the denuded hill slopes.

The hope is that if local people are involved in the projects from the outset they will have a vested interest in protecting the tree plantations, rather than poaching wood for their own fires. You can find out more about and contribute to the project if you visit the Pokhara Museum, in the area.

Interestingly, too, ACAP recently approached the Intermediate Technology Development Group (ITDG: page 367), set up by 'Small is Beautiful' guru Fritz Schumacher, for advice on water power. ITDG advised them on how to set up the first 'micro-hydro' power station, which will generate electricity for a number of local communities and a tourist lodge. Such schemes, and several more in the pipeline, could dramatically cut the need for firewood.

Goa, going, gone?

Despite the fact that there is as yet relatively little in the way of formal nightlife or water sports, Goa has become the favourite beach destination in India for UK tourists – it is even serviced by a direct flight which is a sure sign that mass tourism has arrived. Unfortunately, however, this dream-like place is gradually being devoured by the tourism industry.

The decline began with the hippies in the 1960s, who brought drugs and a soaring crime-rate in their wake. Like many Trailblazers, who travel far and wide in the belief that they cause less damage than package tourists, the hippies paved the way for an influx of tourists as well as uncontrolled land speculation and construction.

Goa now has an active anti-tourist lobby. Nude and topless bathers are regularly harassed. And when a German charter flight arrived at Goa's airport recently, rotten fish had been lobbed into the tourist bus – which had also had its 'Welcome' banner smeared with cow dung.

'We were very polite,' insisted the Vigilant Goan Army's leader, 'and we just handed out our leaflets explaining that there is a certain sort of imported lifestyle that we cannot accept in Goa. Goa should remain as beautiful as God made it.'

Bhutan's pursuit of happiness

It may be some time before a country like Burma opens up to tourism, but with other countries encouraging tourists – among them Vietnam and even Cambodia – Goa and other parts of Asia would be well advised to take note of the way that the Himalayan kingdom of Bhutan handles its visitors.

Opened to tourists as recently as 1974, Bhutan is a deeply religious and conservative country. It imposes a strict quota on the number of visitors (about 2,000) it is prepared to accept each year. Tipping is prohibited, as is the distribution of sweets and pens to children. Monasteries are closed to foreigners following incidents where visitors took photos, even when specifically requested not to.

The policy has been very successful. The country's motto was perhaps best expressed by its king some years ago. It is often thought that the United States is the only country to enshrine the pursuit of happiness in its Bill of Rights, but Bhutan has similar ideals. Bhutan's aim, the King said, should be to work not towards Gross National Product but towards Gross National Happiness.

From Fiji to Bali: islands await tidal wave

Reared on tales like *Robinson Crusoe* and *Swiss Family Robinson*, many people dream of finding themselves on a tropical island, surrounded by glittering seas, coral reefs and coconut palms. As a result, islands throughout the Pacific Basin are coming under pressure from tourists, from Hawaii to the Seychelles (see page 229).

Let's start in Fiji, the South Pacific archipelago of over 800 islands and islets just over 2,000 kilometres from Auckland, New Zealand. Many of the islands are privately owned by large corporations and are kept exclusive and expensive – the local people are apparently either kicked off or employed as domestics. But on the small island of Vatulele, the village of Tamoua Ekubu recognises that tourism – along with tidal waves – is a serious threat. The last really destructive tidal wave was in 1973, and the islanders comfort themselves with the thought that the coral reef gives them some protection. One side of the island is already 'developed', a fact that the villagers welcome, but they do not want another hotel in Vatulele. So far, at least, the powerful village Elders are fairly confident that they can prevent such development.

Elsewhere, however, the tidal wave of tourism can sweep straight in, with no social reef to slow it. Consider the Indonesian Archipelago, strung out 'like emeralds scattered across sapphire blue seas'. The Archipelago consists of 13,667 islands at the last count, and is seen as one of the last great frontiers of tourism.

Best known is Bali, which early Trailblazers always feared

would disappear under a wave of tourists. It's not hard to find examples of tourist impacts: in neon-lit 'Aussie Alley' the pub crawls include beer races for boys and wet T-shirt contests for girls. Worse, no sooner have the Balinese displayed their exquisitely arranged, traditional daily offerings to the gods than they are trampled by uncaring – and often inebriated – tourists. But even here there are signs that some aspects of Balinese culture are proving more resilient than had been feared. In some ways the culture has been strengthened by the tourist invasions, as they try to protect it from being corrupted by outside influences.

The best hope for sustainable tourism may reside in such islands. Even though their ecology is often more vulnerable, they may be in a better position to control the numbers of people arriving – and to manage them once they have landed. A good example of what can be achieved can be found in the Maldives, a thousand rocky islands strung out across the Indian Ocean.

The Maldives are determined not to be swamped with tourists. The government imposed a strict zoning system in 1981, with 200 islands set aside for local people only and another fifty opened up for tourists. Topless bathing is forbidden (Islam is the religion here). Speargun fishing is banned, to protect the islands' fish. And the government also insists that concrete is used for beach building, not coral rubble, which should keep most green tourists happy.

Stemming the flow of tourists may help to create a sustainable industry, but the Maldives are also under threat by issues that they cannot control. The highest point of the islands is just 5 metres above sea-level. If the sea-levels continue to rise as a result of the greenhouse effect, the islands, and their tourism industry, could disappear for ever! Not surprisingly, the people of the Maldives have lobbied strongly at UN conferences for measures to cut back on carbon dioxide and other greenhouse gases.

'Our survival,' explained the Maldives environmental affairs director, 'is very much dependent on what the rest of the world can do to reduce its emissions of greenhouse gases. It is impossible for us to build up all the islands by ourselves.'

THE MIDDLE EAST

Outside the world of pilgrims, most parts of the Middle East do not top the average tourist's wish-I-was-there list. And the Gulf War hit tourism in the region very hard.

One cartoon published in Israel showed a man and a boy in a bus. The man was reading a newspaper whose headline trumpeted: 'Tourists see Martian in Tel Aviv'. The boy was not taken in. 'That doesn't fool me, Pop,' he said, 'there's no such thing as tourists.'

Saddam Hussein's adventures around the Gulf did not help his own country's tourism industry either. Ancient cities like Babylon and Ur in Iraq have always been well placed to build a strong tourism industry, but in the wake of the Gulf War the whole country became a virtual no-go area.

Yet in times of peace the cultural and natural treasures of this entire region beggar the imagination. The Fertile Crescent, stretching from the Levant to the Zagros mountains, south of the Caspian Sea, was the cradle of many of the world's greatest early civilisations. Visit the citadel of Nimrud in northern Iraq, once the capital of the Assyrian empire, or the royal palace of Persepolis, in what used to be Persia, and you get an inkling of the unimaginable cultural achievements of peoples who are now little more than footnotes in our school history books. Clearly, if you are not put off by the political tensions that are such a hallmark of this region, there is a great deal to see and do.

Not surprisingly, however, some of the most impressive sights reflect the deep roots of today's tensions. Throughout Israel, Lebanon and Syria, for example, you can find some of the world's most spectacular castles, among them Belvoir, Blanchegarde and Krak des Chevaliers. The Crusades triggered an explosive period of castle building both by the Crusaders and the Saracens. At Belvoir, a few miles south of the Sea of Galilee, the ambitious building programme almost bankrupted the powerful Knights Hospitaller military order – and drove its master to a nervous breakdown.

Birdwatchers, too, know that Israel has a lot to offer, lying as it does on the migration routes between Africa, the Middle

East, Europe and the Soviet Union. Nearly 500 species of birds can be found in this tiny country, which has been described as the 'Clapham Junction of the bird world'.

But this region has also been the birth-place of a number of the world's great religions – and tourism develops within the constraints imposed by this fact, if it develops at all. Here and there, too, you see evidence that even some governments that are closely allied with the West are prepared – for a variety of reasons – to put their foot down when it comes to tourism.

To visit Oman, for example, you need a 'No Objection Certificate'. The Sultan of Oman is determined that his beaches should not become a replica of the nightmare resorts of the Mediterranean. 'We do not want tourism to destroy our dignity, our habits or our traditions,' explained the Omani commerce minister. So whether you are birdwatching or camel-trekking, your tour operator will be very keen that you should behave. Tour operators know that they could be blamed – and banned from the country – if anyone in their care gets into trouble.

The pursuit of prophets
The hordes of pilgrims who travel to the Middle East each year seem relatively unaffected by the up-and-down nature of the tourism industry there. Jerusalem, for thousands of years the epicentre of political earthquakes, is of unique importance in the religions of Judaism, Christianity and Islam and is a magnet for pilgrims from around the world. The wealthiest pilgrims tend to come from the United States – and Israel has in recent years been publicising its attractions to the 'Bible Belt' of the southern United States, and to the pilgrims of Europe.

But Jerusalem is by no means the region's only religious magnet: Mecca, too, exerts an almost irresistible pull on Muslims. In 1991 the *Haj* attracted more than two million pilgrims to Saudi Arabia. The *Haj* is one of the biggest annual human migrations, with Muslims from around the world travelling to visit the birthplace of the Prophet Mohammed in Mecca and his tomb in Medina.

Although Saudi Arabia is more sensitive than most, many Middle Eastern countries still have deeply mixed feelings about tourism. On the one hand they want the revenues to help build – or rebuild – their economies. On the other, they fear that tourism will corrode morals. In Iran, for example, a tourist campaign was launched just a few months after the death of Ayatollah Khomeini. But President Rafsanjani's spokesmen warned that, though the country wanted tourists, it did not want 'to drag in Western-style immorality and laxity'.

It remains to be seen whether modern tourism can co-exist and even flourish cheek-by-jowl with such religious sensitivities. For the moment, however, Iran need not fear a tourist invasion. In the wake of the revolution and the protracted war with Iraq, Tehran – the country's capital – is an unattractive, smog-wreathed city. Anti-Western slogans cover the walls of many buildings and there are still deep suspicions about Western visitors. Even male tourists are advised against wearing short sleeved shirts or ties. And if that does not put you off, the Iranian practice of 'sporting apartheid' may still do the trick. In the Elburz Mountains, men and women have to ski on separate slopes!

Water wars

Green tourists who like to get to grips with environmental issues while on holiday are well served in the Middle East. Natural resources stretch ever thinner as the region tries to meet the needs of growing millions of people, and some scientists are now predicting a new age of 'resource wars'.

Most people think of oil wars when they think of recent Middle Eastern history. But, as if the volatility of oil politics were not bad enough, we seem to be on the verge of what could become full-blown water wars. Syria, Jordan and Israel are already sparring over the waters of the River Jordan.

In 1990, the Sea of Galilee fell to its lowest-ever level. And there are real fears that if it ever dips below the so-called 'red line', the increased concentration of salts, phosphorus and algae in its waters could render it unusable. Turkey recently agreed to supply Israel with 400 million cubic metres of water a year in huge plastic bags, but the region's thirst can only get worse.

Of course, water is not a new issue in the Middle East. Earlier civilisations are also responsible for over-taxing their environments. In various regions of the Fertile Crescent, for example, you can visit the glittering, barren salt deserts where early farmers over-irrigated their arid soils with brackish water.

In Dubai, meanwhile, they are using water as if there was no tomorrow. This small Gulf state has ambitions to turn itself into the leisure centre of the region and has, for example, created an eighteen-hole golf course, smack in the middle of the desert. Golf courses are always thirsty creatures, but never more so than when located in the middle of a desert. Dubai's course requires a staggering million gallons of water every day of the year to keep the grass green.

Egypt: Land of the Pharaohs

The Middle East's most popular tourist destination is Egypt. For those who come with expectations of an 'Aladdin in Wonderland' world, however, the real Egypt is obvious as soon as they drive out of Cairo airport. You are almost immediately made aware of the country's greatest problem: its population is growing at a prodigious rate. One Egyptian is born every 24 seconds.

Although there are many other things to see, Egypt's main attractions for visitors still lie in its ruins. Mention Egypt and the world thinks of the Pyramids, the Sphinx, King Tutankhamen – the boy king – and Cleopatra, well-known for her extraordinary impact on powerful men.

The tourism industry has been a pearl in Egypt's otherwise lacklustre economy. The boom started in the late 1980s and was fuelled by the success of the government's decision to develop international tourism in the Red Sea area. The region's beaches, scuba diving and coral reefs are seen as a welcome addition to Egypt's undoubted cultural heritage –

not least because most people are likely to visit the pyramids only once in a lifetime.

Pressure from tourists has already led to changes in the way Egypt deals with its wastes, although these are by no means always to the environment's overall advantage. The city of Alexandria, for example, came under pressure to clean up the sewage it was discharging into the Mediterranean. 'Before, they used to pour it into the salted water,' explained a local fisherman. 'But people complained, the people who used the beach, the tourists.' So now much of the sewage flows into the marshwaters of nearby Lake Maryut, where the fish are now being pulled in with ulcerated flesh and deformed tails and fins. The earnings of thousands of local fishermen are now a third of what they were before the city started dumping its sewage into the lake.

Ironically, too, the pressure of tourism has built up so fast in the Red Sea that the Gulf War had a beneficial ecological effect there. The conflict gave the spectacular Red Sea coral reefs time to recover from the close attentions of the 150,000 divers who have visited them each year – and the impact of the hotels and power boats that have followed in their wake. Longer term, the government will have to take tougher measures to limit numbers and implement planning controls if the region is going to withstand the pressure.

Back in the country's tourist heartland, meanwhile, the combination of air pollution and rising groundwater caused by the Aswan Dam, which straddles the upper Nile, is threatening many of Egypt's classical monuments (see page 177). The pearl of the country's economy, it turns out, is being attacked by acid emissions from industry and many other forms of pollution.

The Sphinx recently lost a 600-pound chunk from its shoulder, and archaeologists say that there is a real risk that pollution damage will cause the vast statue to lose its head. Some people are now recommending that the Sphinx be reburied in the sands, where it spent two thousand years in safety.

The Nile, which flows through the heart of the country, remains the life-spring of Egyptian civilisation. But it, too, has become seriously polluted with industrial effluent and huge quantities of sewage. The construction of the Aswan Dam reduced the rate of water flow in the river and forced farmers to buy artificial fertilisers in place of the Nile silts that used to flood their fields every year.

Even so, the Nile continues to provide a vital tourism life-line for the beleaguered country. The problem is that the Nile now often suffers from too much of what many Egyptians have come to see as a good thing. The number of Nile cruisers doubled from sixty-four to 120 between 1986 and 1991, at which time a further sixty were under construction. The tourism slow-down encouraged the government to impose a ban on the building of any new boats, however, and many were soon lying idle in any event. But the pressures are sure to return when the world economy begins to look up again.

Like Israel, Egypt offers breath-taking spectacles for bird-watchers, particularly around the Nile Delta lakes, the biggest of which is Lake Manzala. Given the potential income this could generate through eco-tourism, we must hope that the Egyptians will be encouraged to think twice before ploughing up – or concreting over – their wild places. But the sheer pressure of human numbers makes it extremely unlikely that wildlife conservation will enjoy a high political priority in the foreseeable future.

We read that the Egyptian government, despite its limited resources, had passed a law in 1985 decreeing that 10 per cent of the cost of foreign travel should go to the state, up to a maximum amount. The income was to be used to fund conservation of historic monuments, anti-pollution measures and environmental protection. Unfortunately, we have been unable to substantiate this information. Both the Egyptian Embassy in London and the country's Ministry of Tourism said that they had never heard of such a scheme. If, as seems likely, the idea was never adopted, it is certainly something to aim towards, not only in Egypt but in all the world's most popular tourism destinations.

AFRICA

Rather than attempting to cover each of this huge continent's countries, we will spotlight some of the areas where tourism is well planned, as in the Korup rainforest, Cameroon – or where it is in danger of getting out of hand, as in some of the game parks of Kenya.

For most people travelling to Africa, the main attraction is still its wildlife, coupled with natural attractions like Victoria Falls. Hunters like Teddy Roosevelt and Ernest Hemingway helped to put East Africa on the map as *the* place for big game hunting. Thankfully, given the rate at which the animals were being wiped off the map, hunting was banned in Kenya as long ago as 1977.

Tourists still flock in pursuit of game, but now most of them fire camera shutters rather than bullets. Unfortunately, however, a wealthy few continue to ignore the ban on hunting. Having wiped out most of their own game, shooting down birds like bustards with automatic rifles fired from the speeding comfort of their Range-Rovers, wealthy Arabs have taken to hunting in Africa. Some African countries are keen to instigate a resurgence of hunting because they see it as a good source of income.

This is just one more example of a basic problem facing conservation in Third World countries: money doesn't simply talk, it screams. With a shortage of most resources in most African countries, it is often very difficult to get local people to be concerned about environmental damage, whether it is caused by tourism or other industries. But, here and there, it is possible to see uniquely African solutions emerging, among them Zimbabwe's 'Operation Campfire' programme (see page 224) and Tanzania's *Ecopolis* (see page 55).

Kenya: White mischief

Kenya remains the favourite destination for African wildlife safaris – indeed, tourism has overtaken coffee as the largest source of foreign exchange. And films like *Out of Africa* and

White Mischief have boosted the numbers of tourists arriving in the country's National Parks and wildlife reserves. Already it is clear, though, that Kenya will not be able to sustain the current level of growth, and other countries, among them Tanzania and Zimbabwe, are beginning to attract the attention of tour operators.

Most of the tourism industry in Kenya is privately controlled, but it is not slow in calling on the government for aid. It argues, for example, that the government has been slow in responding to the need for a national development strategy for the industry. The development of a tourism infrastructure, as well as the rapidly expanding population, has created an insatiable appetite for building timber. Lorries stream across the border from Tanzania laden with recently felled forest trees. If Kenya is going to have any hope of running its tourism industry in a sustainable fashion, it will need to enact and enforce much tougher laws, both for development and conservation.

Meanwhile, many game parks are seriously overvisited, and their lodges overstretched. Resentment has built up, particularly against the 'mob', predominantly Germans, who include a three-day safari as a tack-on to a holiday on the coast, and who expect to maintain an air-conditioned, pampered coastal luxury even when in the more rugged safari environment.

In the more popular parks, such as Amboseli and the Masai Mara, wildlife are harassed daily by mobs of tour vans (see page 160). Not only is this pressure threatening fragile ecosystems and eroding the soil, but wildlife experts fear that the over-exposure of the animals to people is leading to stress and confusion. The wild cats in particular are often unable to pursue their instinctive life in a natural habitat. Unless there are enforced limits to the number of visitors or the times of the year when the parks are open, there is a real possibility that such parks will become little more than glorified zoos.

Most park lodges still have a problem with unregulated sewage disposal and the various wastes produced attract carrion eaters like hyenas, vultures, baboons and vervets.

Meanwhile, the unregulated dumping of rubbish in Lake Nakuru from the nearby industrial town of Nakuru has banished many of the pink flamingos for which the area was once famous. Tourists are also put off visiting again when they see dead animals floating in the water.

Where lions earn $74 a day

Mercifully, the news is not all bad. The Kenyan government took a brave step when it appointed Dr Richard Leakey, the leading conservationist, as Director of Wildlife – a move that has inspired a new wave of commitment among conservation organisations and the general public. It has also worried the poachers – Leakey has received so many death threats that he has to have bodyguards. The Kenyan Association for Tour Operators (KATO) has also taken steps to enforce the protection of some areas.

With around a third of Kenya's national income coming from tourism, the country knows it is going to have to work hard to keep the tourists coming. It is estimated, for example, that every lion in the Amboseli National Park brings in $27,000 a year and the National Parks themselves earn $40 per hectare every year – which is perhaps fifty times what the land would bring in if it were cultivated by African farmers.

Apart from visitor pressure, the parks have to contend with an even more deadly threat: poachers (see page 162). In the last fifteen years, the number of Kenyan rhinos has plummeted from 15,000 to 500, and the number of elephants has fallen from 60,000 to 18,000.

If visitor numbers are properly controlled, however, safari holidays can provide a vital shot in the arm for wildlife conservation. The income generated from tourism helps to maintain the National Parks and reserves, paying for anti-poaching measures. Some of the money even gets through to local communities, helping to convince local people that wild animals are worth conserving.

Zimbabwe: Putting wildlife to work

Most African countries still have a good deal to offer the eco-tourist. And in some areas wildlife reserves are defended quite literally to the death – usually of the would-be poachers. In Zimbabwe the so-called 'Rhino Wars' have resulted in rangers shooting over a hundred armed poachers or suspected poachers. As a result, the country still hangs on to the world's largest concentration of endangered black rhino.

Zimbabwe, once dubbed 'Africa's best-kept secret', is now firmly on the wildlife tourism map. In 1990 nearly 600,000 people visited the country, and it was expected that the 1991 figures would show an increase on this of 15 per cent. Initiatives like 'Operation Campfire', which ensures that local people benefit directly from the income wildlife brings, help recruit the active support of villagers in the constant fight against poachers.

Compared to most other parts of the world, many African countries still have staggeringly large wildlife resources. In the Zambezi River Valley, an area nearly twice the size of Belgium, located in northern Zimbabwe, there are 2,000 elephants, 56,000 cape buffalo, 2,000 lions, 230,000 impala and 50,000 warthogs. Unfortunately, however, many of these animals compete for living space with humans. And some, among them elephants, rhinos, hippos, lions and leopards, kill people or livestock and destroy crops. Given that their skins, horns and ivory can be worth a great deal of money, their fate would seem to be sealed.

And that's where Operation Campfire (Communal Area Management Programme for Indigenous Resources) fits in. The basic approach, which involves helping local people to profit directly from wildlife resources, has been tried out by a number of Zambezi Valley councils. The WWF recently looked at two Operation Campfire projects – and came up with some fascinating conclusions.

The Nyaminyami District Council, which pioneered the Campfire programme in 1989, sold hunting permits that year for 14 elephants, 82 cape buffalo and 26 lions and leopards. These permits earned more than $120,000 for the villagers. In addition, they received meat from both sport hunting and herd reduction programmes, while also being paid for wildlife damage to crops and livestock.

According to WWF, the 'wildlife dividend' in 1989 alone increased local household incomes by between 15 and 25 per cent. And, as local people began to see 'their' wildlife as an asset to be protected, WWF noted a drop in both poaching and habitat destruction. In nearby Guruve, by contrast, villagers did not benefit directly, and the scheme is not working so well. The lesson, WWF concluded, is clear: 'If it pays, it stays.'

The Okavango: jewel in Botswana's crown

Another magnet for African wildlife enthusiasts is Botswana, where National Parks account for around one-fifth of the country's area. The jewel in the country's crown, however, is the Okavango Delta. The Okavango is one of Africa's longest rivers, flowing south from the Angolan highlands into the Kalahari, where it spreads out into the delta, a vast area of swampland – and a true wildlife paradise.

Much of this region is extremely arid. In the Gemsbok National Park, a 10-million-acre reserve shared by Botswana and South Africa, years can go by with no rain. Perhaps the most extraordinary inhabitants of the Kalahari are the Bushmen, whose lives were described by Laurens van der Post in his classic *The Lost World of the Kalahari*.

Exquisitely adapted to life in these arid conditions, this ancient race of hunter-gatherers has been persecuted for centuries, hunted down like the Australian Aborigines and shot like so many vermin. Often, ill-considered aid has resulted in the sinking of deep wells, which have attracted groups of Botswana people with their cattle. The result is generally over-grazing, with the diminutive Bushmen becoming third-class citizens – at best – in the land of their ancestors.

Cattle ranching has been a major ecological problem in the region, creating great dust-bowls. When the EEC funded cattle ranching on a vast scale there, the ranchers erected a fence around the Okavango. Not long after, 60,000 dead wildebeest were found starved to death against the wire, stalled on their migratory paths.

Greenpeace has recommended that the Delta, a vast and unique wetland system lying in the north-western part of Botswana, should become a World Heritage Site. In 1991 the government of Botswana invited a delegation from Greenpeace to investigate and assess their proposed water extraction scheme, designed to supply water for a nearby town and for the diamond mining industry. Greenpeace did not come out in favour of the scheme and the government have been reviewing their plans.

Whatever impacts it may have, tourism in the Delta helps to offset the demands made by other industries. The diamond mines in particular are extremely thirsty in their consumption of water. But unfortunately, so far at least, the diamonds are worth more than the tourists. In an effort to increase the value of tourism, fees for entering the Okavango parks have recently been raised. If more money is raised from tourism the value of conserving the Delta could begin to outweigh the value of draining it to provide water for other industries and agriculture.

Tutu Tsiang, Botswana's director of tourism, said recently that the industry would soon diversify beyond wildlife and wilderness holidays. The Kalahari, he noted, has barely been touched. Among other potential attractions, it contains Lake Nagami, which David Livingstone found on his first journey of exploration, and the Tsodilo Hills, which boast some remarkable rock paintings. Like it or not, these areas will be opened up by the trans-Kalahari highway, currently under construction and due for completion in 1994. The road will give access to the Kalahari Gemsbok Park in the south, which you can reach at the moment only from the South African side.

The government sees tourism making a much bigger contribution to the economy in the future, and it remains to be seen if it can succeed in balancing the needs of the tourists with those of the environment. At the moment, Botswana's tourism industry is based on the principle of low intensity and high quality, which almost automatically means expensive holidays. If the industry were to switch to low-cost, package tours, the impact on some of the country's treasures could be devastating.

South Africa: back in business

'If we get Club Med and its German equivalent, Club Robinson, to build group hotels, South Africa is the place of the future for tourism,' said Walter Daman, manager of Germany's South African Tourist Office. In fact the biggest contributor to the future of the country's tourism industry was probably the release of Nelson Mandela, which put South Africa back on the map for many Travellers.

Tour operators have been piling back into the country, and the luxury market in particular has been expanding rapidly. The industry reckons the timing of the political thaw could not be better: South Africa is near-virgin territory, offering new resources to Travellers who are becoming both jaded with existing destinations and more demanding about standards of travel and accommodation. Because wages in South Africa are still low, the country could soon be promoting itself on the basis of providing First World standards at near-Third World prices.

There has been relatively little public debate about environmental issues in South Africa, not because the country has no problems but because racism and apartheid have naturally had a higher priority.

At the same time, however, the country has a good deal to teach other parts of the continent. In the South African state of Bophuthatswana, for example, there is a very progressive approach to wildlife management at work. At the Pilanesburg National Park, as in Zimbabwe's Campfire programme, the objective is to involve local inhabitants. Fences have been removed, along with non-indigenous vegetation, and the area restocked with animals like the buffalo, white rhino, blue wildebeest and eland. The animals are culled and hunting licences are issued, with the resulting income ploughed back both into local economy and into conservation. The success of the scheme has enabled the park authorities to donate some previously endangered animals – most notably the white rhino – to other conservation areas.

As South Africa has begun to dismantle apartheid, some interesting ideas have surfaced in the environmental field. One, put forward by the World Bank and governments in southern Africa, is based around the creation of a series of 'peace parks'. The idea is that these would link previously warring nations politically, economically and ecologically.

As a first step, it was proposed that South Africa's enormous Kruger Park be tripled in size, with some 8,000 square miles of Mozambique territory being included within the park boundaries. If the scheme goes ahead, the huge electrified, elephant-proof fence between the Kruger Park and the newly designated area of Mozambique would be removed. The Kruger Park animals would then be encouraged to repopulate the new areas, which have been devastated by civil war and poaching.

If things go well, future peace park schemes could involve Botswana, Namibia, Lesotho, Swaziland and Zimbabwe. No one is expecting miracles, but the need – and potential – for improvement is clearly enormous!

The Victoria Falls: lunar rainbows

One of the scenic wonders of the world, the Victoria Falls mark the border between Zambia and Zimbabwe. The tumbling waters, which the Kalolo-Lozi tribespeople called *Mosi-oa-tunya* ('the Smoke That Thunders'), send up huge clouds of spray, creating a small rainforest and dancing rainbows in the midst of an arid region. The wall of spray climbs a thousand feet into the sky – and is visible from up to 65 kilometres away. During every new moon, you can see an amazing lunar rainbow.

Livingstone's discovery of the Falls in 1865 opened them up to European hunters, sportsmen and missionaries. In the 1930s, a new power station was built at the Silent Pool in the

Third Gorge – and Zambia later further boosted the hydro-power output of the area. Hopefully, however, the tourism potential of the Falls will help to constrain future development of the vicinity, ensuring that future generations will also experience lunar rainbows in the roaring mists.

In 1991, tremendous investment went into hotels around the Falls in preparation for a visit from the Queen. Even before her visit, however, the area had been well managed – with little or no litter and visitor education centres that include information on environmental issues affecting the Falls and the surrounding country.

The Seychelles: aiming for sustainability

People have been visiting the Seychelles, a collection of around a hundred islands, for a very long time.

The Arabs were probably the first to see the Seychelles, although they did not settle. The Portuguese did. They were followed by the French and the British. Then, in 1976, the islands gained their independence. An economy once based on such products as cinnamon, copra and guano is now increasingly reliant on tourism. As recently as 1972, the islands welcomed just over 15,000 visitors. By 1990, the figure was around 104,000.

Island ecosystems are particularly vulnerable to human intrusion, because their isolation has often led – as in the case of the Galapagos Islands – to unique animal and plant species evolving. The Seychelles government is acutely aware of the need for sound management of its island inheritance. Announcing its 'Environmental Management Plan for the Seychelles, 1990–2000', it said that it hoped to prevent the number of tourists growing any larger. The goal: a controlled 100,000 visitors a year. The consultant who prepared the plan described it as the 'world's first explicit sustainable development plan'.

Several islands have been set aside for conservation. Indeed, the Seychelles already have proportionately more nature reserves than any other country. They also boast two giant tortoises for every islander. Part of the government's motivation stems from the fact that the Seychelles depend so heavily on fishing and tourism, both of which depend for their sustainability and therefore their success on unspoiled environments.

Sadly, in August 1990 two-thirds of one of their three forests, the Vallée de Mai, a World Heritage Site, was destroyed by fire. This disaster helped to focus attention on the delicate ecosystem of the Seychelles – and enabled them to raise £30 million through an international appeal.

Among other measures taken in recent years have been:

- the establishment of marine reserves by the Nature Conservation Board to protect whales and other marine mammals around the islands;
- the introduction of tough fines for fishermen who land any dolphins along with their tuna catch;
- the protection of the triton, a shell-fish which preys on the coral-eating crown of thorns starfish;
- planning controls that mean that new houses must now be built below the tree line, to preserve the appearance of the islands; and
- the imposition of tight controls on the further import of cars, in an attempt to reduce the jams that choke the capital.

Now, however, even Aldabra, one of the most inaccessible and – as a result – least spoiled islands is to be opened to tourism. Declared a World Heritage Site in 1982, Aldabra is the only terrestrial environment dominated by reptiles. It is home to some 150,000 giant tortoises, more than are found even in the Galapagos. The Seychelles Island Foundation plans to host small (a maximum of eight at a time) groups of 'selected rich foreigners'.

The island is considered dangerous for unaccompanied tourists (the coral has been described as 'concrete with razor blades in it'), and visitors will be taken around by a ranger. The plans are to plough back the proceeds from the tours into conservation and science and between foreign visits to allow in small groups of Seychelles residents and scientists.

Despite all these positive moves, it is no surprise to find that the Seychelles still has problems. These include soil and coastal erosion, the dumping of waste in rivers, industrial pollution and threats to the islands' coral reefs. But these problems pale into relative insignificance when compared with Madagascar, just over 1,000 kilometres away.

Madagascar: lemurs on the menu

Madagascar is thought to suffer the worst soil erosion of any country in the world – and the causes are all too visible. These include the devastating deforestation caused by slash-and-burn agriculture, the burning of trees for charcoal, cattle grazing and – sometimes – what can only be described as mindless destruction.

These problems would be worrying enough anywhere, but they are particularly alarming here because of the spectacular and unique wildlife for which Madagascar is rightly world famous.

An old Madagascan proverb says that 'all who live together under the sun are plaited together like one big mat'. Unfortunately, however, this sense of interconnectedness has yet to embrace the huge island's wildlife.

The government is keen to encourage eco-tourists, but even before the country ground to a halt in a mire of political unrest in 1991 national conservation efforts seemed little more than tokenism. Lemurs are perhaps the main attraction, but many visitors are shocked to find that some Malagash like to see lemurs on the menu – rather than in the wild.

One of the most popular reserves in Madagascar is Berenty, near Fort Dauphin in the south of the island. It is a small pocket of dry forest owned by a Monsieur de Heaulme, known locally as 'Monsieur Tourism'. A sisal farmer, he has found that this reserve of around 145 hectares earns more money than thousands of hectares of sisal plantations. It is a pity that this was only a recent discovery because the sisal plantations have long since replaced vast tracts of Madagascar's dry forests.

If Madagascar continues on its suicidal course, small pockets like the Berenty reserve may be the only places where remnants of the huge island's exquisite diversity of unusual plants and animals can be found.

Namibia's Skeleton Coast

An interesting approach to tourism can be found along Namibia's Skeleton Coast – 'an unexplored paradise of breathtaking beauty, wide open spaces, distant horizons, unspoilt beaches, rugged mountains, deep canyons, smoothly contoured sand dunes, unexpected water-holes and lonely animals', as one brochure puts it.

Part of the Namib Desert, the Skeleton Coast Park dates back to 1963 when – mainly for political reasons – this tract of coastline some 30–40 kilometres deep and 500 kilometres long was set aside as a future nature reserve. Since the Park was created in 1971, development has been kept to an absolute minimum and public access has been limited.

Recently opened to tourists, the area has populations of desert-adapted elephant, black rhino, giraffe and lion, in addition to a spectacular coastline. The name 'Skeleton Coast' reflects the horrendous toll in lives caused by shipwrecks in this remote area, among them the *Dunedin Star*, *Montrose* and *Suiderkus*.

Once wrecked, with their ships falling victim to the ice-cold and fast-flowing Benguela Current, with its vicious crosscurrents, heavy swells and dense sea fogs, the chances of early castaways ever finding their way back to civilisation were almost zero. In the end, most of their skeletons found their place among the bleached bones of whales, the rusting hulks of whalers, coasters, liners and gunboats, and the even older – and even more romantic – wooden remains of galleons.

Although tourism in the region is still very limited, Amy Schoeman, actively involved in the conservation of the area for many years and author of *Skeleton Coast*, was made acutely aware of the damage that visitors can cause. 'Few people realise how sensitive the surface of the desert is to vehicle tracks, especially the harder surfaces of the gravel pans,' she noted. 'Tyres break the hard top layer and leave tracks which, in human terms, could be permanent. According to experts, tracks on the harder surfaces could take anything from 700 to 1,000 years to disappear.'

To ensure that environmental impacts are kept to the minimum, the Namibian government has let the rights to tourism in the area to a single operator, who therefore can – and must – keep close control over visitors. The criteria for success are closely geared to conservation. Groups entering the area are limited to fifteen people and a great deal of effort is made to ensure that wildlife habitats are not disturbed. All rubbish is bagged and brought out. Interestingly, too, the local tribe, the Himba, share in the proceeds of the operation.

Cameroon's Korup Rainforest Park

One of the most exciting rainforest conservation projects in the world is Cameroon's Korup Rainforest National Park. First brought to public attention by Phil Agland's award-winning film *Korup*, the forest was soon the subject of international campaigns by Earthlife and the World Wide Fund for Nature.

The proximity of the rainforest is clear as soon as you get off the plane at Douala airport. The experience has been described as rather like walking into the bathroom with the shower on – in Douala, London's annual rainfall can fall in the space of a single hour. Mount Cameroon is rated the second wettest place on earth, after a Hawaiian island.

Around half of the country is covered by rainforest, although – as is the case right around the earth's tropical belt – the forest is under intense threat. Korup, in the English-speaking south-west of the country, is reckoned to be the greatest concentration of animal species anywhere in Africa, sheltering a quarter of Africa's primate species and over 250 species of bird.

Scientists and conservationists have flocked to Korup from

all over the world, but the forest underscores the difficulty of promoting eco-tourism in such areas. Not only is Korup a nightmare to get to, but once inside the forest it can be much more monotonous than might be imagined. It is rarely poss-ible to see more than a hundred feet in any direction and many of the animals keep well out of sight. But an experi-enced guide will ensure that you see enough to make the experience one to remember, including green mambas, tree hyraxes, hornbills and pangolins.

Definitely not a holiday for the Tripper or Termite, particu-larly when it comes to eating 'bushmeat', the local word for monkey and other jungle game. But it's important that some of us do visit such areas – and pay a reasonable amount of money for the experience. Otherwise the extraordinary gen-etic wealth they contain will be almost certainly lost for all time.

When in Ghana, stay with Ghanaians

Further to the west, Ghana provides another fascinating example of how low-impact tourism can be developed. Insight Travel, a very small operator (see page 330), working exclusively with Ghana, organises what it calls 'host-based holidays', which means that you stay with local people in order to maximise the benefit to the host community. They also encourage their clients to fly with the national airline – and to make the most of locally available food, transport and entertainment.

Another innovative Ghanaian initiative is Bristol Bond (see page 370), which involves the twinning of the British city of Bristol with the Fete tribal district in the Central region of Ghana. The link between the two places began a long time ago, with the cocoa trade – and, more infamously, the slave trade.

Bristol Bond is another small organisation that is in the early stages of setting up environmental and community pro-jects in Ghana and has formed educational and cultural links between the two countries. There are plans to include tourists in some of the projects in the near future. If the scheme works, it could help to ensure that Ghanaians keep a reasonable degree of control over their tourism industry – unlike the Gambians.

The Gambia: more than a smile for sugar mummies

In contrast to some of its neighbours, Gambia has embraced tourism with a vengeance. The country, a former British colony, has been described as a long, quizzical smile in the bulging face of west Africa.

Tourism is now the second largest foreign exchange earner after peanuts. But the contribution of tourism (15 per cent) has trailed a long way behind that of nuts (85 per cent), because of the way in which the tourism industry is structured. One 18-kilometre stretch of beach, for example, has no less than twenty four-star hotels, all owned or part-owned by expatriates. And the Gambia imports most of the food and services it offers to tourists. Worse still, the vast majority of tourists have pre-paid their bed, board and transport back home, where most of the money stays.

Package tourism was introduced to the Gambia in 1968 when a large Swedish tour operator, Vingressor, bought a five-year monopoly to operate charter flights on an exclusive basis. Sex tourism is popular here, but with an unusual twist. Young Gambian men operate as 'professional friends', taking up with Western women on holiday. Many eventually accompany their 'sugar mummies' back home, particularly to Scandinavia.

Gambia is only 30 miles wide at its widest and 193 miles long, with a population of around 1 million people, which means that the 100,000-plus visitors coming to the country each year are hard to miss. Swamped, many Gambians have become dependent on tourist handouts and aggressively pursue tourists for money. But here, too, interesting tourism projects are beginning to emerge.

Morocco and Tunisia: tourism is a thirsty business

Further north, the countries of Morocco and neighbouring Tunisia are receiving a rising flood of visitors, predominantly attracted by the warm climate. Instead of staying in bush camps, these people mainly stay in hotels and holiday complexes.

By the late 1980s, Morocco was hosting 2 million visitors a year, while Tunisia – which had been better marketed – was welcoming 3 million. Longer term, there seems to be every prospect of the northern coastline of Africa developing a parallel crust of holiday complexes facing those of the southern coast of Europe.

In Morocco, tourism is now established as the country's second largest source of foreign income – after the $1.3 billion sent home by Moroccan workers overseas – but by the end of the 1990s the holiday industry is expected to top the list.

In common with other predominantly desert regions, the industry's demand for water is likely to become a major problem. The water demand from hotels, swimming pools, air conditioners, gardens and, inevitably, golf courses far exceeds other local needs.

As in so many other parts of this huge continent, tourism is seen as a saviour for weak economies, but it will need to be extremely well planned and managed if it is not to cause more problems than it helps to solve.

EUROPE AND SCANDINAVIA

Europe is the heart of the world tourism business, and recent events suggest that travel within the region is going to explode in the coming years. We aim to give you a glimpse of some of the developing tourism pressure points in Europe from its crowded Costas to its rural retreats. After focusing on some of the underlying trends, we kick off in Britain and

Ireland, before moving to France, Spain, Italy, Turkey, Eastern Europe and Scandinavia. Along the way, we stop off to take a look at the 'Mayle Trail' in France, the wildlife of the Alps and Pyrenees, the problems facing the Mediterranean and, in Spain, the growing concern about animal cruelty during bullfights and fiestas.

Boom will follow gloom

Although Europe's share of international tourist arrivals slipped from 70 per cent in 1970 to 64 per cent in 1990, the number of tourists visiting various parts of the continent rocketed from 113 million to 271 million over the same period. In the wake of the Gulf War, however, the European tourism business was plunged into gloom.

The European Tour Operators' Association (see page 352) said that visitor numbers would be down by at least a third, worse even than the period after the Libyan crisis in 1986. With up to three million American and Japanese holidaymakers turning their back on Europe, the industry said that empty hotels had cost it $40 billion – and many tour operators were forced to lay off up to a third of their staff. More UK hotels were going bankrupt, we were told, than at any time since the 1973 oil crisis.

But even the combined impact of world recession and Saddam Hussein will probably turn out to have been little more than a blip on the inexorable growth curve of the European tourism business. Europeans are, always have been and probably always will be great travellers. The British are amongst the most active, with more than 60 per cent taking at least one holiday a year. The Germans occupy the number one spot, however, and they are second only to the Americans as world tourism's biggest spenders.

Not surprisingly, given that West Germany led the way in green politics in recent years, some of the greener Germans have been using their indisputable spending power to help put pressure on environment-wreckers in destinations like Ibiza (see page 247). At home, the West Germans had made considerable progress in cleaning up such tourist attractions as the Rhine and the Black Forest, long affected by acid rain pollution. But the country is also now having to share the burden of cleaning up the grossly polluted environment in what used to be the German Democratic Republic.

The French, meanwhile, despite the fact that they are much better placed to travel around Europe, make only a third as many foreign trips. But then, with France being the world's most popular tourist destination – in 1989 it received 12 per cent of total world tourism – perhaps it is simply a case of the French being happy with what they have on their doorsteps?

If you are looking for the most footloose people in the region, however, look to Sweden. A higher proportion of Swedes go on holiday than any other nationality. Indeed, the general trend in Europe is for the Southern Europeans to stay at home, while the Northern Europeans spend a considerable proportion of their holiday budgets on trips south. On present trends, it looks as if the northern habits, rather than the southern, will spread across the continent – triggering another boom period in European tourism.

Britain and Ireland: why not stay at home?

Inevitably, as more and more of us travel during the same periods of the year, the likelihood of major tourist attractions having to hang out the 'Full up' sign grows rapidly.

Martin Brackenbury, a top executive at the largest UK tour operator, Thomson Travel, warns that if current trends continue a 'worldwide ticketing system' will be needed. The busiest resorts and attractions will have no option but to turn away would-be visitors, asking them to come back tomorrow – or next year.

The best holiday option, the Greens tell us, is to stay at home. The tourist boards of England, Northern Ireland, Scotland and Wales agree: they spend millions of pounds each year on advertising campaigns designed to offset the attractions of 'abroad'. Faced with overloaded airports, typhoid scares in Spain, pollution problems in Italy and forest fires in France, many Britons have decided to explore the attractions of their own country.

Half the people who holidayed in Britain in 1990 took some kind of activity break. The most popular recreations, according to the tourist boards, are hiking, hill walking, rambling and orienteering – with Scotland proving to be the favourite location for such activities. The next most popular activities include swimming and visits to castles, monuments and churches.

About two-thirds travelled by car, with all the problems that that implies in a heavily populated country. In Britain, the West country is the most popular destination; throughout the holiday season endless columns of cars, caravans and other holiday traffic clog the motorways and scenic routes alike. Some of the most popular villages, like Clovelly in Devon, have even begun charging for visitors to enter. And, further north, the Lake District is another 'honeypot' which often teeters on the verge of going solid.

Much of Britain has become increasingly sordid in recent years, as tides of litter and rubbish mountains have been allowed to build up in our cities, while sewage pollution (see page 109) leaves many holidaymakers fearing that each visit to the seaside around our shores could be their last! Despite the government's environmental White Paper – and its continuous claims that the environment is getting steadily cleaner – many people prefer to believe the evidence of their own eyes.

Despite all its problems, however, Britain still has many areas of superb landscape and wildlife interest. We may not have attractions quite on the scale of Niagara or the Victoria Falls, but the discerning visitor can find just as much to fire the imagination around Yorkshire's High Force. Hundreds of nature reserves are protected by organisations like English Nature, the Royal Society for the Protection of Birds and WWF – in addition to the enormously energetic local nature conservation trusts. If you are visiting an area, check with the local trust to find out about the best places to go.

Even (possibly) imaginary wildlife can pull in the tourists. The Loch Ness Monster, for example, nets the Highlands up to £25 million a year, attracting some 500,000 visitors flocking from all over the world hoping to catch a glimpse of Nessie.

Whether Nessie exists or not, Scotland certainly has a lot to offer with its long coastline, wild country, sea lochs, islands, dunes, salt marshes and amazing 'seabird cities'.

If you intend to take a walking holiday, consider staying in one of the growing network of 'camping barns', once home to cattle and sheep but now converted for use by walkers and other holidaymakers. From Derbyshire's Peak District National Park to the Northern Pennines, this provides a sympathetic use for old buildings – and stops them being converted into holiday ghost-homes. The conditions may be spartan, but the barns, promoted by the Youth Hostels Association and the Countryside Commission, provide a cheap way of seeing some of Britain's most beautiful countryside.

Green attractions are on the increase around the country, including the Centre for Alternative Technology (page 366) outside Machynlleth in Wales and the National Centre for Organic Gardening (page 367) at Ryton-on-Dunsmore, near Coventry.

And in Melmerby, near Penrith in Cumbria, there is the award-winning Village Bakery, supplying organic bread and cakes baked in a wood-fired brick oven. 'Good Food from a Sustainable Environment' is the motto of this operation, licensed by the Soil Association and occupying a converted eighteenth-century barn overlooking the village's undulating green. Like a number of other green businesses founded along 'Small is Beautiful' lines, however, the Village Bakery is having to cope with exploding demand for its products.

But, longer term, perhaps the best hope of keeping Britons at home may well be the Center Parcs twenty-first century version of the traditional holiday village. Located in places like Sherwood or Elveden Forests, the Center Parcs villages are based around big glass domes (see page 174). The result: near-tropical conditions all year round. Not everyone's cup of tea, and particularly unlikely to appeal to Trailblazers, Travellers or Trekkers. But for families with children, the Center Parcs formula can be a godsend.

Meanwhile, millions of foreign visitors continue to come to these islands, in search both of our unique cultural heritage and of the landscapes made famous in such television series as *Poldark*, *Bergerac*, *Inspector Morse* and James Herriott's *All Creatures Great and Small*. But if we are to have any hope of sustaining their interest, we are going to have to pull up our environmental socks.

Maybe after Britain has been in the European Community for rather longer, with ever-increasing pressure from the European Commission to clean up its act, it will be able to follow Eire's lead. The Republic of Ireland promotes itself throughout Europe as the 'green, clean island'. For obvious historical and political reasons, however, it tends to be more popular with the rest of Europe than with the British.

The landscape is certainly green, but the Irish (particularly their farmers) still have a good deal to learn about environmental conservation. And the country's growing tourism industry is itself causing a number of environmental controversies. For example, a £2.7 million European Community grant for the development of a National Park and interpretive centre sparked an uproar in the Burren region of County Clare. The Burren Action Group has welcomed the National Park proposal, so long as it helps to protect the 6,000-year-old farming traditions of the area. But the controversy was ignited by the plan to site the associated interpretive centre and parking lots below Mullaghmore Mountain.

The Dingle Peninsula has also been in the eye of an environmental storm. This has been whipped up by plans put forward by a hotel across the bay to develop a marina. Despite intense local opposition, which includes posters in almost all the shops, the developers look set to win the battle to build along the shoreline. But Eire still has some way to go before it faces the sort of environmental problems that tourism causes in warmer parts of Europe.

France: on the Mayle trail

If any one country in Europe stands out as the tourism destination *par excellence*, it is France. Environmental issues are not yet top of mind there, but the country's ability to create and maintain tourism magnets helps it to stay at the top of the list of world tourism destinations.

From the châteaux of the Loire to the waterfront of St Tropez, from the cellars of Champagne to the treasures of the Louvre, tourists can't get enough of the country. But sometimes, as in the case of the Lascaux Caves (see page 120), tourist attractions can have too much of tourists.

The pace of development has been rapid in many areas of the country. Since 1989, for example, the number of hotels in the Dordogne has increased from around 140 to more than 230, while the number of campsites and self-catering properties has more than doubled.

Inevitably the Channel Tunnel is going to have a major impact on the north of France, and further south, too. Le Touquet, to take just one example, is preparing for the boom with nearly forty hotels being built along a 50-kilometre stretch of coast. But there is considerable wariness about low-budget British tourists. The locals dread what they see as the 'Boulogne daytrip mob', and are hoping to outprice them in order to prevent the region from getting locked into a down-market spiral.

Even slightly more upmarket tourists can sometimes prove too much of a good thing. Peter Mayle, whose book *A Year in Provence* created such a surge of interest, is not the most popular man in the area he made famous. As hundreds of thousands of people poured in to follow the 'Mayle Trail', local residents took great delight in making sure that a significant proportion of the pilgrims were directed to the Mayle household.

Many French people, not surprisingly, have mixed feelings about tourism. One farmer was overwhelmed by tourists – most of them British – wanting to see a tomb mentioned in another runaway bestseller, *The Holy Blood and the Holy Grail*. The tomb was located near Arques and Rennes-le-Château, the epicentre of the mysteries discussed in the book. The road alongside it became blocked with cars as people flocked to ponder its inscription *Et in Arcadia Ego*. Not long after, the farmer on whose land the tomb stood reacted in typical Gallic fashion and blew it up. But his problems are not completely resolved because some people now stop off to view the rubble!

If you want to get a sense of what France used to be like, one place to visit is the Ecomusée of the Grande Lande, near Sabres, some 90 kilometres south of Bordeaux. Here you can see how people lived before electricity, cars and televisions arrived on the scene. You can only get to the *quartier* of Marqueze by taking a small train into the forest. Once you arrive you can wander around a couple of dozen wattle-and-daub buildings. Among them you will find a thatched sheepfold, thatched chicken coops, water-mill, charcoal kiln, beehives and examples of resin tapping, or *gemmage*. Pine trees naturally exude resin, and in the Grande Lande they have been tapped like rubber trees. A few aspects of modern times have caught up with many *gemmeurs*, however: you will find that they now use plastic bags rather than clay pots to catch the oozing resin.

The Alps: eroding pinnacles of pleasure

Anyone who has visited Europe's hills and mountains will have found them increasingly alive – with tourists. An estimated 40–50 million people ski, sledge or tramp through the Alps alone each year. To be fair, however, the Alps stretch across such a huge area of the world map that the visitor can find overloaded resorts and many less-trafficked areas. The Alps are 1,200 kilometres long and 300 kilometres wide, running through seven countries that speak four different languages.

Even so, at peak periods, the pressure of numbers can be intense. In Chamonix, France, visitors to Mont Blanc outnumber the locals by four to one in August. The Benedictine monks are abandoning their Hautcombe monastery, near Chambéry, because tourists disturb their prayers. In Switzerland, meanwhile, there are something like 250,000 holiday establishments, with a further 750,000 guest-houses projected by the year 2010 – mainly catering for skiing and other winter sports.

The alpine skiing industry is now an enormous business, with some 40,000 ski-runs and 14,000 ski-lifts serving 12 million skiers. The cumulative environmental impacts of skiing are considerable – and growing (see page 142).

Inevitably, all this development and activity is leaving its mark on the mountains. Already under pressure from other forms of development, from forestry operations and from industrial and traffic pollution, some parts of the Alps may well need to have a ceiling imposed on further development.

The staging of the Winter Olympics has exacted its toll on many resorts. In the Austrian Alps, where the Winter Olympics were held in 1964 and 1976, forests were cleared to create 68 hectares of ski-runs. In 1983, significantly, those very same slopes were hit by a disastrous mudslide. A conference on alpine protection subsequently recommended that the Winter Olympics be banned in the Alps, while a number of groups have recommended a total ban on all new skiing developments.

Although it seems unlikely that such a ban will be imposed in the foreseeable future, a number of positive initiatives are now under way to try to contain the damage being done. The Austrian government, for example, has been seeking EEC funding for a new rail-tunnel through the mountains. And the Swiss have imposed bans on heavier lorries, with speed restrictions – although one result was to divert much of the traffic through Austria!

There is a great need for a regional response to the problems of such huge areas. At the same time, there is plenty of scope for local initiatives. Some of the most interesting existing initiatives focus on tree-planting schemes, with the largest reforestation programme in the Alps being undertaken by Alp Action (see page 354). In its 'Green Roof for Europe' campaign, Alp Action plans to plant 180,000 trees in vulnerable locations – and is helping to conserve threatened species as different as the Apollo Butterfly and the bearded vulture.

The Pyrenees: on the slippery slope?

Further west, in the Pyrenees, you can still see considerable numbers of relatively rare birds like griffon vultures and golden eagles, spiralling in the thermals like jet-liners stacking up over Heathrow. If you are exceedingly lucky, you may also catch sight of the very rare pink-gold lammergeier, also known as the bearded vulture. Once hovering on the brink of extinction, the lammergeier is making a slow comeback. The vast bird dines on bones, generally the left-overs from the meals of griffon vultures, breaking them up by dropping them from a height of 30–50 metres on to the rocks below.

But if you visit the border between France and Spain you are likely to stumble across the lines of gun-pits, trenches and watch-towers that blast into action each year against migrating birds. Every year, tens of thousands of hunters bang away at the birds, with one and a half million pigeons alone ending up on the table. Inevitably, there have been occasions when bird-watchers and hunters have come to blows.

As the number of visitors grows, so will the disputes between different groups of people who want to use the environment in different ways. In the wake of poor snows in recent years, ski resort developers have been moving ever-higher into the mountains of France, Andorra and Spain – putting further pressure on the forests and wildlife.

Despite the *Plan Ours* (Bear Plan), announced by President Mitterrand in 1984, the brown bear – one of the mascots of the Parc National des Pyrenées – has been hunted into invisibility. About the only place you can hope to see a bear is Etsaut, where the Parc National maintains a permanent exhibition on the bears and their role in the local ecology and economy. The bears here are stuffed. In a nearby village, you can see a live brown bear in captivity, but any self-respecting green tourist would give such an exhibit a wide berth.

The Pyrenees still rank among Europe's most beautiful regions, yet as the borders between countries like France and Spain become ever less important, the pressures from hunting, skiing and the associated development will almost certainly continue to grow.

A greener Spain?

No country demonstrates the problems of mass tourism better than Spain. Over 50 million visitors a year visit this country with a population of just under 40 million. In 1989 the country was the world's third biggest tourism earner, after the USA and France. The money injected into the economy has fuelled an extraordinary development boom.

Not surprisingly, there are clear signs that tourism has hit the environmental buffers in Spain. In 1990, for example, there was a sharp fall in the number of British tourists – the most frequent visitors from outside of Spain – arriving in the Costa del Sol, the Costa Brava and the Balearic and Canary Islands. Many went elsewhere because they were fed up with holidaying in a building site, or in poor quality (but highly promoted) resorts. Even so, in most areas the cranes have continued to swing into place the building blocks for the next generation of tourist developments.

At the same time, the Spanish Tourist Office launched an España Verde – or Green Spain – campaign. But environmentalists and green tourists who thought that the goal would be to develop more sustainable forms of tourism were disappointed. They soon found that, while the idea was certainly to reduce some of the pressure on the coastal areas and attract tourists into areas of northern Spain that have not yet been spoiled, environmental conservation measures did not seem to be part of the package.

When challenged on the point, however, the Spanish Tourist Office denies that Spain is willing to sacrifice its coastline – or other areas – for a quick profit. It protests that resorts like Benidorm were developed to fulfil the needs of a particular market at a particular time, providing thousands of holidaymakers with their first trip abroad. Whatever the facts of the matter, Spain does appear to be starting to pull its socks up a bit.

Benidorm is a useful illustration of the scale of the pressures imposed by mass tourism. In the space of a single generation, the resort grew from being a small village to a holiday centre catering for 4 million tourists a year. The British have been the most frequent visitors. As in other places, British visitors wanted low prices and somewhere sunny that nonetheless had many of the characteristics of UK seaside resorts. So local tourism officials in Benidorm were understandably left in a state of shock when they carried out a survey – and found that three-quarters of British visitors never wanted to return. As a result, the Benidorm authorities started working on a new image for the resort in the 1990s, part of which involved employing their first 'ecology counsellor'. They now say they are spending around £1 million a day to clean up the beaches and have put in hand a number of other important environmental measures.

In Marbella, meanwhile, a new mayor sensed which way the wind was blowing and decided that enough was enough. The Mediterranean resort had been one of the region's most popular fleshpots, but it had lost its glamour as prices soared and standards plummeted. Grime and crime made Marbella less and less attractive, with the authorities attacking the jet-set visitors as 'social parasites'. The new mayor may have been dictatorial in style, driving the prostitutes off the streets and recruiting hundreds of the town's unemployed into a marathon litter and rubble clean-up campaign, but he won widespread support.

The British can hardly be blamed for all the Mediterranean's ills, but it is perhaps significant that the Germans tend to pay almost twice as much as the British for the same sort of package tour. Maybe Mediterranean holiday resorts would invest more heavily in improvements, including environmental clean-ups, if they had more money to do so?

Ibiza: will the Las Salinas victory stick?

One of the most hopeful recent campaigns was mounted in Ibiza, one of the Spanish Balearic Islands, by Friends of the Earth Europe. Ibiza has seen enormous changes over the last twenty years as the numbers of tourists arriving each year rocketed. But the campaign also shows how hard it can be to protect threatened areas against tourism development –

whether it involves hotels, villas, swimming pools or golf-courses – particularly in a location that has become economically dependent on tourism.

The campaign was designed to protect Las Salinas, an area of salt flats, beaches and dunes threatened by a series of developments. Eventually, a total of nearly sixty local citizens' groups were involved in the campaign, which began in May of 1990 and lasted until January of 1991. Neil Rock of Friends of the Earth Europe (FoEE) recalls that one action involved residents sending 2,000 letters to the President, Sr Gabriel Canellas, asking him to include Las Salinas in the catalogue of protected areas. 'The letters were not answered,' says Rock.

When the San José municipal council refused to even consider requests that building permission be refused, a series of protest demonstrations was launched and a petition with 8,000 signatures, the largest ever produced on Ibiza, was presented to the President of the Balearic Parliament.

Suspecting that, once again, they would get nowhere, the campaigners linked up with another member of the FoEE network – Germany's BUND – and began to lobby the German travel trade. And FoEE also submitted a strong protest to the European Commission, arguing that the government of the Balearic Islands was incompetent to rule on the matter, because some of the politicians were also involved, directly or indirectly, in the development plans.

Again, FoEE failed to get a reply, this time from the Chairman of the Environmental Committee of the European Parliament. So, demonstrating the benefits of an international network, they promptly began to lobby members of his party in Scotland. Eventually, the European Commissioner for the Environment put the matter before the Council of Ministers, and the Commission registered the 420-page report submitted by Amigos de la Tierra (FoE Spain). The Spanish government was asked to investigate the matter and, on 10 January 1991, the European Council of Ministers included Las Salinas in the provisional European catalogue of protected spaces for birds. On the same day, the Spanish government also declared Las Salinas a protected area.

A fantastic victory, on the face of it, but Neil Rock and his colleagues are not resting on their laurels. 'The laws at Balearic Island level might not be enforced,' he warns, 'as local politicians and property speculators – with compromised persons often occupying both positions – have already declared their intention of modifying the law on protected spaces to protect their own interests.'

At the time of writing, a battle was already in the making between local families and the owner of a discotheque under construction just 25 metres from the boundary of the newly protected area.

Fiestas of cruelty

Countries that open themselves up to tourism, as Spain has done, inevitably expose themselves to challenge from visitors with different standards. Sometimes this is a question of the quality of hotels or transport, sometimes a question of what is done with wildlife areas and, increasingly, it is also a question of how animals are treated.

Spain boasts some 2,500 *fiestas* each year, but there is growing concern about the level of cruelty to animals seen at these events. It is no longer just a matter of bullfights, which have long been controversial (see page 168). Instead, campaigners and film-makers (most notably the makers of ITV's *Fiestas of Blood*) have been focusing public attention on what has been described as 'a latter-day equivalent of the Spanish Inquisition, using animals instead of people'.

Viewers of *Fiestas of Blood* saw horsemen riding beneath a line of live chickens strung up by their feet from a washing line. As the riders passed beneath the line, they ripped off the chicken's heads, one at a time, and tossed them into the crowd. These fiestas may not be everyday occurrences, even in Spain, but they help to entrench a distinctly un-green view of our responsibilities to nature and other species.

Elsewhere in Spain, drugged bulls are stabbed with meat hooks and shot with blowpipes. In Italy, too, it is not hard to find examples of outrageous cruelty to animals. One amusement there involves burying cockerels up to their necks and then bashing them with poles.

It won't be long before towns that permit such cruelty will find themselves pilloried not only in the media but in the European Parliament too. No one disputes that different countries have different cultures and different traditions, but is it far-fetched to imagine that in the years to come Spain's fiestas of cruelty to animals will be viewed with the same abhorrence as badger- or bear-baiting?

The Mediterranean

The classical civilisations of Egypt, Greece and Rome were all born and flourished around the Mediterranean. Not surprisingly, the Mediterranean basin now attracts around a third of all international tourist traffic – and is the world's favourite destination. The Eastern Europeans began to arrive in 1990 and the Russians will also soon be seeking their place in the sun.

Now scientists involved in the Mediterranean Action Plan, designed to bring the heavily polluted sea back to life, are warning that if present trends continue as much as 95 per cent of the coastline could be developed just forty years from now. The Mediterranean Basin, they say, may well have to support more than 500 million residents, rising from the current 320 million, with another 200 million tourists and 150 million cars annually. Each year, it is predicted, these people will eat 45 million tonnes of meat and 250 million tonnes of grain – in addition to consuming one billion tonnes of oil. Pull out your pocket calculator and work out the scale of the resulting sewage effluents and car emissions!

Horrified by this prospect, French conservationist Jacques Yves Cousteau has argued that all new development should be stopped immediately. He has also suggested that nearly half of the existing developments be razed to the ground and their sites returned to nature.

If, instead, the inexorable growth does continue, then we can expect to reach a point where many beaches are closed because of pollution; traffic jams set solid in areas like the Riviera; and the fish you eat in Mediterranean restaurants, if you can get it at all, comes from the other side of the world rather than the fished-out sea that laps at the concrete margins of the resort you have travelled so far to enjoy.

Italy: the merchants of Venice

If you believe UNESCO, Italy is home to 40 per cent of humanity's artistic treasures. It is also highly industrialised and criss-crossed with fume-hazed *autostrade*. The country's population density – at 120 people per square kilometre – is nearly double the continental average. As in many other parts of the continent, the natural and cultural heritage that tourists come to see is under constant attack. Air pollution caused by traffic fumes, domestic heating systems and industry is corroding monuments, *palazzi* and churches alike.

The best place to get a sense of the pressures that are eroding Italy's historic treasures is Venice. For years the city, dubbed *La Serenissima* (for the most beautiful city in the world), was thought to be in imminent danger of sinking under the waves. Now it is thought to be in more immediate danger of drowning under a flood-tide of tourists. Part of the problem is that the city has gone for quantity, not quality. Anything up to 100,000 tourists wash in each day, and many of these people spend relatively little much-needed cash in the city itself.

In 1989 a single Pink Floyd concert brought 200,000 people into a city with just five public toilets. Venetians awoke the next day to find many of their canals and alleys awash with urine and excreta. In fact cleaning up the mess was so far beyond the resources of the city authorities that the army had to be called in.

In the space of just five hours during the May bank holiday in 1987, 630 tourist coaches poured 36,000 tourists into the city, while the ferries discharged another 30,000. The crowds were so appalling that, for the first time in the city's peacetime history, the causeway connecting it to the mainland had to be closed.

Once the heart of a Mediterranean empire, Venice is tough:

it has survived the attentions of Attila the Hun and the ravages of the bubonic plague. But one of its latest problems underscores the way changes in its social structure now threaten to undermine its environment. Sewage pollution and industrial effluent have recently been the cause of plagues of a giant seaweed, *Ulva rigida*, in the lagoon. The seaweed eventually rots and strips the water of oxygen – suffocating the fish whilst aphids, flies and midges feed on the putrefying remains and reproduce in huge numbers. A few years back, the weed even forced the airport to close, for fear that the incoming aircraft would skid on the runway. 'Once the tide used to cleanse the lagoon,' explained Gianpietro Zucchetta, an ecology specialist working with the National Council for Research. 'Now it brings in more pollution. The lagoon hasn't got a chance.'

In addition to the problems of pollution, Venice is increasingly becoming a museum piece rather than a lived-in city. There are now only around 7,000 Venetians living in the city; the remaining 80,000 'residents' comprise mainly rich Italians and foreigners who have bought homes but spend little time in them. With fewer people living in and caring for the city and fewer resources to maintain the city's infrastructure, the city is crumbling. If the canals are not dredged, mud and sewage accumulates, blocking the sewers and causing sewage to seep through the walls of the houses. Few tourists can see behind the picturesque surface to the decay underneath – where the sewage causes the walls to disintegrate.

No one disputes that Venice is a transcendentally beautiful city, nor that people should be allowed to enjoy it. But the sheer number of people wanting to do so at peak periods raises the question whether anybody and everybody should have the freedom of the city.

Other Italian cities, such as Florence, also sometimes seem to be in danger of drowning in a sea of tourists. In the summertime the waste-bins are overflowing by 7 a.m., so Coke cans, paper cups and all sorts of other junk end up in the River Arno. It then flows out into the Adriatic and, eventually, into the Mediterranean – simultaneously the world's favourite sea and, in some areas, one of its most polluted.

'The Adriatic is dying,' warned one of the country's leading environmental groups, Lega per L'Ambiente. Each year since 1986, the organisation has sent its 'Green Boat' around the coast of Italy to monitor and report on pollution levels. The idea was expanded in 1988, with the introduction of a 'Green Train', a joint venture between the environmentalists and the Italian State Railway. The train has travelled around the country, stopping for a few days in each town to measure the air pollution and other problems.

Even with a fairly lively environmental movement, Italy is still having great difficulty in pushing such issues to the top of its political agenda, however. So what hope for countries where the movement is still embryonic – or, at best, in its carry-cot?

Turkey: 'Go, before it's gone . . .'

When Turkey woke up to its tourism potential and began to promote itself internationally, the country rapidly shot to the top of the list of popular, low-budget Mediterranean destinations. Again and again, the rallying cry for the travel agents and tour operators who promoted the country had a subliminal message: See Turkey before it's too late!

The transformation wrought in some of the country's less developed areas was little short of miraculous. Thousands of villages had been effectively marooned for centuries, without electric power, telephones or even adequate drinking water, but by the end of the 1980s there was hardly one left that did not have these facilities.

Inevitably, there has been a down side to this development. In 1988 alone Turkey increased the number of licensed beds available by over 430,000. The subsequent rash of buildings, many of them standing half-finished for long periods, scarred the natural beauty of coastal areas, churned up dust and produced decibel levels that deafened residents and visitors alike.

The biggest controversies, however, have focused on the impact on wildlife, and in particular the Mediterranean monk seal and the loggerhead turtle. To date, though, most of the successful environmental campaigns have been led – or heavily assisted – by campaigning groups from other parts of Europe.

In the case of the turtles, which are supposedly protected by a number of EC directives, Turkey's rush to develop had long overridden any environmental objections, wherever they came from. Developers sent their bulldozers growling over the turtle nesting grounds – and then built holiday villages there. Motor boats and plastic bags added to the day-to-day problems the turtles faced, while newly hatched baby turtles ended up under vehicle tyres or as easy pickings for predators, distracted from their dash to the sea by bright lights inshore.

It is still unclear what the outcome will be, but – under sustained attack for several years – the Turkish government is beginning to take action. Indefinite building bans have been imposed in five main areas: Dalyan, Fethiye, Patara, Göksu and Ekinçik. The quality standards imposed on hotel developers are being tightened and the World Bank has given Turkey a loan to improve its sewage facilities.

Longer term, Turkey plans to diversify into nature and skiing holidays. Before it does so, however, it should look carefully at some of the mistakes that have been made elsewhere in Europe, particularly in the Pyrenees and Alps.

Eastern Europe: the Russians are coming!

Thanks to a law passed by the Supreme Soviet, Russians – and other residents of what used to be the Soviet Union – will soon be able to travel abroad without let or hindrance. The East Germans and other travel-starved East Europeans are already at it. No sooner had the Berlin Wall fallen than the East's smoking, clanking Trabants and Wartburgs began turning up in Greece and in the car-parks at the Mestre end of the causeway that leads to Venice.

Many European Russians are likely to make a beeline for Spain's Benidorm and other Mediterranean resorts. According to British Airway's *High Life* magazine the resorts may already busily be printing hat-bands and badges urging *Potseluy menya bystro!* – Russian for 'Kiss me quick!' But there will also be a surge of interest in Europe's cosmopolitan culture – and in the delights of that forbidden paradise, the United States.

And as the Eastern Europeans and Russians pour out, so the rest of us will probably start pouring in to see for ourselves what lay on the other side of the Iron Curtain. Whether you are interested in skiing, bear hunting, city culture, run-down country houses or smokestack industries, Eastern Europe has it all. Indeed, the ex-communist countries increasingly recognise that tourism may be the best way of earning the foreign exchange they so desperately need. Worryingly, however, none of them have environmental planning systems worthy of the name.

As a result, we are likely to see historical cities like Prague hit by a tide of hamburger, pizza, fried chicken and jeans shops. And German speculators are already busily shopping for palaces and villas to turn into tourist havens. Now, too, one of Europe's most important wildlife habitats, the Danube Delta, is under threat from increasing tourism in addition to its problems of disastrous agricultural policies and grandiose development plans.

Elsewhere, the region has enormous potential for well-managed tourism. Lake Baikal, in Eastern Siberia, for example, contains around one-fifth of the world's fresh water – and a wealth of species found nowhere else on this planet. But here, too, pollution is a problem – and the environmental pressure is illustrated by the fact that the average size of some of the key species of fish is now much smaller than it was.

There are hopeful sparks in the gloom, however. A Soviet tour agency – Ecotour – organises 'ecological cruises' along the great Siberian river Lena. And the German SDP has proposed a designated bicycle route along the Baltic coast to Czechoslovakia. But many tourists will be put off by the examples of gross pollution that these countries will find very difficult to either hide or clean up in short order. Some tourists may of course be attracted by the pollution – and some of the old smokestack industries of Eastern Europe could become a lasting symbol of the bleak era that produced them.

The political volatility of much of this region – highlighted by the Soviet coup and counter-coup, and by the civil war in Yugoslavia – will also make it difficult for Eastern Europe to compete. Once the West's initial curiosity is satisfied, these countries will have a tremendous task on their hands to ensure that they win their share of the West's increasingly demanding tourists.

Scandinavia: Santa's radioactive reindeer

Although the Swedes, Norwegians and Finns all figured in the world's top twenty tourism spenders for 1989, their countries did not figure among the top twenty tourism earners. Even so, these are still popular countries to visit. While Sweden and Finland attracted roughly similar numbers that year – 882,000 tourist arrivals for Finland, 837,000 for Sweden – Norway pulled in more than twice as many (1.9 million).

In fact, the Norwegian Tourist Board has said that one of its major goals for the 1990s is that the country should become a leading destination for green tourists. Significantly, perhaps, the Norwegians claimed that the Winter Olympics at Lillehammer would be the world's first 'green' Games – all the buildings were being designed and constructed to be as environment-friendly as possible.

Skiing is a major attraction, with cross-country skiing a long-established sport (see page 142). The cross-country version, dubbed *langlauf* by the Germans, needs much less infrastructure than does down-hill skiing. There is generally no need for ski-lifts, snow ploughs or large-scale forest clearance to make the pistes. This is a sport which does not need purpose-built resorts, since it happens all over the country.

Apart from its fjords and midnight sun, Norway – like much of Scandinavia – can boast vast areas of natural beauty. The country is expensive to visit, but counts among its attractions sandy beaches, deciduous forests, steep mountains and even the most northerly point on earth which you can reach by car. At Hustadvika, where the North Sea penetrates the fjords and inlets, Norway is also planning its first underwater National Park. Already the area has become something of a Mecca for scuba diving enthusiasts.

Sweden also offers a wide range of beach holidays. Despite the country's international reputation for environmental consciousness, though, much of its sewage goes directly into the sea, largely because the resorts have not yet geared themselves up to the numbers of visitors they now welcome each year.

Beaches may not be what first comes to mind when you think of Scandinavia, but Santa Claus might be. In 1984, for example, the Finnish government decided to use Santa Claus to market Lapland as a province of 'peace and goodwill' and, after a few years, they had managed to fill their hotels. Later, however, an unholy squabble broke out between rival factions in Greenland, Iceland and Scandinavia, each claiming that Santa Claus came from their country.

Wherever he comes from, however, his reindeer will be glowing rather more at present than Rudolf's nose did. The radioactivity that spewed out of the stricken nuclear reactor at Chernobyl polluted huge areas of northern Europe and Scandinavia. The reindeer of Lapland were particularly vulnerable, because of the way the lichen and grass they eat concentrated the fall-out. Real or not, the image of Santa glowing as he comes down our chimneys at Christmas is a powerful reminder of the way environmental problems are no respecters of borders in our ever-more interconnected world!

CANADA AND THE USA

Ever since Columbus 'discovered' the Americas some five hundred years ago, ever-larger numbers of tourists have been flooding in. But the business has really taken off in the last few decades. In 1970, 37 million international tourists arrived in the Americas. By 1980, the figure had reached 54 million – and by 1990 it had soared to 84 million.

The United States, not surprisingly, turns out to be the most popular destination, accounting for nearly 52 million arrivals in 1990 alone. Canada came second, with just over 15 million, followed by the Caribbean, with nearly 11 million. By contrast, the combination of twelve South American countries (from Colombia down to Argentina) attracted just over 8 million, only a few hundred thousand people ahead of the figure for Central America – where Mexico accounted for an overwhelming 79 per cent!

In this section we focus on Canada and the United States, before heading south in the final leg of our round-the-world journey to look at some of the trends in Central and South America (see pages 278–98).

Dances with tourists?

Following the success of Kevin Costner's film *Dances with Wolves*, interest has grown in the world of the native American Indians (the so-called 'Red Indians') who occupied much of the continent before the whites came. If you can find out something about their culture, do. They certainly saw their world very differently.

Read too, the testimony attributed to Chief Seattle of the Duwamish people – an impassioned plea to the US President in 1855 for the Indians' way of life. At a time when the authorities were making every effort to buy up the Indian territories, the short document was called *How can one sell the air?* One passage that will ring down the centuries, and which should be a text for any self-respecting green tourist, runs as follows:

> All things are bound together.
> All things connect.
> What happens to the Earth
> happens to the children of the Earth.
> Man has not woven the web of life.

He is but one thread.
Whatever he does to the web,
he does to himself.

There are many places on the continent where you can visit Indians on their own terms, or follow trails which they walked before the prairie schooners and railroads came. In the South, for example, the Natchez Trace follows an ancient Indian track from Nashville via Jackson to Natchez. It runs nearly 500 miles through rolling countryside and swampland. As you pass through, imagine how the world looked to Indian travellers just a few centuries ago.

Neighbours: Canada and the USA

Canada and the United States, which together account for 13 per cent of the world's land mass and stretch from the high Arctic to the sub-tropics, have long boasted of sharing the world's longest undefended border. But this is not to say that there are no disputes between the two huge neighbours; far from it.

A century ago, the two countries almost came to blows over rights to water for irrigation from one western river that flowed across the border. This led to one of the oldest anti-pollution treaties on record, signed in 1909. Even so, the border region has seen some of the world's worst environmental problems.

A couple of decades ago, for example, Lake Erie was so polluted by phosphorus from sewage, soaps and fertilisers that it was turning into a green, soupy mess. Oxygen-starved areas formed in the lake waters where no fish could survive – and it was widely believed that Erie was dying. Today, although the clean-up of the Great Lakes is far from over, Canada and the United States have together spent some $15 billion on Lake Erie. Green slime no longer coats its beaches, its waters no longer taste foul and the fishing is getting better all the time.

Canadians, you will soon notice, tend to blame the Americans for many of their environmental ills. Incidents like the occasion when the effluent in the Cuyahoga River, which flows from the States into Lake Erie, burst into flames make it easy to understand why. But Canadians, too, contribute to these problems and the government's drive for environmental citizenship is not before time. So let's start out by looking at some of the things visitors hope to find in Canada.

Canada: in the footsteps of Grey Owl

Canada is the second largest country on earth. If you stand on its eastern tip, near St John's, you are nearer to Britain than you are to Vancouver. Eleven of the smaller US states would fit into Newfoundland and Labrador alone. From Newfoundland right across to the Yukon, Canada is brimming with wildlife and wild places. These great unspoiled tracts rank among the western world's last great wildernesses.

In the middle of the country lies Saskatchewan – where the Prince Albert National Park covers a million acres. And the Grasslands National Park attempts to preserve the short-grass prairie of the Great Plains, supporting endangered species such as the pronghorn antelope, the prairie falcon, rattlesnakes and the black-tailed prairie dog.

In the Prince Albert Park, you are near the old stamping grounds of Grey Owl – remembered by lovers of the great outdoors as the father of Canadian conservation and as a stalwart campaigner for the beaver. Grey Owl was a world-famous figure in the thirties, with tens of thousands of people, including some of the crowned heads of Europe, flocking to hear him give his lectures in his Red Indian buckskins. On his death it was discovered that Grey Owl was not a Red Indian at all, but an Englishman from Hastings. In the end it hardly matters: his memorial can be found in the thriving beaver colonies which he did so much to protect.

Canada's great cities – Montreal, Toronto, Calgary and Vancouver – are generally safe, clean and easy to get about in. They also provide ready access to the great outdoors, whether you are planning to go camping, canoeing, fishing, skiing or wildlife watching. Indeed, Grey Owl would be pleased to see how some leading Canadians today are carrying the torch for sustainable development.

'The world is facing an environmental crisis of unparalleled magnitude,' the country's Prime Minister Brian Mulroney told the UN General Assembly. 'Nature is sending us an urgent message that we ignore at our peril. The signs of this crisis are all around us: shortages of timber, exhausted soil, desertification, depleted fish stocks, seals dying in the North Sea, beluga whales washing ashore in the St Lawrence River.'

In its Green Plan, published in 1990, Canada committed itself to setting aside 12 per cent of its total area as protected spaces. Among other things, it said it would establish at least five new National Parks by 1996 – and establish half a dozen new marine parks. Even more important, the government pledged that it would establish the Canadian Environmental Citizenship Program, to help develop an 'environmentally literate society'. This was a particularly welcome step. As the pace of economic development continues to build across North America, the role of green consumers, green investors and green tourists will become ever-more important.

Islands on the edge: the Queen Charlottes

The tensions between environmental exploitation and sustainable tourism have been sharply defined on South Moresby Island, in the Queen Charlotte Islands – a forested archipelago the size of the Falklands some 90 kilometres off British Columbia's Pacific coast. The Queen Charlottes are islands on the edge in several senses: perched at the western edge of the continent, they are also at the edge of most people's consciousness and on the edge of environmental disaster.

South Moresby Island was faced with the prospect of clear-fell logging in an area which Jacques Cousteau had dubbed 'the Canadian Galapagos'. The area's rich wildlife reflects the fact that the last major Ice Age, which covered much of North America with glaciers some 10,000 years ago, left the islands unscathed.

Thanks to the stand taken by local Haida Indians and by a small number of dedicated environmentalists from Victoria and Vancouver, South Moresby's predicament became headline news. Eventually, the provincial government of British Columbia said it would work towards establishing a National Park on the island. This Park is now included on the federal Green Plan action list. But this victory was a bitter-sweet one for the environmentalists. Continued clear-felling, it was announced, would be allowed on Lyell Island, close to the loveliest region of South Moresby.

'In aesthetic terms,' said Brian Johnson, a British conservationist involved in the campaign, 'the Lyell Island decision was akin to protecting Hyde Park while designating the Serpentine as a refuse tip.' Some of the finest stands of temperate rainforest anywhere in the world would be cleared, with the scars visible from almost every part of the Juan Perez Sound – a major deterrent to sea-going tourists.

Ironically, the campaign established that tourism, including wilderness-based recreation, was already worth more to British Columbia's economy than timber – and that, properly managed, it could grow several-fold on a sustainable basis without destroying the natural resource on which it rests.

Alaska: the battle for America's last frontier

Head north and east from British Columbia and you are in Alaska, the largest US state. The state's name comes from an Aleutian word meaning 'great land' – and the Aleutians knew what they were talking about. If you laid Alaska atop the lower forty-eight states, it would stretch from Florida to California. Often described as America's last frontier, the state is rich in fish, oil, coal and timber. It is also an environmental paradise, as long as you are dressed and equipped for the often hostile conditions.

For years, the Alaskans thought that their traditional world and the new industrial world could live happily side by side. But the *Exxon Valdez* disaster changed all of that. 'People are going to have strong feelings about this for a long time,' said the state's environment commissioner. 'Every time people here go to a fishing hole, they will think of the spill and they will be angry.'

More than a third of the huge state is now designated as National Parks, wildlife refuges and forests. But the pressures are building in a number of areas. For example, there has been a raging controversy over whether the oil industry should be allowed to move into the vast Arctic National Wildlife Refuge, just east of the last mega-find in Prudhoe Bay. Environmentalists are concerned that the inevitable development would have a major impact on the region's wildlife, including caribou, musk-oxen, polar bears, golden eagles and wolves. Because the permafrost confines biological activity to a layer of earth just a few feet thick, they argue that oil spills can have a much greater impact here than in other parts of the world.

Nor is the oil industry alone in taking this sort of flak. The logging industry – not surprisingly – is also under fire. 'We have a saying about the timber industry,' said the founder of the Southeast Alaska Conservation Society. 'They take the best. Then they take the best of the rest. And then they leave us, the public and the nature lovers and the Alaskans, the scraps.'

The potential for developing eco-tourism here is as huge as the state itself. And the success of this vast continent, stretching from Newfoundland to Alaska, will be critically important in determining whether tourism can be greened in the rest of the world. America may be slipping behind in the race to export manufactured goods to world markets, but it still exports lifestyles – the 'software' of Western culture – with great success. Maybe in the years to come we will see eco-tourism joining Madonna and the Mutant Turtles on the export success list? To get an idea of how likely this is, let's swing through the United States, from east to west.

Niagara: pay as you view

If you follow the Niagara River north from Lake Erie to Lake Ontario, you come to the Niagara Falls, one of the continent's most impressive natural spectacles. The Falls, which draw millions of visitors every year, also form part of the boundary between Canada and the USA.

The falls fell into the hands of tourist promoters as long ago as the early 1800s. Travellers were hounded for their money and amazingly by 1860 there was no longer any point around the Falls where the view could be seen without paying for the pleasure.

Sadly, the pressure of development was such that the Niagara Falls soon became 'America's first environmental disgrace'. At nearby Love Canal (so named to tempt honeymooners to come to the Falls), it was discovered that an entire housing area had been built on an old toxic waste dump. Local people and their pets kept falling ill because the chemicals were seeping to the surface. The area was declared a Federal Disaster Area in 1978 and the entire community had to be evacuated.

As you make your way around the Falls, your guide is unlikely to allude to the sort of environmental idiocy illustrated by Love Canal. Instead, your attention is likely to be drawn to the rainbows which form all through the day. Green tourists may be less happy, however, at night. The Falls are illuminated in garish red, blue and – yes – green.

The east coast: from Nantucket to New Jersey

As you travel down the east cost of the United States, you continually come across evidence of the colonial period – and of the way in which early Americans viewed the natural wealth that greeted them when they arrived in the New World.

The economic mainstay on Nantucket, an island 40 kilometres south of Cape Cod, is now tourism. But once it was whaling. Most of the houses on the island are built of white cedar, but on Main Street the whale oil tycoons – with names like Coffin and Starbuck – built grand Georgian and Regency town houses.

The first ship to hunt sperm whales left the harbour in 1712, at the dawn of a boom period which lasted for around 150 years. Many families added viewing platforms to their houses, so they could watch for the returning whalers. If the sails were blackened with soot, the furnaces had been in action and the holds would be full of oil cooked out of the blubber. If, instead, the sails were white, the voyage had been a failure. Eventually, as in almost every other corner of the earth, the whaling industry destroyed its basic natural resource. More and more sails came back white. The last whaler sailed in 1886.

Today, the east coast is better known for its spectacular coastline – and as the home base for countless thousands of yachts. The ports of Maine, Newport and Marblehead, for example, clink with the noise of the rigging and other tackle as the huge pleasure fleets rock at anchor.

Riding the green wave

Less adventurous Americans take to the waves in increasingly gargantuan cruise liners. With millions of Americans booking cruises each year, there are cruises catering to almost every taste (see page 97). And while many cruise lines are still struggling to absorb the implications of the green wave which has swept around the world, you can now book passage on cruise ships whose owners are already doing their utmost to keep their environmental record spotlessly white.

Salen-Lindblad Cruising, based in New York, claims to be setting the pace with its 164-passenger *Frontier Spirit*. Food waste will be frozen for later disposal, non-biodegradable trash will be stored, glass will be ground into sand and all other trash will be burned in a high-tech incinerator. The cruise ship also features an on-board sewage plant and bilge oil separator. Passengers who toss things into the sea, Salen-Lindblad says, will be fined.

Many New Yorkers do not range so far afield in their leisure hours, however. They head for the string of beach resorts, among them Coney Island on Long Island, which stretch down the coast into New Jersey. But year after year there has been evidence that the sea has been abused to such an extent that even a day at the seaside is becoming a high-risk exercise.

In the summer of 1988, for example, there was a scandal when medical waste and hypodermic syringes – suspected of being used by AIDS sufferers – were washed ashore on Long Island. The news washed on to the covers of national news magazines and a massive clean-up operation was launched. Refuse bobbing in the currents is now being tracked by orbiting satellites and vast holding tanks are being built to contain the contents of overflowing sewers during heavy rainstorms.

But don't expect clean beaches anywhere near New York just yet. One New Jersey beach was recently hit by a three-mile oil slick that was found to contain a plastic bag containing a severed human head. It turned out to have belonged to a jockey from the Belmont racetrack.

Travel further south, however, and there are some stunning beaches, many of them located in state or National Parks. The beach at Virginia's Chincoteague, for example, is just across from a bird sanctuary and offers miles of platinum-coloured sands. Beaches such as these are sufficiently far away from 'civilisation' that you are unlikely to encounter the hazards of many American beaches, from rafts of foam plastic cups to blaring radios.

Florida: alligators and Mickey Mouse

Even on a clear day it is possible to see air pollution as you make your way south towards Florida. Pollutants have changed the legendary blue mists of the Blue Ridge Mountains and the great Smoky Mountains to a whitish, man-made haze. By the time you get to Florida's Everglades National Park, you are unlikely to have left the air pollution behind, but the most obvious environmental perils are of a very different nature.

Here you will see evidence of probably the world's largest nature rescue programme, designed to save at least some of this giant area of wetlands on which some 4 million people now depend for their water. As the demand for water has grown, and development, much of it tourism-related, has bitten ever deeper into the Everglades, the entire ecosystem has shown increasing signs of stress. Since the 1930s, about 90 per cent of the marsh and wading birds have gone.

You can still see alligators sliding through the waters, thanks to vigorous conservation efforts. But, as local conservationists point out, the reason you can see the great reptiles so easily is that there is so little water left in the swamps. And phosphate pollution from fertilisers used by sugar cane plantations and farms is also now killing off many of the native cypress trees and marsh grasses.

None of this has stopped the tourists flocking in, of course. Florida, for example, is still the favourite long-haul holiday spot for British tourists visiting America. Although the concrete horrors of the Miami beach-front come most readily to mind, Florida is far from being the state-wide desert of high-rise blocks that some people believe it to be. Here, too, you can find places that are resisting the tide of change. To the north are the two lovely islands of Sanibel and Captiva, the only places in the US where neon light is actually forbidden. There should be more. Parking is not allowed on the road – and no building may be over two storeys high.

And in the Florida Keys is the outstanding Cheeca Lodge Hotel, which in 1990 received the Gold Key Environmental Achievement Award from the American Hotel and Motel Association – and hosted President George Bush's Earth Day '90 speech to the nation. What did it do to win the award? Among other things, it created a snorkel trail explaining different aspects of the shallow marine meadows off Cheeca's beach; it organised Camp Cheeca, a children's ecology programme; it hosted a dinner for environmentally aware Floridians, raising $10,000 for the Cousteau Foundation; it treats waste water to make it usable for irrigation in the hotel grounds; and it recycles plastic, glass and aluminium. 'Cheeca Lodge is located in one of the most pristine and environmentally precarious regions of the United States,' explains Helmut Horn, president of the Coastal Hotel Group which owns the lodge. 'We believe it is imperative to have a solid and work-able awareness programme. If we fail to protect our natural resources, our own industry will wither and die.'

However, the biggest tourist attractions in the region centre around Disneyland and Sea World. Disney developments are not universally welcomed: in France, for example, the new Disneyland outside Paris was described by one critic as a 'cultural Chernobyl'. Not that that will stop even the French turning up for their day with Mickey Mouse and the rest.

A greener shade of Disney

Don't go to Disneyland – or to Sea World – if you are looking for solitude. Half the world and their families will be there. But of their type, these huge tourism complexes are amaz-ingly well organised. More than 50 million visitors passed through the gates of Disney World and Disneyland in 1989 alone. Along with the Tokyo Disneyland, these parks now account for over half of Disney revenues. Indeed Disney World in Orlando is the most popular vacation destination in the USA.

To preserve the illusion of a perfect world, all the 'works' are underground, the lawns are cut at night and a com-puterised irrigation system is hidden under green mush-rooms. But even this apparently flawless facade is not impervious to cracks. In 1990, Disneyland was fined for violating thirty-eight toxic waste laws. It was alleged to have removed 14,000 gallons of paint thinner, solvents and other toxic waste from its Disneyland theme park in Los Angeles to dumps in Wyoming and Utah that were not permitted to handle the waste. Under the eventual settlement with the Environmental Protection Agency (EPA), Disney accepted responsibility for the violations, but the EPA agrees the viol-ations were unintentional.

And it's fair to say that Disney has long been concerned with conservation. Half of Disney World's 114 square kilo-metres is to remain undeveloped, and there is also an 18,500-hectare nature reserve – which is closed to the public. The company also appointed a marine biologist as head of environmental affairs. He was soon at work reviewing building specifications, with both electrical energy and water conservation in mind, and specifying materials and equipment that are less environmentally damaging for new developments.

Environmental affairs departments have been set up throughout the company and guidelines issued to all employees. Disneyland now says that it recycles glass beverage bottles, as well as other items such as cardboard, laser printer toner cartridges, office paper, batteries and scrap metal. None of the polystyrene foam cups at Disneyland use CFCs – and real progress has been made towards converting company vehicles from gasoline to cleaner burning compressed natural gas.

But when we called Disney while researching this section, it was clear that the company is still acutely sensitive about its environmental image. We were told that we could not publish anything about the company without clearing the copy with them first – and they were not prepared to send information on the status of their initiatives.

The 'world's sixth ocean'

We found Sea World, just across the way from Disney's Epcot, rather more friendly. Walt Disney's original concept for Epcot, a model city where scientists could test out future technologies and life-styles, may have been heavily watered down, but the scale of his achievements is indicated by the vital statistics of Epcot's 'Living Seas' Pavilion (see page 166). Billed as the 'world's sixth ocean', it was Disney's first venture based on living animals.

Clearly, such attractions can have a huge educational effect – and they also have the indisputable advantage of concentrating tourists in a relatively small space.

But, at the same time, Sea Worlds and their ilk do display animals – among them dolphins and killer whales – that would be much better off in their natural habitats. At the same time, too, they may help to create unreasonable expectations in the minds of visitors.

One of the authors, for example, visited Tokyo's Disneyland and saw robot versions of almost all Africa's animals inside five minutes, not to mention cannibals. It will be interesting to see whether National Parks and wildlife reserves – where the wildlife is thinner on the ground – suffer as a result!

America's National Parks

Most green tourists, we suspect, still prefer to see animals in their natural surroundings, rather than in an artificial habitat, however brilliant the engineering. And here North America is extravagantly blessed, with National Parks scattered across the continent.

The thirty-seven National Parks within the North American system include national monuments, historic sites and national wildlife reserves. In many Parks, you will find that you will be asked to pay a fee – a good idea, since much of the money goes to protecting and managing the Park.

America's Yellowstone Park, created in 1872, is generally considered to have been the first National Park in the world. It is difficult to exaggerate the plight of American wildlife a hundred years ago. There were only twenty-three bison left at the turn of the century – and the arrival of the National Parks in the States was too late for the passenger pigeon, which once darkened the skies for days but was hunted into extinction (see page 139).

If you are used to National Parks in countries like Britain, you will find their North American counterparts very different. Visitors are looking for a true back-to-nature experience. In fact, Yellowstone does not allow cars, offering a mono-rail instead. And some Parks even go as far as banning phones and TVs in park accommodation.

The scale of the National Park system is suggested by the fact that if you took a trip around the Parks of north-west America and Canada alone, you would cover some 9,000 kilometres. Inevitably, the most popular US Parks, such as Yosemite and the Grand Teton, have received such heavy use that many of the qualities for which they were established are in serious danger of being destroyed. Land, water and air pollution are reaching dangerous levels in some places.

Fragile ecosystems are being trampled. Crime and vandalism are also becoming a major problem in some areas.

Indeed, the popularity of the major Parks is such that at the height of the season you have to book a visit six weeks in advance. Some camping sites are fully booked as soon as the computer booking service opens for business. In addition to the computer booking system, some Parks offer places on a first-come, first-served basis – but even these sites are generally full by 10 a.m.

And there are concerns that some of the Parks are too small to do what they were designed to do. A recent study suggested that at least seven out of eight National Parks in western North America are too small to maintain minimum viable populations of several species found within them. So in future we may see attempts to link up some existing Parks – or to return some land nearby to conservation.

The Rockies: 'roof of America'

Some of the most spectacular scenery can be found in the Rockies, covering an area six times that of the Swiss Alps and linking the states of New Mexico, Utah, Colorado, Wyoming, Montana and Idaho. The 'roof of America' is liberally sprinkled with National Parks and other protected areas, but those who know say that if you visit only one US National Park in your life you should make it the Rocky Mountain National Park. It may be commercialised on its edges, being only 80 kilometres from Denver, but it is so huge that in its interior wildlife abounds.

Inevitably, there are tensions between tourism and conservation. Yellowstone tourists, for example, may find themselves in grizzly or black bear territory. The bears have been attracted in to open-pit garbage dumps, tourist roadside food offerings and even tourist picnic baskets and campsite food caches. Some tourists have been mauled – and a few killed – by the bears. Some of the bears, in turn, have had to be shot by park rangers. Others have been hauled off by truck, trailer and helicopter to remote back-country areas, far away from the tourist centres. Because they are dangerous, the bears, which once roamed from the Arctic Circle to Mexico, are now confined to three major locations, two of them US National Parks. Some bears have ranges of several thousand kilometres, so even a Park as big as Yellowstone may not be big enough for them. Longer term, we may have to decide whether Parks are for bears or for people – and the problem for the bear lobby is that people bring more money.

The Grand Canyon and Canyonlands

Even so, throughout the Park system, we are seeing limits imposed on visitor numbers. At the Grand Canyon, campsites are scarce and the potential crowding impacts so great that they have had to limit commercial and private party rafting trips to about 2,000 a year. They also have a 'carry in, carry out' policy that results in all refuse (including human waste) being taken, by the rafting party, off the river and deposited in a disposal site approved by the National Park Service. Raft operators can lose their licence if they ignore the rules.

Over at the Canyonlands National Park, as in most other parks, a related debate is about which activities to allow. In some Parks, off-road vehicles, including all-terrain bikes, have been limited to roads. And there is still a raging debate about the use of helicopters for sightseeing. Many people see them as particularly invasive of their privacy, in what they believe should be a rock-and-water wilderness free from modern machines. The pilots retort that they provide a service for those who do not have the time – or physical ability – to raft the river or hike along the Canyon. The issue here may be whether everyone has a right to see something regardless of whether or not they are prepared to do so at an appropriate time – and pace.

All the Parks are more accessible than they were. Consider California's Yosemite, given Park status in 1890. If you travelled there from Los Angeles in 1885, according to the diary of Sir Arthur Sullivan, you had to put up with a fourteen-hour train journey, followed by another fourteen hours in a stage coach 'in boiling heat and smothering dust'.

Around 4 million people visit Yosemite each year, three-quarters of a million of them arriving in August alone. Even so, we are told, Yosemite is in a better state today than it was thirty years ago – and there are very few Parks in the world about which you can say that.

But there are inevitably concerns that the Park is in danger of being turned into a 'Disneyland' experience. These were reinforced in 1991 when the Japanese electronics giant, Matsushita, took control of MCA, the California-based conglomerate that owns both Yosemite and the company that operates the Park's lodging facilities, restaurants, shops and services. Conservationists will be watching developments very closely indeed.

From the saucers of Sedona to Seattle

In Arizona, meanwhile, at least one nature reserve is facing a very different form of pressure. 'New Age' believers have been making pilgrimages from all over the States to experience Sedona's seven 'vortices' – points through which they believe energy is transmitted from the centre of the earth to the heavens. They also believe flying saucers stop off in Sedona for repairs.

Unfortunately, the vortexes are in a 28,000-square-kilometre nature reserve. The New Agers rearrange rocks to form what they call 'medicine wheels', up to 60 metres in diameter. The local rangers say they are destroying the landscape and that they are sick and tired of putting the rocks back to where wave formations left them aeons ago.

And you don't have to be a New Age flying saucer aficionado to leave your mark on the landscape. If you are lucky enough to find yourself on the flanks of Mount Rainier, the huge snow-capped volcano that looms on Seattle's horizon (and an easy day-trip from the city), you will find it hard to miss the damage caused by thousands of hiking boots. Every year, over a million visitors flock to see the mountain which a local pioneer dubbed 'Paradise'. As you watch the grey marmots and mule deer, you may reflect that the mountain's extremely vulnerable sub-alpine meadow ecosystem is going to need all the help it can get. When the highly specialised and sensitive vegetation is destroyed, the thin soils rapidly erode, leaving bare rock. A study revealed over 900 of these bare areas, particularly around viewpoints.

This is one place where you may find yourself welcoming the helicopters. They swoop in over the tree tops carrying great sacks of gravel to repair the paths. Because commercial choppers are so expensive, at over $8,000 a day, military Chinooks have often been used – with the flights doubling as training for their pilots.

It is in places like this that you get a real sense of the huge effort that is now being developed worldwide to save our great natural treasures. At the Mount Rainier National Park headquarters, as Robert Francis put it, 'you can sense the enthusiasm and pioneering spirit among those involved in a world class project that could save one of North America's natural jewels.'

California: America, only more so

It's the place everyone wants to go to and it's showing the scars of too many people doing too much with too little respect for the environment that provides such a dazzling backdrop to their affluent lifestyles.

The Golden State of California remains one of the most popular tourist destinations in the world, hosting well over 100 million visitors every year. The state's attractions and geographical diversity ranges from Yosemite and Mount Whitney to the stark beauty of the Mohave Desert. The spectacular Pacific coastline is a must-see.

Though many North American cities are interchangeable, San Francisco has a character all its own. Its steep hills, cable cars, rickety Victorian houses and ever-present Bay are a tour operator's dream. The history of the city's Golden Gate Bridge also shows that development is not always an environmental disaster. When the bridge was first proposed, objectors said it would disfigure the landscape – while timber firms feared that the increased tourism via the bridge would expose their devastation of California's forests! Indeed it did and the public reaction to the denuded landscapes north of the Bay forced tighter controls on the loggers.

But the pressure of development – and the pollution that hazes cities like Los Angeles and fouls some of that spectacular coastline – has sadly tarnished what many early pioneers saw as a utopia. The main ingredients in smog are ozone, sulphur dioxide and a number of petrol-engine emissions. The worst smogs in the country are found in cities like LA and Denver, Colorado during temperature inversions, periods when atmospheric conditions trap pollution in the city air for days or even weeks. Often, a sickly, yellow pall hangs over the city. Even healthy young people find their eyes streaming, while the old and infirm can suffer greatly.

Now thousands of Californians are moving to Arizona, Oregon and Washington, fleeing from the traffic congestion, pollution and, increasingly, the crime and drug problems. California, as one environmentalist put it, is 'America, only more so'.

The affluent worked up about effluent

There is no question that Californians need to keep the pressure up on polluters. Surfers at Malibu Lagoon state beach have been known to emerge from the waves with red welts all over their bodies. 'I feel like I've just taken a bath in battery acid,' said one. 'Look, the water's got a better head on it than Budweiser beer.' More obvious are the discarded needles and condoms. Now surfers are taking aggressive action to protect both their sport and the marine environment.

Surfers at North Jetty, located at the mouth of northern California's Humboldt Bay, also suspected local polluters of causing sinus infections, sore throats and skin rashes. So they formed the Surfrider Foundation in 1989 to fight pollution from two nearby pulp mills. Led by a thirty-year-old surfing attorney, Mark Massara, Surfrider's legal team showed the court videos of black plumes of effluent spreading out into the sea. Now the mills are promising not only to clean up the effluents and to print their legal compliance reports on recycled paper, but also to provide solar-powered showers for the surfers!

Meanwhile, the millionaire residents of Malibu Beach – among them Madonna, Rod Steiger, Olivia Newton-John and Larry Hagman – found themselves in the limelight when they tried to block a new sewage treatment plant. The environmental planners said that the septic tanks that dispose of the stars' wastes were antiquated, so that sewage was seeping into the very sands on which the stars lolled in the sun. The stars were not against sewage treatment, but they were worried that if the Los Angeles planners put in a sewage system, massive development projects would not be far behind. This is a paradise-for-some-versus-progress-of-a-sort-for-the-many story. Some, like Hagman, JR in the long-running series *Dallas*, have already bought houses further up the coast in the hope of escaping the human wave.

Although population growth is not as rapid in North America as it is in many parts of Central and South America, the sheer resource-intensiveness of American lifestyles – as promoted in shows like *Dallas* and *Dynasty* – is imposing growing strains on the environment. Many parts of California, with their endless swimming pools and hissing lawns, now face imminent water shortages. As water is imported from ever-greater distances, so the pressures on western rivers grows. So much water is now taken out of the Colorado, for example, that it no longer reaches the sea.

Here, as elsewhere in the world, the focus must increasingly be on environmental sustainability. Although Canada probably has the edge when it comes to sustainable development policies, there are signs that the US tourism industry could go green. 'Travel agents, too, are passengers on Planet Earth,' explained Voit Gilmore, president of the American Society of Travel Agents. 'Not only do we hear the rising crescendo of concern over environmental threats to the earth, we see with our own eyes the over-impacting and over-stressing of tourist destinations.'

Eco-tourists have a whale of a time

As green concerns mount, whale watching (see page 163) is booming across North America. Each year, more than 2 million people go whale watching on special boats – and as many again do it from the shore for free. California, Hawaii and Canada each draw over 200,000 whale watchers a year. Newfoundland is a good place for whale watching and whales also pass along the American and Canadian west coasts on their way from feeding grounds in Alaska to breeding areas in the lagoons of Mexico. They swim past California in mid-January.

Often, you can help whale conservation directly. If you visit Cape Cod, you can 'adopt' a whale and help fund local whale conservation work in the area. Biological Journeys and Oceanic Society Expeditions are well-known whale-watching organisations on the west coast, while Eco-summer Canada Expeditions offer eight-day kayaking tours to the Johnstone Strait.

In Alaska, you can watch humpback whales, porpoises, seals and sealions. Ashore, courtesy of a ship charted from Biological Journeys, you can see coastal grizzlies and Alaskan brown bears gorging on salmon. Vancouver Island, on the other hand, is famous for its resident killer whales.

A whale-watching park was established on one of the San Juan islands, off the west coast of Washington State. There you can hire a kayak and paddle around looking for killer whales. There is a toll-free whale-sighting telephone number – and a local billboard advises: *Call Bill if you find a stranded whale on your beach and don't know what to do.* Constant vigilance is needed, given that the islands are on the Alaska oil tanker route, with the continuous danger of a massive spill.

Many consumer market experts are predicting that the nineties will be the Earth Decade – or the Green Decade. A recent Gallup poll showed that 76 per cent of Americans think of themselves as 'environmentalists' – and businesses of all kinds are responding to the new market demand. One area where we are seeing rapid growth is in 'low-environmental-impact' travel.

One popular journey offered by Breakaway Adventure

Travel of Cambridge, Massachusetts, takes small groups of tourists deep into the Amazonian rainforest, where they live for six days with indigenous tribespeople. This experience, Breakaway notes, was 'previously only available to hard-core explorers, anthropologists and missionaries'. Let's end our round-the-world tour by looking at what Central and South America have to offer.

CENTRAL AND SOUTH AMERICA

Attracted by places as diverse as Acapulco, Antigua, the Amazon and the Andes, some 22 million tourists – if you believe the region's notoriously inaccurate statistics – spent an estimated $13 billion in the Caribbean and Latin America in 1987 alone. But precious little of that money filters through to the poorest of the poor – or to the cause of environmental conservation.

Apart from its natural attractions, the continent offers a huge array of archaeological and cultural treasures. Many of the archaeological sites found in Mexico, for example, are in the Yucatán Peninsula, which was the heart of the world of the Maya. Here you can visit a wide range of Mayan ruins, some of them almost deserted. Guatemala's spectacular Tikal, thought by many to rival the Pyramids, receives perhaps 100,000 visitors a year, while the ruins of the city of Tulum, on the east coast of Mexico overlooking the Caribbean, are visited by nearly a million people. Some of the best examples of conservation in action come from the smaller countries, among them Belize, Costa Rica and Ecuador.

But, despite local success stories like the Galapagos Islands (see page 288), conservation is not a priority for most of these countries, mired as so many are in foreign debt. Faced with the need to make massive repayments to Western banks, is it any wonder that some governments turn a blind eye to 'environmental crime'? So jaguar shoots are laid on for tourists in Paraguay, while in Colombia there are markets where visitors are encouraged to buy both animal skins and live animals, among them birds and small primates caught in the wild, many of which are endangered.

It is dangerous to generalise about any continent, but it is particularly risky to do so with South America, which stretches from the Equator to Tierra del Fuego, cheek-by-jowl with the frozen wastes of Antarctica. The Andes alone run nearly 8,000 kilometres from Venezuela to southern Patagonia, while the Amazon Basin covers a distance of 3,000 kilometres from the Andes to the Atlantic. And the wildlife interest is almost as great when you get down to the Falkland Islands (or *Malvinas*, if you are Argentinian), where tourists now go to see King penguins, sealions and elephant seals.

Rather than attempt to cover the whole canvas, we have tried to sketch in some local highlights which give a sense of the underlying trends.

THE CARIBBEAN

Most visitors who lie on the Caribbean's beaches soaking up the sun have little idea of the region's history. When Christopher Columbus (known as Cristóbal Colón in South America) discovered what he thought was Asia five hundred years ago, he had actually stumbled across several Caribbean islands. As America celebrated the quincentenary of its 'discovery' by Columbus, various campaigning groups linked up to ensure that the other side of the story was heard – a story of colonisation, disease, slavery and, in some places, outright genocide. More recently, tourism development has brought different problems, including pollution.

Learning to say no
For centuries the staple industry on many islands has been that of sugar, but tourism now occupies pride of place in the Caribbean economy. Columbus would hardly recognise most of these islands today. Some feel as if they have been eaten alive by the tourism industry, while others – notably Cuba – have turned their backs on tourism in recent decades. But even Cuba is beginning to open itself up again to visitors as

communism's star fades around the globe. And no one who knew the pre-revolutionary Cuba will be surprised to hear that the island is already beginning to pay a high price for the much-needed foreign exchange, with prostitution and other social problems booming alongside the new developments.

From mainland Belize and the Cayman Islands through Cuba, Jamaica, the Bahamas, the Turks and Caicos Islands, Puerto Rico and the Virgin Islands to the Lesser Antilles (stretching from Antigua to Trinidad), the Caribbean has become one of the world's main winter vacation resort areas. The region has become a playground for the huge populations of America and Canada – and, increasingly, for South Americans from as far away as Argentina. Each year some 170 million residents are joined by another 100 million tourists.

Jamaica, the largest of the English-speaking islands, illustrates the way that the glittering world of tourism can exist alongside abject poverty. Long a wintering spot for the likes of Noel Coward and James Bond author Ian Fleming, Jamaica now appeals to a wider market, with tourism the biggest foreign exchange earner. Even so, the island ranks as one of the most indebted nations on earth. Life for most Jamaicans is an unappetising combination of chronic unemployment, declining living standards, low wages and high prices. In fact, most Jamaicans have been getting poorer for the last decade.

In some ways, however, Jamaica is better placed than many other Caribbean islands to cope with the pressures brought by tourism. Its sheer size has enabled it to avoid the worst ravages of beach-front saturation – and its government has emphasised competing attractions in the island's wooded and mountainous interior.

But some of the region's social problems are glaringly obvious here. The availability of drugs, for example, especially the locally made *ganja*, has been a strong attraction for some visitors – and an intense irritant for many in the tourism industry. In recent years the government has tried to crack down on the drug trade and the tourist board now warns that 'arrests are made daily at Jamaican airports, with many European travellers going directly from elegant resorts to drastically inelegant Jamaican jails'.

The decade of the environment?

If more Caribbean nations become committed to the cause of conservation, we may see a political backlash unless they take social equity issues into account at the same time.

An example of the inequities that could emerge – or be reinforced – is the National Park on St John, in the Virgin Islands. The land that was to become the Park was originally donated by the Rockefeller family. Following the ending of sugar cultivation in the area, much of it had been taken over by bush vegetation. To get the area back to its pristine state, however, the Park authorities banned farming and cattle grazing – forcing the farmers to slaughter many of their cattle when drought set in, rather than turning them out to feed in the bush.

Ironically, the main long-term beneficiaries of the Park turned out to be the Rockefellers, who built a hotel and tourist facilities to exploit the growing tourism interest, whereas the local people found themselves left with the menial tasks, like taxi-driving and serving in cafés and restaurants.

The Virgin Islands, which include some of the most heavily developed areas in the region, began a $3 million international publicity campaign in the summer of 1989. The campaign focused on images of underwater life, flowering plants and migratory birds, to emphasise the new commitment to protecting the environment. But there is still a strong sense that if such islands err, they will almost always err on the side of over-development.

In wealthy Bermuda, however, the local community has been pressurising the authorities actively to manage tourism. Here, too, tourism is the number one earner, but tourists have had to fit in with the local standards, not vice versa. There is very little litter, very few graffiti and no billboard advertising. In recent years, too, there has been virtually no unemployment, poverty or crime. Only four cruise ships a week are allowed, and there is no berthing at weekends. The ships that do arrive are promptly linked to mains sewerage and developers onshore can only build a new hotel if one of equal size closes down.

Most Caribbean resorts are still some way from turning

away tourists rather than accepting all comers and the consequent damage to their environment. But some islands are becoming uneasily aware that the wind may be shifting. Although visitors will continue to look for sun, sea and sand, they sense that visitors will also be looking for – and insisting on – environmental quality.

In the Windward Islands the government of St Vincent and the Grenadines has declared the nineties 'the Decade of the Environment'. An environmental task force has been sifting through the issues and doing its best to convert the public to the cause of environmental protection. It is also focusing on visiting yachtspeople, many of whom complain about the rubbish in the Caribbean waters but are perfectly content to dump their own wastes at sea.

CENTRAL AMERICA

Mexican environmentalists are acutely aware that their country, just across the border from the United States, is likely to experience another tourism boom once it becomes part of the North American trading bloc. Further south, the pressures may not yet be quite as intense, but countries like Belize, Costa Rica and Guatemala are also having to wrestle with the environmental and social impacts of a rise in tourism.

Down Mexico way

Out of every hundred tourists arriving in Mexico, an astounding ninety-two will be Americans, five will be Canadians and only three will be Europeans. The tourism industry is making a strong pitch to attract more Europeans, emphasising the country's cultural and ecological riches. But although in 1975 about two-thirds of the tourists visiting Mexico came to see its great wealth of cultural sites, by 1989 the figure was down to 10 per cent, and the majority were coming for the beaches rather than the ruins or natural history.

Even without tourists, Mexico has environmental problems enough. In 1940 the Lacandona rainforest covered nearly 13,000 square kilometres. Since then some 60 per cent of the area's trees have been lost to fires and farming. But tourism-related development has also contributed significantly in some areas to the widespread problem of deforestation, to the mushrooming shanty towns and to pollution problems that have often appeared to be running out of control.

One of the biggest tourism centres in the region is Cancún, the country's main beach resort, which is as big as flashy Acapulco and is developing a less-than-totally-green reputation to match. Described in the promotional literature as 'the world's first completely planned vacation resort', it is full of high-rise blocks and casinos. Cancún is an example of the Mexican government's preferred approach to tourism development, to build huge mega-projects to concentrate the impact. The liberalisation of the country's investment rules will inevitably lead to further development – indeed, another fifteen 'Cancúns' are apparently already on the drawing-board.

Inevitably, the sheer pace and scale of development is causing both social and environmental problems. South of Acapulco, for example, on the west coast, Mexico has built a totally new tourist resort called La Crucecita. Designed as a world-class beach resort, it expects 2 million tourists a year by 2018. But many people were forced to sell their property at pathetically low prices to make way for the new resort. When it became clear that the same plots were subsequently changing hands at incredibly inflated prices, there were vociferous – but ultimately unsuccessful – protests.

Here too, however, there are some signs that the links between environmental quality and sustainable tourism are increasingly recognised. The government of the state of Guerrero, for example, has continued an ambitious clean-up of Acapulco Bay, a programme that began in the 1980s.

And eco-tourism is also beginning to take root. One Mexican project that could well appeal to eco-tourists is the Sian Ka'an Wilderness Adventure. Based on a 1.3-million-hectare UNESCO biosphere reserve of largely undisturbed tropical forest, wetlands and marine habitats, the project offers visitors the opportunity to see – and help fund the conservation of – both resident and migrant songbirds, wading birds, manatee, monkeys, crocodiles and jaguar. But to find the regional magnet for eco-tourists you have to cross the Mexican border with Belize.

Belize and Costa Rica: test-beds for eco-tourists

Once called British Honduras, Belize may be the second smallest state on the mainland of the Americas, after El Salvador, but it is emerging as a pioneer in eco-tourism. Which is not to say that the Belizean environment is untouched. Far from it.

Along the border with Mexico uncontrolled development has burgeoned, while the run-off of pesticides from farmland has been a considerable problem in some areas. And the northern mangrove swamps, which can slow shore erosion and serve as nurseries for huge numbers of fish, have been extensively cleared for development. But with vast forests the country still has a huge wealth of wildlife, including deer and jaguar, puma, tapir, the American crocodile and manatee, as well as many species of turtles, tortoises, birds, reptiles, insects and fish.

Perhaps Belize's main claim to fame, however, is its coral reef. Stretching the entire length of the coastline, this is second only to the Great Barrier Reef of Australia (see page 198). Sadly, like the Great Barrier Reef, Belize's reef has also been under growing pressure.

The Hol Chan Marine Reserve was recently established to control diving and fishing in order to protect the area's natural resources against the ravages of uncontrolled tourism. But a great deal of damage has already been caused by snorkellers standing on the coral or holding on to outcrops for better views. On all the easily accessible areas of reef white patches of dead corals can clearly be seen, especially on the large brain coral heads.

Following pressure from the conservation lobby, however, the government has now made eco-tourism a priority. Although there is as yet no National Parks authority, a string of parks and wildlife reserves – administered by the Belize Audubon Society – now covers around a third of the country land area. The country is also working on its first national tourism plan, which will give a high priority to the conservation of tourism attractions like the Mayan ruins and the country's forests, rivers, lagoons and reefs. The aim is to create a better climate for investment in the right sort of tourism development, and to encourage visitors both to stay longer and to spend more.

An innovative development along these lines has been Chan Chich Lodge, built in the forecourt of a Mayan temple. But even though guests pay $100 a night, the income still does not cover the costs of protecting the surrounding forest. The developer, one of Belize's richest businessmen, can afford to make up the shortfall. He bought 700,000 acres of forest from the main colonial timber company when the country achieved independence. But it is unlikely that such an approach can be adopted across a continent which not surprisingly produces many fewer millionaires per head than North America.

Belize entered the conservation business early, with the establishment in the 1960s and 1970s of bird and wildlife sanctuaries, and there are now a number of eco-tourism experiments underway. One place where conservation is being given top priority is the Rio Bravo area, in the far north-west of Belize. In 1989 Gerald Durrell helped to launch the international campaign, Programme for Belize (see page 361) which asked people around the world to buy an acre of forest for £25 and donate it to the conservation project. As more of the area is acquired, it will be protected from illegal hunting and tree-felling. Interestingly, a number of companies have helped with the project. Tate & Lyle, which has long-standing links with the sugar cane industry in the region, has encouraged its employees to back the initiative. British Airways has helped with free air transport, while Coca-Cola Foods gave around 170 square kilometres of land alongside the protected area to the project – following intense opposition to its plans to create a citrus plantation there.

Sandwiched between Nicaragua and Panama, Costa Rica also has a reputation for its conservation achievements. Again, although it stretches from the Caribbean to the Pacific, this is a small country – just over 280 kilometres across at its widest.

Although Costa Rica accounts for only around 0.001 per cent of the planet's land surface, it has long served as a land-bridge between the Americas – and, as a result, it is one of the most ecologically diverse countries on earth, now containing around 5 per cent of the world's biodiversity. It is said that it has more bird species than North America and Canada combined, more butterflies than the whole of Africa and more orchids than Indonesia.

Ironically, the country – whose name means 'Rich Coast' – is one of the world's poorest and has a huge foreign debt problem. Partly as a result, although you need a permit to cut down rainforest trees here, Costa Rica turns out to have an even higher rate of deforestation, in terms of the percentage of its total land area cleared, than Brazil. Nevertheless, it does have fifteen National Parks and sixteen nature reserves – some of them privately owned. And the government's resolve to protect the environment will hopefully have been strengthened by surveys showing that nearly a third of visitors to the country say they have come to see its natural wonders!

One of the key figures in Costa Rican eco-tourism is Professor Dan Janzen, an American conservationist who has been fighting to reforest the Santa Rosa for nearly thirty years. He remains optimistic. As he told the *Independent on Sunday*, 'Costa Rica is becoming a hot tourist spot. But fun-in-the-sun tourism won't ever be that big here, not because there aren't wonderful beaches – there are – but because eco-tourism is going to out-compete it. People will come here principally to see the forest, because it's one of the last places on earth where you still *can*.'

One of the country's key attractions is Tortuguero, or the 'Land of the Turtles'. Located on Costa Rica's Caribbean coast, this is the region's largest nesting area for the huge green sea-turtles, which have their annual *arribada* – or arrival – between July and October. If you are lucky, you can watch the giant female turtles hauling themselves ashore and dragging their bulk up the moonlit sands. Because the turtles are deaf and extremely near-sighted when on land, you can watch them lay their eggs without them even being aware that you are there. But don't use torches: the turtles are sensitive to light and can be distracted from the central task of ensuring the future of their species.

SOUTH AMERICA

The Amazon, the Andes, archaeological sites and palm-fringed beaches – the South American continent has them all. The global campaign to save rainforests has focused world attention on the plight of the Amazon, but other areas are equally threatened by the politics and poverty of the region.

The Andes forms the backbone of the entire western side of the continent and we start by focusing on the two countries that have inherited much of its cultural heritage: Ecuador and Peru. We then turn to look at Brazil and how it is managing its vast ecological heritage, before focusing on some positive initiatives coming out of Venezuela.

Ecuador: Incas and iguanas

Astride the Equator, Ecuador is the smallest of the Andean nations. One of South America's largest oil producers, the country will have to exploit reserves in its Amazon region if it is to continue exporting oil into the next century. Conservationists are already warning that oil-wells have polluted streams, with oil spills killing freshwater pink dolphins in the lakes of the Cuyabeno Wildlife Reserve in north-eastern Ecuador.

The oil companies are promising to protect the fragile rainforest environment, but their critics warn that the development of the oil fields will attract settlers into the region. This influx will, in turn, lead to further development and further environmental destruction.

More positively, Ecuador is famous for the extraordinary wildlife of the Galapagos archipelago, 1,000 kilometres off its coast. Another key attraction of this entire region is the culture of the Quechna-speaking Indians, descended from the peoples of the Incan empire. Tourists are particularly drawn by their fiestas and markets featuring highly coloured woven clothing and a wide range of handicrafts, many of them made from the wools of the alpaca, vicuña or llama.

Travelling by bus, truck or, in some cases, by motorised dug-out canoe, you can take in ruins like the Inca fortress of Ingapirca, near Cuenca, hike through the country's popular but remote park, the Parque Nacional de Cotopaxi or visit innovative tropical forest projects – like Rio Mazan (see page 361) – which are struggling to save Ecuador's wildlife.

But the rest of the world usually thinks of the Galapagos archipelago when it thinks of Ecuador. This group of more than sixty volcanic islands is warm enough to be comfortable for tropical birds, yet at the same time its waters are cooled by the Humboldt Current so that it is also home to species such as penguins and seals, which are normally found much further south.

Sometimes called *Las Encantadas*, or Bewitched Islands, the Galapagos have attracted countless sailors, pirates, scientists and now tourists to their shores since their discovery in the sixteenth century. The sailors took an estimated 300,000 of the giant tortoises for fresh meat, finding that they would live for a long time even if stacked unfed on deck. In the late 1700s Captain Cook took a giant tortoise from the Galapagos to the Island of Tonga in the South Pacific – it died in 1966. Other early settlers introduced rats, pigs, goats and a range of other animals and plants to the Galapagos, a practice which has devastated many of the islands' unique species.

At the same time, however, the Galapagos proved inhospitable to all but the most hardy settlers, so many of the islands have remained a sanctuary to the sort of species that alerted

Charles Darwin to many of the basic principles of evolution.

Best known for their marine iguanas and giant tortoises, the Galapagos are a paradise for snorkellers. The seas around the islands abound with colourful fish and crustaceans. And whether in the water or on the land, most of the animals are astonishingly fearless, so that visitors find themselves much closer to wildlife than they are used to. In general, though, the animals are allowed to touch you – but not the other way around.

The main centre for visitors is Isla Santa Cruz, which offers the best range of facilities – including the Charles Darwin Research Station. Here you can get to know Galapagos giant tortoises and Darwin's finches while walking the winding paths through arid-zone vegetation such as prickly pear and other cacti, salt bush and mangroves.

Inevitably, there has been huge pressure from the boat owners and tour operators to allow ever-greater numbers of visitors to follow in Darwin's footsteps. But the islands' appeal lies in their relatively unspoilt nature. So, to keep the pressure down to manageable levels, the Galapagos National Park authorities have talked of limiting visitor numbers to 26,000 a year. But when we enquired of the Corporación Ecuatoriana de Turismo in Ecuador, we were told: 'There is no official limit to the number of tourists that may visit the Galapagos. There is, however, a managed capacity closely monitored by the National Park Service. Should there be visible harm, the site could be closed until it recovers.'

Every boat, including visiting yachts, must have a guide and all the guides have to be trained naturalists and keep a close eye on visitor behaviour. This is just as well, since in the 1970s the land iguanas were being fed so much food by the tourists that they became fat, stopped foraging for food and began to show disturbances in their breeding cycles. Another problem surfaced when marine turtles died after swallowing plastic bags, many dumped by tourist boats, having apparently mistaken the transparent bags for jellyfish.

Although there has been some erosion of the most popular paths, particularly on Bartolomé, Caleta Tagus, Santa Fé, Plaza Sur and North Seymour, there is as yet little evidence that the animals are being seriously disturbed. Indeed, nesting booby birds and marine iguanas alike all show near-indifference to the clicking cameras. The sealions on Isla Lobos, however, are thought to be more nervous than they were – and will sometimes nip tourists who get too close.

If you are planning to visit the Galapagos, make sure you go in a small group – the local fishing boats are better than the luxury cruisers – and follow the rules laid down by the authorities.

Peru: the 'gringo trail' and Shining Path

The history of the Incas is an extraordinary and tragic one. Visitors who have seen their amazing buildings are often astounded to hear that the Incan empire proper lasted for only around a hundred years. Although Inca civilisation developed over a number of centuries, its full flowering and expansion dates from scarcely a hundred years before the Spanish *conquistadores* arrived. Then, in an early – and unintentional – version of germ warfare, the European explorers brought diseases like smallpox and common cold, which swept ahead of them, devastating communities that had no natural immunity.

The new arrivals often built their cities atop the ruins of buildings put up by the Incas and even earlier cultures. But Peru is the unrivalled treasure-house of this archaeological wealth. In fact the ancient Inca capital of Cuzco, in Peru, has been described as the 'archaeological capital of the Americas'. But perhaps the country's most famous site is Machu Picchu, the 'Lost City of the Incas' discovered by Hiram Bingham, an American archaeologist, in 1911.

Inevitably, many areas are in the process of becoming over-commercialised. Back in the 1970s, for example, Machu Picchu was heavily littered and what has since become the Inca Trail was rapidly degenerating into a linear cesspit in places. Although it took years to get government permission to remove the rubbish, the South American Explorers' Club and the Peruvian Andean Club set to work in 1980. Interestingly, they recorded the country of origin of the cans they found along the trail. Half, not surprisingly, had Peruvian labels, but 37 per cent came from West Germany, 7 per cent from France and the remaining 6 per cent came from various other 'gringo' countries. Today, by contrast, hikers pay a fee to use the Inca trail, there are designated camp-sites and the ruins are usually spotlessly clean.

Visit Lake Titicaca, on the other hand, which is the highest navigable lake in the world, and you will sense the pressures building. Among the most popular tourist attractions here are the floating islands of the Uros people. Their islands are built from many layers of *tortora* reeds. As the reeds at the bottom of each island rot away, others are added from the top. It is anyone's guess how long such communities will last before disintegrating or becoming museum pieces. Already most of the island people have taken to begging, abandoning traditional activities like fishing and weaving.

If you cross the border at Titicaca from Peru to Bolivia, you may fit in a visit to the highest ski slope in the world, outside Bolivia's capital La Paz. The mountain range has not yet been equipped with skiing infrastructure and even if it was it is unlikely that it would become a major destination because the high altitude very quickly makes people breathless. The views are spectacular, enhanced by jewel-like lakes dotted around the valley floor. But the glistening green and turquoise colour of the lakes is not, as you might imagine, natural. Instead, it results from minerals, including highly toxic arsenic, in the effluent from tin mining.

Also under pressure are the unbelievable Nazca Lines, vast geometric lines drawn in the Peruvian desert, but only visible from the air. Some of these patterns – created by removing dark stones to reveal the lighter desert floor – are abstract geometrical shapes, but others are clearly meant to represent animals. Studied for decades by Maria Reiche, a German mathematician, they include a 180-metre-long lizard, a 90-metre-high monkey with curled tail and a condor with a 130-metre wing span. Unfortunately, as more and more people visit the Nazca Lines, and some drive across the desert, the shapes are being blurred or even destroyed completely.

Indeed, it is one of the ironies of environmental conservation that sometimes the least disturbed ecosystems and archaeological sites are found where most people never think of going – or are afraid to venture. In Peru the horrors perpetrated by the Maoist Shining Path (*Sendero Luminoso*) guerillas have made the central Peruvian Andes one of the least visited places on the continent. The link between the number of visitors and level of environmental degradation is underscored in such areas.

Like a number of other South American countries, Peru has a huge potential for tourism, yet it seems tragically likely that when the twenty-first century rolls around Peruvians will be living in the same desperate conditions of poverty and disease – or worse. Paracas, for example, on the country's eerie, beautiful Pacific coast, is generally considered to be one of the finest wildlife reserves in the southern hemisphere. But this isolated paradise is being despoiled by corrupt politicians, unthinking tour operators, quarry-the-seas fishing companies and even escaped criminals.

With terrorism and crime adding to the intolerable burdens already laid on such economies, it is difficult to see them easily reversing the downward path of the centuries. And the spread of cholera can only make matters worse. But if they are to have any sort of future, they must be helped to invest in sustainable tourism ventures. The first steps in this direction can be seen at the Tambopata Reserve, which aims to help indigenous people to preserve some of the Amazonian forests of Peru – and to revive traditional patterns of use, including the rediscovery of Indian lore about medicinal plants.

Brazil: the ecology samba

If you know nothing about Brazil's recent economic history, you might well vote the country 'the most likely to succeed' in tourism because of its many attractions. But the facts suggest otherwise. The Brazilian tourism industry remains relatively undeveloped and the national economy has been in turmoil in recent years, with inflation often running at over 1,000 per cent! More optimistically, Brazil's current President, Collor de Mello, has shown more interest in the environment than his predecessors – to the extent of employing Jose Lutzenberger, a prominent rainforest campaigner, as his environment minister.

Brazil is the world's fifth largest country – and South America's biggest. It covers almost half the continent and its sheer scale is suggested by the fact that it shares borders with every South American country, except Chile and Ecuador. Its natural resources are vast, but its 'boom-and-bust' economy has resulted in high levels of unemployment and dramatic disparities in wealth. The richest 4 per cent of Brazilians own over 40 per cent of the country's wealth, while the poverty found in the country's *favelas*, or shantytowns, is quite as bad as you will find in the poorest countries of Africa and Asia.

The Brazilian environmental protection agency, Ibama, has been trying to pursue a get-tough policy with anyone who destroys the country's rainforests. But even Ibama admits that less than 20 per cent of the fines it imposes on ranchers and loggers for illegal land clearing are ever paid. There has been a recent drop in the area of rainforest burned every year, although environmentalists fear that this has simply been a knock-on effect of the economic recession. When the recovery comes, they warn, the burning will reduce even larger areas of forest to ashes.

A controversial figure in the debate about Amazonia's future has been Gilberto Mestrinho, governor of the region's biggest state – Amazonas. 'I'm a conservationist, not a preservationist,' he said recently. 'I believe that man should use nature with intelligence to take out of her what he needs to live, and I reject the views of ecologists who want to put a giant condom over the forest.' Hugely popular with voters, Mestrinho notes that Amazonas has 16 million people who 'have the right to a comfortable living – it was they who voted me governor, not the monkeys and trees.'

Here again, population growth is a key issue. Surprisingly, even though the rate of population growth remains high, Brazil is still one of the world's most sparsely populated countries. But you wouldn't guess it if you found yourself in the coastal strip, particularly in cities such as Greater São Paulo and Greater Rio, the latter often called *a cidade maravilhosa*, or 'the marvellous city'. These teeming hives have huge populations – and pollution problems to match.

When an alligator appeared in the Tiete, the main river running through São Paulo, the Paulistas (the local people) were amazed that it survived the pollution. It is reported that the river is so toxic that the gases are corroding nearby office equipment. A clean-up campaign has just been launched, kicked off by a campaign by the local radio station.

Most people have seen photographs of the Corcovado (statue of Christ) which towers over Rio de Janeiro. If you stand alongside the statue and look across the city to the sea, you will be looking at Guanabara Bay – and, though you will be too far away to see, the Bay's waters are heavily polluted with industrial waste and sewage. The whales that once frequented the Bay have fled, while the dolphin population is sharply down too. Bathing on Rio's world-famous beaches is generally considered to be hazardous to health. New sewage treatment plants are being planned, but even they will only cut the amount of sewage discharged into the Bay by around one-third.

Of course, none of this stops the people of Rio – known as the *cariocas* – having fun. Each year, the city girds its loins for the Carnival, usually held in February. The samba clubs practise all year for the event. It's one of life's huge paradoxes that out of the corrugated and cardboard *favelas* there comes the greatest show on earth. Every year the Carnival has a different theme – and in 1990 the theme was ecology.

Brazil certainly needs an Ecology Samba to get its people thinking about what is happening to their environment. The country has been devastating its forests – and massacring the Indians who live there – for centuries. In fact the international environmental movement gained a new martyr when Chico Mendes, the tireless campaigner for the rights of the rubber-tappers who create wealth from the standing forests, was gunned down in 1988. He joined a long list of people murdered for their stand against the wave of destruction that has been sweeping the country – and others have been murdered since.

It is tempting to think, given the sheer size of so many of Brazil's natural resources, that the country can continue in the same old way for a few centuries more. But even the 6,275-kilometre Amazon, the world's longest river and carrying about a fifth of the world's fresh water, could be threatened.

For years, Brazilian law has required that at least one-third of forest land be put to use. Generally those who buy land burn the forest, plant grasses and raise cattle – or grow coffee. Unfortunately, Brazil's soils are not like those in Europe and the fertile plains of North America. They rapidly dry out and erode, or turn brick-hard. As forests are turned to semi-desert, scientists – and local people – are beginning to notice that the climate is changing. The rains come less frequently, for example, speeding the process of rainforest destruction.

But perhaps the most interesting area to look at from the tourism angle is the Pantanal, a vast area of wetlands which is about half the size of France. Frequently flooded by the River Paraguay and its tributaries, the Pantanal is best seen from April to September. Apart from the infamous carnivorous piranha fish (careful not to trail your fingers in the water), visitors can see *capybaras* (pig-sized amphibious rodents), anacondas, ant-eaters, monkeys and giant otters – together with a huge spectrum of birds, among them parrots, toucans, eagles, vultures and humming birds.

The Pantanal featured in Brazil's first ecological 'soap opera', screened by the Manchete TV network. The series has done a great deal to raise public interest in environmental issues, but – paradoxically – it has also increased the Pantanal's problems. As a result of *Pantanal*, a home-grown *Dallas*, many viewers have been left with a highly idealised picture of what the Pantanal ecology is all about. Worse, from the conservationist's point of view, visitor numbers leaped from 15,000 in 1989 to more than 100,000 in 1990.

Inevitably, developers are racing to capitalise on the Pantanal's new-found popularity, building hotels, restaurants and other facilities. And with the development come all the familiar problems: in 1990, for example, at the height of the show's popularity, volunteers collected 8 tonnes of litter from the Pantanal's marshes!

With visitors able to walk straight into bird-breeding colonies, conservationists are increasingly alarmed that the survival of birds like the blue hyacinth macaw will be endangered, along with that of animals like the spotted jaguar, maned wolf and giant otter. Tourism is by no means the only threat to the Pantanal. As in many other regions of the world there is growing pressure to drain these wetlands and turn them over to agriculture. In addition the marshes are being increasingly polluted by the fertilisers used by local farmers and by the toxic mercury spilled into the water by gold-miners.

Add that to the toll taken by hunters and fishermen and it is apparent that tourism for all its faults could relieve some of the pressures facing the area. Potentially it provides one way of exploiting the Pantanal without destroying it for ever. Many environmentalists now believe that the Pantanal's best hope for the future lies with the people who live there – and with sustainable tourism.

For some two hundred years, a small community of ranchers – perhaps 3,500 strong today – has lived in the marshes, which are mainly privately owned. Worried by the pressures they could see building up on the area's ecology, a group of ranchers formed the Society for the Defence of Pantanal in 1985. 'The *pantaneiros* are the ones with the most skill and know-how to protect the area,' said the head of the forest police for Mato Grosso do Sul. 'They were born and raised on the land – and they understand its limits.'

Venezuela: wildly wealthy

It remains to be seen whether Brazil has the vision to hand over such large areas to those who understand them best, whether they be small-scale ranchers or Indians. Its past record does not hold out much hope, but eco-tourism and sustainable tourism projects could play an important role in paving the way – and in stopping the developers who, to paraphrase the song, would happily pave Paradise and put up a parking lot.

To the north, Venezuela – known as the 'Gateway to South America' – provides some interesting examples of the role that 'green' or sustainable tourism could play in meeting this vast continent's social and ecological objectives.

Venezuela's north coast on the Caribbean was the first part of South America to be explored and settled by Europeans. In fact the country's name originally meant 'Little Venice' and was coined by the early Spanish explorers who, finding the native Indians living in houses built over the water on stilts, were reminded of the Italian city of Venice.

Like much of South America today, Venezuela was once a poor, backward and feudal agricultural nation. But the discovery of oil in 1917 triggered a process of industrial development that led to Venezuelans enjoying the continent's highest per capita income by the early 1970s. Unfortunately, since the collapse of world oil prices in the mid-1980s, the country has had to look for other sources of income.

The devaluation of the country's currency has made Venezuela more affordable for foreign tourists – and visitors have found it almost as rich in wildlife as it is in oil. The range of habitats extends from the high Andes, across the flood plains of the vast Orinoco River to the coral beaches of the Caribbean. Some 45 per cent of the continent's bird species can be found here – and many of them are unique to Venezuela.

Inevitably, however, the oil price collapse has dented conservation, too. The government has drastically cut the amount it spends in this area. As a result, despite the best efforts of the environmental authorities, conservation organisations like Fudena (the Venezuelan version of the World Wide Fund for Nature) warn that many of the parks are beginning to suffer from uncontrolled tourism.

'In the Morrocoy coastal park in the Caribbean,' says James Bedding, the *Observer*'s Travel Writer of the Year in 1990, 'the rubbish left by visitors threatens the coral reefs. In the vast Canaima Park, an area the size of Belgium that contains virtually untouched rainforest, the threat is the construction of a

new road to Brazil that could bring uncontrolled tourism.'
And if you visit the 'orchid island', a popular stop for those
making trips in dug-out canoes up the foaming brown Carrao
river to the foot of the staggering Angel Falls, you will find
that the orchids have all but disappeared.

The news is not all bad, though. Determined to preserve
as much as possible of this wild heritage for the future, Venezuela has long been a pioneer in conservation. Its oldest Park
dates back to 1937, set up in the cloud forest of the coastal
cordillera that separates the Orinoco plains from the Caribbean. Today, some twenty-eight National Parks have been
established, covering around 9 per cent of the country.

Around the country, the endangered spectacled bear peers
out of posters headlined: *Save me!* If any South American
country is going to make a success of saving both its wildlife
and its longer-term economic prospects, it is likely to be Venezuela. And the approaches it develops to ensure that tourism
is an economically and environmentally sustainable industry
could be of enormous value to the rest of the continent, which
has the potential to become either a man-made desert or a
working model of how we can work with – rather than against
– the grain of nature.

6
THE TOUR
OPERATOR

So what are the tour operators actually doing to address the environmental agenda? To find out, while we were writing *Holidays that Don't Cost the Earth*, SustainAbility carried out an environmental survey of UK tour operators. Our questionnaire was sent to around 200 firms, representing a good range of large, medium and small tour operators. In particular, we targeted those firms we felt had a high public profile or were known to have launched interesting environmental initiatives.

Around 40 per cent of the firms replied. We have not been able to use all of the replies because of their uneven quality, but we are grateful to the respondents for their efforts in completing the questionnaire. Although we rang many of the firms to cross-check the information, we cannot guarantee the information supplied by these companies. Even so, we feel that the results (see pages 310–37) give a reasonable indication of the state of the industry's thinking in 1991.

In most firms it was clear that environmental issues had not yet been seriously addressed. Worse, the recession not only reduced the number of people booking holidays but also, as a result, put the brakes on a number of the early green tourism initiatives. Interestingly, very few of the firms that responded – whom we assume are among the better performers – had an environmental policy statement worthy of the name.

But when we held a workshop on tourism and the environment, it was clear that companies were increasingly aware that this issue would be on the agenda in the 1990s. And several of the firm responding to the questionnaire said they were in the process of preparing their first environmental policy.

'We need a world policeman'

However, if we believe what the travel agents and tour operators told us, they are becoming increasingly schizophrenic. Although some of the greener operators were convinced that tourism was an environmentally flawed industry from the outset, most of the operators saw enormous benefits flowing from tourism. 'Too many to list,' as Thomson put it.

Others were a little more specific. They talked of contributions to education and understanding; of employment; of the revitalisation of areas plagued either by poverty or suffering from an exodus of the young, or both; the protection of ecosystems that would otherwise be lost; and the discouragement of poachers, loggers and miners in National Parks and wildlife reserves.

But they were also aware of the huge range of problems that tourism can bring. 'Too many to list,' said Thomson again. Others pointed to the loss of wilderness, the pollution of rivers and seas, the destruction of coral reefs, the development of sprawling concrete jungles of egg-box hotels, the over-extraction of water, the traffic congestion, the disruption of traditional cultures and the promotion of greed, the spread of 'beach bum' and 'Dallas-style' lifestyles, the encouragement of crime and the spread of sexual diseases. And that was just for starters. 'We need a world policeman to oversee tourism,' concluded one tour operator.

So tourism potentially has a great deal to offer – but the way it is being managed raises a real question-mark over its long-term future. The danger is that tour operators will continue to pursue their short-term 'See it now, before it's gone' goals, rather than look for ways of promoting sustainable tourism.

'Tourism has a stranglehold'

When we asked the agents and operators about their influence in the countries to which they send holidaymakers, one message came through loud and clear: money is the name of the game. They insisted that if green tourism brings less money in the short term, as it generally does, it will be rejected. But don't let that convince you that this is an industry without influence. These were some of the comments we received which suggest otherwise:

- 'Tourism is now placed much higher on priority list – and political attitudes are changing accordingly.'
- 'Though the small operator may not have a major impact, the package tour operator definitely does.'
- 'In Greece, tourism has almost a stranglehold.'
- 'In Rwanda, the handful of mountain gorillas earn more foreign currency than any other industry in the country.'

Clearly the tour operator's influence can be considerable. But when we asked whether this influence could be used in the greening of host countries and resorts, one operator replied: 'Only by cutting our own neck'. Others felt that any efforts they made would be akin to spitting into the wind. 'It's all very well for the British to be educated to look after a Greek island,' said another, 'but you should see the way the Greeks behave!'

Others pointed out that this is an intensely competitive market, allowing little margin for 'luxuries' like environmental care. One green tour operator even recalled losing clients when 'we became too intense' about the environment. But the firm was pressing ahead, nonetheless.

Don't be put off. Remember how green consumers woke up the supermarkets to environmental issues? By quizzing our tour operators – and anyone else who helps us to get away on holiday – green holidaymakers can do a great deal to promote similar changes in the tourism business. Let's now look at some of the specific questions we should be asking the tour operators, travel agents and other companies that want our custom.

Choosing Your Tour Operator

Before you book your holiday, ask your travel agent for details of the environmental performance of the tour operators they recommend. Don't be put off if the reaction is 'Oh, we've never been asked about that before. We wouldn't know where to begin to look for the answers!' If you cannot get a satisfactory answer, try another travel agent.

Try out some of the smaller operators too – don't just go for the names you know, which are likely to be the big companies. If you check through our survey (pages 309–37) you will see that the small- and medium-sized holiday firms did best. It's no accident, because this is where most of the real innovation is happening. These are the people who are listening to their customers, rather than tailoring their holiday packages to the lowest common denominator.

Read the tour operators' brochures, and if the information you want isn't there, *ask*. Badger before you book. Remember that by putting your money into a company, country or resort you will be supporting their activities, good or bad.

Next, take notes when you travel. Ask questions when you arrive. Criticise poor performers – and make sure you praise those who try hard to make sure your holiday does not cost the Earth. And when you return home voice your opinions about the destination and the companies that took you there, looked after you and brought you back.

Be part of the solution, not just part of the problem. More specifically, seek out and support travel agents and tour operators who have initiatives in most of the following areas:

1 Information for tourists

This should include:

- a written environmental policy in the company brochure – and details of how it is being carried out

- general guidelines on what the tourist can do to minimise environmental damage and to blend in with local cultures

- fact sheets on environmental issues and projects relating to specific destinations, and information on what can be done to help

- details of endangered species – animal or plant – and the laws and regulations concerning the export of products made from them

- advice on the potential environmental impact of sporting and leisure activities – and on how to minimise them

2 Community projects

The company you support should:

- participate in local initiatives and projects in tourist destinations, for example litter clean-ups

- help to plan resorts to suit local needs, not just the needs of tourists

- support local crafts, so long as these don't rely on endangered or banned species for raw materials

- encourage communication between local people and visitors, to help promote a better understanding between them

3 Environmental and conservation projects

The company should:

- promote environmental organisations and initiatives in its holiday brochures

- make donations to environmental projects and organisations, perhaps linking donations to the number of bookings or profits

- give active support to conservation and environmental projects focusing on nature, culture or architecture, both worldwide and in tourist destinations

- consider setting up environment projects where none exists

- encourage clients to monitor environmental problems and improvements – and provide feedback to operators

- make sure that all tour groups abide by local regulations or relevant codes of conduct

4 Transport

The company should:

- be aware of the environmental impact of the transport systems it uses

- put pressure on the transport companies it uses, such as airlines and car rental firms, to ensure they move towards better fuel efficiency, recycling and other environmental measures

- consider switching to more environment-friendly alternatives, such as public transport, using trains rather than planes – or supporting local transport systems, where practicable

- enforce strict guidelines for coach operators to ensure that they do not drive too fast, do not leave their engines on whilst the coach is stationary and ensure that the vehicles are well maintained

- create a policy for hire cars, which should be diesel-powered or fitted with catalytic converters and be fuel-efficient

- provide guidelines on greener motoring

- make sure that coaches or cars do not drive into sensitive areas, for example the heart of medieval towns

- provide information on local bicycle hire companies, where appropriate

5 Planning and development

The company should:

- promote greater pedestrianisation in town or city centres – by supporting and encouraging local government initiatives, or even suggesting them

- help to ensure that sewage facilities in resorts are adequate for the increased numbers brought in through tourism

- use and improve on existing facilities, rather than constantly switching to new resorts or encouraging new developments
- make sure that any new development is sympathetic to the environment, using traditional local materials and in local styles

6 Hotels and accommodation

The company should:

- use local accommodation where possible, so that the income goes to the local economy rather than being siphoned off to international corporations
- request that large hotel chains carry out an environmental audit of their operations – and that they make the necessary improvements when it is completed
- question the need for modern conveniences, for example air conditioning, particularly in less developed countries
- encourage energy and water efficiency, particularly where these resources are in short supply, and support initiatives that use alternative energy sources, such as solar power
- specify that the recycling of waste is – or will soon become – a requirement
- support innovative green accommodation, either where it already exists or is planned

7 Governments and tourism agencies

The company should:

- alert governments and national tourism agencies to their interest in environmental initiatives
- specify measures that should be taken by

governments if they are to continue bringing tourists – and therefore tourist revenue – into the country

- establish straightforward, above-board contact with government ministers in the countries visited

- protest to national governments, tourist bodies and in international circles about any corruption encountered, especially where money for environmental projects is affected

8 Leisure activities

The company should:

- be aware of the potential environmental impacts of any leisure activities it promotes or organises

- check all operators it uses – or whom its clients are likely to use – to make sure that they are behaving responsibly

- provide guidelines for tourists on how to minimise damage

- actively discourage activities that are excessively damaging to the environment, favouring activities with a minimal impact

9 Company greening

The company should:

- produce a written environmental policy statement

- carry out an environmental audit of its activities, implementing changes where necessary

- look at the best of the competition to see – and, where appropriate, emulate – what they are doing

- start greening its office(s), including initiating a recycling scheme for paper, glass and cans, cutting down on waste and using recycled paper for office stationery and brochures where appropriate

- operate a staff and client suggestions scheme for
  environmental improvements in running both the
  office and company's holidays

10 Communications

The company should:

- be in a position to provide information for clients
  who enquire about its environmental initiatives

- create a code of practice for tour leaders

- keep a regular flow of information to travel agents
  to make sure they are well informed about
  environmental issues

- report other tour operators if they are not complying
  with environmental or conservation regulations

- present a real picture of the host country rather than
  a 'packaged' and 'distorted' version for tourists

TOUR OPERATOR QUESTIONNAIRE RESPONSE

The survey results outlined on pages 310–37 cover a range of large, medium and small-sized companies. The results relate to the position in mid-1991. Growing numbers of the better firms are involved in one or more of the projects profiled on pages 354–65. Our star ratings are largely subjective, with a star awarded to firms we consider to be tackling the green agenda in depth.

Large tour operators

	Type of holiday	Destinations	Annual no. of customers
Abercrombie and Kent Sloane Square House Holbein Place London SW1 8NS Tel: 071 730 9600	A variety of holidays; particularly well known for sport and adventure	Almost worldwide	6,000– 7,000
Citalia (England) Ltd Marco Polo House 3–5 Lansdowne Road Croydon CR9 1LL Tel: 081 686 0677	Package tours by air, rail, coach or car as well as independent arrangements	Italy	50,000
Exodus Expeditions 9 Weir Road London SW12 0LT Tel: 081 675 5550	Walking, adventure and overland holidays	Worldwide	4,000
Field Studies Council Preston Montford Montford Bridge Shrewsbury SY4 1HW Tel: 0743 850674	Short courses in a wide variety of subjects, all with the purpose of encouraging 'environmental understanding for all'.	Ten residential centres in England and Wales and one day centre; also some destinations overseas	19,989

Staff	Environmental policy and initiatives:
65 full time	• A full statement on the company's activities in the environment is currently being prepared • For every client travelling to Africa a £5 donation is given to Friends of Conservation (FoC) and special safaris are organised periodically which provide larger donations • Permits FoC to send a leaflet to every client booked to travel to Africa and allows them to have free advertisements • Clients are informed in pre-tour documents about any conservation work being carried out in the country to which they are travelling • Claims to take into account the environmental impact of activities it offers, which include sailing and hot-air ballooning; 'catch-and-release' game-fishing is promoted, for example, and scuba diving ground operators are vetted on their approach to conservation issues **Seems particularly good in East Africa, but its approach elsewhere is reported to be more superficial.**
65 full time; 3 part time; 45 full time in Italy	• The company contributes £2 to the Venice in Peril Fund for every booking made • Responded when asked for information about beach pollution **Has not yet done very much.**
80 full time	• Claims to have taken a responsible attitude to culture and environment since the company set up in 1974 • Very concerned about companies publicising their environmental claims as long as there is no way of checking the claims • Has no written guidelines but does encourage group leaders, local operators and clients to minimise their impact on the environment • Has investigated some of the environmental implications of its holidays **Not very active.**
200 full time; 50 part time	• The company's environmental policy is stated in its brochures for schools • The environmental impact of transport offered is being considered; motorised transport is used as little as possible and vehicles are run on unleaded petrol • The company has links with many other environmental organisations, including Wildlife Link, RSPB, the Council for Environmental Education and County Trusts **Focuses particularly on conservation and wildlife.**

	Type of holiday	*Destinations*	*Annual no. of customers*
Flamingo Tours 167 Acton Lane Chiswick London W4 5HN Tel: 081 995 3505	Safaris and beach holidays	Kenya and Northern Tanzania	Not given
Guerba Expeditions Ltd 101 Eden Vale Road Westbury Wiltshire BA13 3QX Tel: 0373 826611	Adventure camping holidays	Most African countries	3,000
Japan Travel Bureau 10 Maltravers Street London WC2R 3EX Tel: 071 379 6244	Based mainly in Japan where it organises European package holidays: also Far Eastern travel from European countries	Worldwide	147,000 Japanese to Europe in 1989
Olympic Vacations 30–32 Cross Street Islington London N1 2BG Tel: 071 359 3500	Inclusive tours, fly-drive, cruises, motoring, motorail, skiing and tailor-made holidays	France, Cyprus, Greek Islands	120,000
Sunsail Ltd The Port House Port Solent Portsmouth Hants PO6 4TH Tel: 0705 210345	Sailing holidays with yachts; dinghies; windsurfing	UK, France, Italy, Yugoslavia, Greece, Turkey, Caribbean, Bahamas, Thailand	35,000–40,000

Staff	Environmental policy and initiatives:
Over 250 full time	• Member of East African Wildlife Society • Despite some demand from customers does not offer hunting safaris • Company drivers advise clients on issues such as rubbish, noise, not harassing animals and not driving off-road in parks • Offers a wide range of activities, including golf, deep-sea fishing and horse riding, which it considers have 'very few negative aspects' **Quite aware but not yet very active.**
70 full time; 2 part time	• Aims to show clients 'the real Africa' and is careful not to leave mess behind • The company brochure is printed on recycled paper, although this is not 100 per cent recycled because a better quality finish is required **Has not undertaken any specific initiatives and appears to think that the impact of tourism on the environment is limited to overload.**
144 full time	• Pays particular attention to staggering travel seasons **Interested in environmental initiatives but has not yet undertaken any**
50 full time; 40 part time	• Involved in turtle protection in parts of Greece and Cyprus • Official supporter of 'Care for the Wild' **Aware, but not very active.**
150 full time; 250 part time	• Staff and clients are briefed on environmental impacts of the company's operations, for example about not mooring yachts on coral beds • The company is associated with conservation organisations in Turkey and Greece but it is unclear how it supports them • All yachts have holding tanks for sewage, and information is provided by the company on pumping sewage tanks and bilges • Rubbish bins have been installed by the company in some of the areas in which it operates **With more customer demands would do more.**

	Type of holiday	Destinations	Annual no. of customers
Thomson Tour Operations (includes Horizon Holidays) Greater London House Hampstead Road London NW1 7SD Tel: 071 387 9321	All-inclusive package holidays	Worldwide	About 3 million
Travelscene 11/15 St Ann's Road Harrow Middlesex HA1 1AS Tel: 071 427 8800	Shortbreak city holidays and specialist Austrian holidays	Wide selection of countries worldwide	80,000

Medium-sized tour operators

Allegro Holidays 15a Church Street Reigate Surrey RH2 0AA Tel: 0737 221323	Holidays to 'unspoilt areas' for individuals rather than groups	Portugal, Spain, Corsica, Italy, India, Sri Lanka, Egypt	10,000
Alternative Travel Group 1–3 George Street Oxford OX1 2AZ Tel: 0865 310399	Walking holidays	Italy, France, Spain, Portugal	2500

Staff	Environmental policy and initiatives:
929 full time; part time not known	• Offers to make a donation to Friends of the Ionian when holidays to Greece are booked and has devoted a page in the company catalogue to them • Has guidelines for activities geared to the resorts and handled there rather than at central office • Has investigated the environmental impact of activities but did not provide details **Has done quite a lot of research, but it is not clear to what extent the company has acted on the results.**
55 full time; 6 part time	• Has held discussions with several tourist boards with the idea of formulating an overall environmental policy • Plans to highlight environmental award-winning resorts in its catalogue **Has not put anything into practice but does have strong views on what should happen and a good understanding of the issues.**
10 full time; 4 part time	• Green Flag member • Has asked for advice on environmental issues from the Association of Independent Tour Operators (AITO) **To date has not undertaken any environmental initiatives – and seemed very defensive.**
10 full time; 40 part time	• Gives about £5000 per annum to RSPB and WWF • All excursions are led by a guide and groups stay in local accommodation • Groups are kept small and are never more than sixteen people • The company believes that operators should invest in the areas where it sends people and is planning to carry this out with a hotel in a National Park • Has invested quite heavily in researching and maintaining footpaths • Invests in staff training and is apparently the only travel company to have had two mentions in the National Training Awards • Very critical of companies jumping on the bandwagon and getting credit despite having a superficial approach **Has been active for some time.**

	Type of holiday	Destinations	Annual no. of customers
*Arctic Experience 29 Nork Way Banstead Surrey SM7 1PB Tel: 0737 362321	General and special interest tours and expeditions to the Arctic and sub-Arctic	Iceland, Greenland, Spitsbergen, Canada, Alaska	2,500
Bales Tours Ltd Bales House Junction Road Dorking Surrey RH4 3HB Tel: 0306 885991	Escorted tours	Worldwide	10,000
*Cox and King's 45 Buckingham Gate London SW1E 6AF Tel: 071 834 7472	Inclusive package holidays and individual fit packages. Also wildlife, botany and photography special interest tours	Worldwide although specialises in India and South America	Not given

Staff	Environmental policy and initiatives:
9 full time	• Green Flag member as well as collaborating with the Wildfowl and Wetlands Trust and the Whale and Dolphin Conservation Society • Donations are made to the Trust and brochures contain details of how to join • Some tours escorted by Trust staff; others by world authorities such as David Bellamy or Magnus Magnusson • Has recently launched a sister company called 'Discover the World' which offers tours led by leading environmentalists and which will provide special itineraries for members of the Wildfowl and Wetlands Trust, the Whale and Dolphin Conservation Society and the David Shepherd Foundation • Group sizes are kept to as small as possible • Information is included in the company brochure on the environmental benefits and problems relating to tourism • Guidelines are given to clients to encourage them not to drive off marked tracks or to leave litter **Aware and active**.
24 full time; 1 part time	• Clients are given written guidelines on how to minimise their impact on the environment as well as a briefing from tour leaders, particularly in relation to vulnerable areas such as the Galapagos Islands, Amazonia and the Himalayas; this includes changing trekking routes to avoid erosion • The company claims to support conservation initiatives raised by their local agents, but it was not clear what these were **Aware, but not very active**.
18 full time; 1 part time	• Green Flag member • Environmental policy permeates the company ethos, but is not in written form • Makes regular donations to environmental organisations, for example buying one acre of rainforest in Belize for every client booking on a wildlife holiday through Programme for Belize (see page 361); and for each client travelling on one of the whale-watching holidays in Baja California, the Galapagos Islands or Alaska, it will sponsor field studies on the Amazon river dolphins conducted for the Whale and Dolphin Conservation Society • Produces brochure on recycled paper **A strong contender, but will need to put a written environmental policy in place.**

	Type of holiday	Destinations	Annual no. of customers
*CV Travel 43 Cadogan Street London SW3 2PR Tel: 071 581 0851	Mediterranean villa holidays and long-haul small hotel/villa holidays	Greek Islands, Spain, Italy, Portugal, South of France, Caribbean, Far East, South and East Africa, USA (Palm Beach), Indian Ocean	8,000
Cycling for Softies 22 Lloyd Street Manchester M2 5WA Tel: 061 834 6800	Cycling holidays	France	3,500–4,000
*EcoSafaris UK Ltd 146 Gloucester Road London SW7 4SZ Tel: 071 370 5032	Wildlife, ecological, historical and cultural holidays both for groups and for independent travellers	Worldwide, but specialises in Africa, Asia and Canada	1,000-plus
*Explore Worldwide Ltd 1 Frederick Street Aldershot Hampshire GU11 1LQ Tel: 0252 319448	Fixed itinerary tours for small groups, including adventure, sailing, trekking, wilderness experiences, wildlife and natural history	Europe, Africa, Asia, Australasia and North, South and Central America	8,000

Staff	Environmental policy and initiatives:
15 full time	• Green Flag member and supporter of Greek Animal Welfare Fund • Recognises that it is in the company's interest to help protect destinations • Works with local people in some resorts to support the use of traditional materials in villas and promote local crafts • Educates local people about rubbish disposal and has organised a series of beach sweeps as part of a drive for conservation of the coastline, particularly in Corfu • Involves company in the planning stage of new properties **Well informed and quite active.**
8 full time; 32 part time	• Tours are designed so that cyclists stick to the roads rather than use tracks • Uses recycled paper in the office **The company has not undertaken any initiatives, but cycling holidays are environmentally desirable.**
10 full time; 2 part time	• The company has a written environmental statement and provides guidelines for its clients on how to minimise environmental impact • Associated with the Kasanka Trust project for Kasanka National Park in Zambia • Has supported WWF, RSNC, RSPC and other environmental charities • Is involved with the Durrell Institute for Conservation and Ecology at the University of Kent • Has a policy to avoid pressure points, to be selective about choices of venues and to help conservationists where it can • Keeps groups small and makes sure they respect National Park regulations and local customs • Has an expanding walking holiday programme which it describes as Eco-Walks **Aware and active. (EcoSafaris was taken over by Worldwide Journeys in 1991. It has stated that it will continue with the same policies and we have therefore kept the entry.)**
21 full time; 35 part time (tour leaders)	• Member of Tourism Concern • Has given donations/support to WWF, Friends of the Earth (FoE), Living Earth Foundation and to a university expedition to Belize • Designs its small group tours to make minimum demands on a country's infrastructure, using local transport and accommodation in limited numbers • Uses local buses, trains and taxis, and local accommodation, sometimes staying in people's houses • Aims to promote mutual understanding through contact with the local people – guides and ground agents are used *(contd)*

	Type of holiday	Destinations	Annual no. of customers
(Explore Worldwide contd)			
*Greek Islands Club 66 High Street Walton-on Thames Surrey KT12 1BU Tel: 0932 220477	Self catering, sailing, sporting and cultural activities	Greece and the Greek Islands (Ionian)	4,000
Headwater Holidays 146 London Road Northwich Cheshire CW9 5HH Tel: 0606 48699	Active holidays in France and cross-country skiing in France and Norway. Specialises in discovery of little-known unspoiled places	France and Norway	Not revealed

Staff	*Environmental policy and initiatives:*
	• All tour leaders follow a code of practice, which includes briefing clients and ensuring that they too follow this code • Launched some 'Responsible Traveller Guidelines' at The Green Show, 1991 **Very aware and active.**
15 full time; 80 part time	• Green Flag member • Founded 'Friends of the Ionian' (see p. 358) which aims to unite efforts to conserve the Ionian Islands and reduce the environmental impact of tourism • Has initiated monthly beach 'clean-ups' on some of the Ionian Islands and encouraged other tour operators to join in • Provides information packs in each villa about rubbish separation, water conservation, local culture and waste disposal • Is keen to create a fruitful dialogue between tour operators and the Ionian communities; in Zakynthos, Kefalonia, Ithaca and Paxos it has organised a selection of cultural activities for tourists, ranging from free Greek language courses to Greek dancing courses **The Club is very aware of the problems of tourism and its impact on the environment – and is actively involved in making this impact more positive.**

11 full time; 2 part time	• Green Flag member
	• Has helped to set up walking trails in association with local authorities
	• Is keen on rail travel
	• Holds discussions with local people and decision makers about the effects of the holidays on them and their land, although it is not clear what results from these talks
	• Has a written environmental policy which includes:
	  - No guided groups, clients make their own way in twos and fours
	  - No more than three or four rooms are taken in any one hotel, so as not to overload with one party
	  - Hotels and local tourist authorities encouraged to support regional crafts and folklore and make them accessible
	  - Clients are sent detailed notes about their destinations and are given additional information by their representatives
	  - Information on local country codes is included in briefing and it is a booking condition that these are followed
	Active, but policy not printed in brochure.

	Type of holiday	Destinations	Annual no. of customers
Impact Holidays Devonshire Chambers 10 Devonshire Street Carlisle Cumbria CA3 8LP Tel: 0228 45252	Coach holidays with camping, apartment or hotel accommodation	Spain, Italy, France	20,000
Journey Latin America 14–16 Devonshire Road Chiswick London W4 2HD Tel: 081 747 8315	Economy journeys, expeditions, group tours and flight-only arrangements	Latin America	1,200
*Moswin Tours Ltd Moswin House 21 Church Street Oadby Leicester LE2 5DB Tel: 0533 714982	Specialist tours and cultural holidays mostly to Germany	Germany, Switzerland, Austria and France	3,500
Scantours Ltd 8 Spring Gardens London SW1A 2BG Tel: 071 839 2927	Made-to-measure individual holidays, mostly by air	Scandinavia and the USSR	10,000
Sunvil Holidays 7 & 8 Upper Square Isleworth Middlesex TW7 7BJ Tel: 081 568 4499	Summer sun, fly-drive, walking and special interest	Greece, Cyprus, Italy, Portugal, Hungary, Azores, Cape Verde	12,000
The Travel Club Upminster Essex RM14 2TT Tel: 04022 25000	Package tours for summer and winter sun	Portugal, the Balearics, Switzerland, Italy, Austria, Crete, Madeira, Cyprus and the USA	25,000

Staff	Environmental policy and initiatives:
18 full time; 50 part time	• Staff training aims to boost environmental consciousness **Although aware of some issues (it points out that coach travel is more fuel-efficient than travelling by air), the company is not very active.**
36 full time; 5 part time	• No environmental initiatives or guidelines provided for tourists, but tour leaders are briefed on codes of behaviour **Not yet very active.**
12 full time; 2 part time	• Green Flag member • Since 1981 has ruled that company coaches may not drive into areas of medieval buildings, or towns – clients have to walk • Provides a professional forester to lead walks in the Black Forest and explain about environmental issues • Plans to accommodate tourists in beautiful but crumbling guest houses, particularly in the former East Germany, to enable the owners to preserve and renovate the buildings • Aware of the negative effects of skiing and does not encourage it • Provides booklet for each tour which includes environmental guidelines, where possible **Seem to be particularly innovative and active.**
6 full time; 2 part time	• Managing Director of Scantours is Chairman of ABTA (page 351) and sits on their Environmental Committee **Has not yet done much, but response indicated that it was becoming more aware.**
20 full time; 3 part time	• No stated policy, but company has donated money and given advice to the Laona Project (page 360) in the Akamas area of Cyprus, which aims to restore dying villages **Very little information provided.**
35 full time; 15 part time	• Green Flag member • Uses recycled paper for luggage labels and photocopying **Seemed unaware that tourism has a long-term impact on the environment (except for skiing) and is not active.**

	Type of holiday	*Destinations*	*Annual no. of customers*
Trek America Trek House, The Bullring Deddington, Banbury Oxon OX15 0TT Tel: 0869 38777	Adventure camping holidays	USA, Canada, Alaska and Mexico	7,500–8,000
Wildlife Explorer 'Manyara', Riverside Nanpean, St Austell Cornwall PL26 7YJ Tel: 0726 824132	Luxury tailor-made private safaris	Tanzania	300
WST Charters Priory House 6 Wrights Lane London W8 6TA Tel: 071 938 4362	Independent travel and flexible tailor-made packaged holidays	Turkey, Israel, Egypt	12,000

Small tour operators

A.C.E Study Tours Babraham Cambridge CB2 4AP Tel: 0223 835055	All-inclusive educational holidays	Many different parts of the world	2,500
Association for Active Learning 9 Haywra Street Harrogate Yorkshire HG1 5BJ Tel: 0423 505313	Anglo-French study tours and family activity holidays	France and UK	600–700

Staff	Environmental policy and initiatives:
40 full time; 150 part time	• Advises clients about the rules and values of National Parks, monuments and other public lands it uses and attempts to educate its clients to minimise their impact on the environment • Uses public transport when in cities and its own mini-vans (which use unleaded petrol) in National Parks • Becoming more active in recycling and cutting down on office waste **Aware and fairly active**
15 full time	• Tours keep to designated areas in National Parks **Seemed unaware of the environmental impact of tourism.**

6 full time	• Member of Tourism Concern
	• Has been involved in projects initiated by the parent company STA Travel, including the following:
	  – working on a group environmental policy
	  – sponsoring of a conference on Tourism and the Environment in the Himalayas, through Tourism Concern
	  – initiation of 'The Reluctant Tourist' column in the *Independent* in which readers' letters are published; copies of the letters will to be inserted into ticket wallets and a travel award given to the best entry
	  – initiation of a company-wide project to recycle paper, glass and aluminium cans
	
	STA Travel seem to be keen on making changes but these may not all filter through to WST Charters.

5 full time; 15 part time	• Runs a number of natural history programmes, including two tours for the Royal Society for Nature Conservation (RSNC) **Displays some awareness of the issues, but has taken little direct action.**
1 full time; 1 part time; 1 volunteer	• French partner has organised two 'Université de la Nature' courses **Not active and showed a very limited understanding.**

	Type of holiday	Destinations	Annual no. of customers
Becks Holidays Southfields Shirleys Ditchling Hassocks West Sussex BN6 8UD Tel: 0273 842843	Self-catering self-drive holidays	France	1,500
*Bird Holidays Dudwick House Buxton Norwich NR10 5HX Tel: 0603 278296	Birdwatching holidays	European destinations and North Africa; planning long haul	300
Andrew Brock Travel Ltd 10 Barley Mow Passage London W4 4PH Tel: 081 995 3642	Specialised tours including art history or botanical trips, Himalayan trekking and French canal holidays	India, France	2,500
*Detours 80 Stuart Road Wimbledon Park London SW19 8DH Tel: 081 946 6295	Development education tours. Leaders take a small group to look at the broader cultural aspects of developing countries	Indonesia, Thailand, Nepal, India, Ghana, Ethiopia, St Lucia, Ecuador	200
ExplorAsia 13 Chapter Street London SW1 Tel: 071 630 7102	Trekking, wildlife and cultural holidays; package and private itineraries	Mostly India and Nepal	700

Staff	Environmental policy and initiatives:
1 full time; 1 part time	• Does not expect to initiate any action – thinks the host country should take the responsibility **Not active.**
2 part time	• All the company profits go to the RSPB • The 1992 brochure will carry a written environmental policy • Has participated in projects in Crete in co-operation with Wildlife Travel • Tours are led by professional conservationists • Demonstrates to the locals that the tourists are there to watch birds so that they see the birds as a useful financial resource **Active and aware.**
5 full time; 3 part time	• None **Showed no interest in environmental issues.**
1 full time; 10 part time	• Member of Tourism Concern • Tours benefit development and conservation agencies in the destination countries, either by generous donations or by using and paying for their facilities • Cultural guidelines on each tour are provided and time is spent with local people in countries visited • Contributes to the Environmental Education Centre in Indonesia and the National Trust in St Lucia, as well as running trips for supporters of the aid agency CARE, which has reforestation and water projects in Ecuador and Nepal • Four- or five-star hotels are avoided in favour of local accommodation and ground operators who respect the environment **Well informed and active.**
5 full time; 1 part time	• Associated with the Tiger Mountain Group of Companies which has its own registered charity, the International Trust for Nature Conservation • A few customers have remarked on wood-burning on treks and now the company tries to use kerosene where it can **Aware of issues, but so far does not appear to have done a great deal.**

	Type of holiday	Destinations	Annual no. of customers
Grass Roots Travel Ltd 8 Lindsay Road Hampton Hill Middx TW12 1DR Tel: 081 941 5753	Guided and independent safari holidays	Kenya, Tanzania, Rwanda, Zaire, Zimbabwe, Botswana, Seychelles, Mauritius	500 approx
Greco File Ltd Sourdock Hill Barkisland Halifax HX4 0AG Tel: 0422 375999	Travel consultancy	All areas to Greece	1,000–1,500
***High Places** Globe Works Penistone Road Sheffield S6 3AE Tel: 0742 822333	Trekking, walking and climbing holidays	India, Ecuador, Iceland, Greenland, Egypt, Borneo, Poland, Costa Rica, Chile	200–300
Himalayan Kingdoms 20 The Mall Clifton Bristol BS8 4DR Tel: 0272 237163	Activity holidays, particularly trekking in the Himalayas	India, Nepal, Sikkim, Bhutan, Mongolia, Tibet, Pakistan, Turkey, China	250

Staff	Environmental policy and initiatives:
1 full time; 1 part time	• Is a member of and has contributed information and finance to East African Wildlife Society, East African Ornithological Society and World Wide Fund for Nature • Has helped in the gathering of statistics about vehicle impact in National Park reserves • Encourages clients to be sensitive to wildlife; all clients in Kenya receive the East African Wildlife Society publication • Uses ground operators, drivers and guides who are aware of the problems of environmental exploitation and will not sacrifice everything for 'the client's ultimate photograph' • Restricts group sizes to ten people • Advises clients about the broader issues of the country they visit – for example, the significance of tourism to economies via foreign exchange **Aware and quite active.**
4 full time; 1 part time	• Green Flag member and subscriber to Friends of the Ionian • Has specified that tour operators should use hired cars that take unleaded petrol and are well maintained **Well informed, but not doing very much.**
3 full time; 4 part time	• Member of Tourism Concern and claims to be the first tour operator to print its guidelines on trekking in the Himalayas in its brochure • The company's environment philosophy is printed on the first page of its brochure • In 1991 donated a free holiday as a prize for fund-raising draw for the Rio Mazan Forest Conservation Project in Ecuador • Tries to minimise 'wear and tear' of its activities • Never uses purpose-built hotels • Brochure is printed on recycled paper **Aware and active.**
4 full time; 15-plus part time	• Member of Tourism Concern • Very good set of guidelines for tourists on protecting the environment and respecting local culture and traditions, which are included in a dossier of information sent out to all clients • Organised a 'Clean up Everest Camp' trek in 1988 **Has carried out a practical initiative, but it would be worth asking if they are still involved.**

	Type of holiday	Destinations	Annual no. of customers
*Hosking Tours Pages Green House Wetheringsett Stowmarket Suffolk IP14 5QA Tel: 0728 861113	Wildlife photographic tours	Falklands, Kenya, Tanzania, Yemen, Belize, Canada, Rwanda, Zaire, India	60
Ilkeston Co-op Travel 12 South Street Ilkeston Derbyshire DE7 5SG Tel: 0602 323546	Adventure escorted tours	Venzuela, Peru and the US	6,000
*Insight Travel 6 Norton Road Garstang, Preston Lancs PR3 1JY Tel: 0995 606095	Tailor-made host-based holidays for individuals or small groups	Ghana	30–50
Island Holidays Ardross Comrie Perthshire PH6 2JU Tel: 0764 70107	Guided wildlife and archaeology tours for small groups	Falklands, Crete, Orkney/Shetland, Cuba, Spitsbergen, Christmas Island, Antartica, Alaska, New Zealand	100

Staff	*Environmental policy and initiatives:*
2 full time; 2 part time	• Annual donations are made to the Falkland Islands Association and for each booking on the Belize tour a donation is made to save the country's rainforest • Clients are recommended to attend a pre-tour meeting where they are briefed on environmentally sensitive issues • Director of Hosking Tours is also vice-president of the British Naturalist Association • The company monitors changes to the environment in its destinations and passes on information to relevant people • Has pressurised authorities in the Falklands to rope off some of the penguin colonies **Aware and active; it is particularly commendable that it monitors and reports changes.**
5 full time	• None **Did not seem interested in environmental concerns. We sent a proof of this entry to the company and their response was: 'We do not wish to be included in this guide.'**
1 full time	• Member of Tourism Concern • Holidays are planned around minimising environmental and cultural impact • Company philosophy is based on visitors learning from the country that they visit; their slogan is 'Don't be a tourist, be a guest' • Provides a booklet entitled *Getting into Ghana* which includes information on Ghanaian etiquette, local foods and how public transport works • Visitors stay in local accommodation • Once in the country trips use locally owned public transport • Maintains contact with the Ghanaian Tourist Board and is careful not to overrule the wishes of local people **Has a progressive environmental and ethical policy that is followed through.**
1 full time; 1 part time (partners)	• Member of Green Flag and Falklands Foundation • Follows countryside codes and provides advice if necessary • Groups are small to encourage greater responsibility and to minimise environmental impact • Clients are advised on souvenir purchasing to avoid trade in endangered species • Recycled stationery is used wherever possible **Although the company provides advice, it does not yet appear to do very much itself.**

	Type of holiday	*Destinations*	*Annual no. of customers*
Magic of the Orient 418A London House 19 Old Court Place London W8 4PF Tel: 071 937 5885	Tailor-made long-haul holidays	Hong Kong, Indonesia, Malaysia, Singapore, Thailand, Vietnam, Philippines, Laos, Cambodia, Borneo, China	1,500
Mountain Goat Holidays Victoria Street Windermere Cumbria LA23 1AL Tel: 09662 5161	Weekly and short break walking and gardening holidays, primarily for 55-plus age group in the Lake District, as well as Yorkshire, Scotland and Northumber-land	UK	10,000 plus
Naturetrek Chautara, Bighton Nr Alresford Hants SO24 9RB Tel: 0962 733051	Bird-watching, botanical and other natural history treks and adventures	Worldwide	300 plus
*Papyrus Tours 9 Rosehill Court Bessacarr Doncaster DN4 5LY Tel: 0302 530778	Wildlife tours	Kenya, Tanzania, Zimbabwe, India, USA and France	150

Staff	Environmental policy and initiatives:
2 full time	• Discourages travel to overdeveloped resort areas and encourages it to rainforests of Borneo • Abides by general principle of 'Leave only footprints, take only photographs' **Has not taken any specific action and does not issue guidelines.**
5 full time; 25 part time	• Supports the Upland Initiative with the Lake District special planning board to regenerate over-used fells and to maintain the environment • No written guidelines but leaders encourage clients to keep to the countryside code • Uses diesel mini coaches, which are more fuel efficient than petrol-powered vehicles **The company is aware of some of the problems in the Lake District, but gave few details in its response to the questionnaire.**
2 full time; 40 part time	• No formal environmental policy, but the company says that environmental ethics are incorporated throughout the literature and 'preached by the tour leaders' • Guidelines to clients include: no camp fires, burning loo paper, no collection of plant specimens and no free handouts, etc. • It has made donations to environmental projects, including the Annapurna Conservation Area Project, the Ethiopian Wildlife Conservation Organisation and the Australian Wilderness Society • Actively promotes environmental organisations in annual newsletter and encourages membership • Claims to subcontract only to companies with a similar level of environmental awareness and where possible to educate local staff, but it is not clear how awareness is checked • Maintains regular contact with the environment ministers or equivalent in all Third World destinations • Compiles detailed ornithological and botanical reports at the end of each trip, which are sent to the relevant natural history society in the country visited **Very active, but traces of complacency throughout the questionnaire.**
2 part time	• Has a policy of 'recycling any surplus profit into conservation initiatives' • Supports numerous other environmental organisations, such as the Ranthambhore Society in India, the Kenya Wildlife Trust, the Elsa Trust in Kenya, the Daphne Sheldrick Wildlife Trust and Leicester University students doing research • All clients who go to East Africa become members of the East African Wildlife Society at the company's expense *(contd)*

	Type of holiday	Destinations	Annual no. of customers
(Papyrus Tours contd)			
Peregrine Holidays Ltd 41 South Parade Summertown Oxford OX2 7JP Tel: 0865 511642	Special interest holidays to see birds, flowers and archaeology	Greece, Turkey, Morocco, New Zealand, Norway, Spain, France, Costa Rica, the Gambia, Botswana, Egypt, Hungary, Austria and Poland	300
Safari Consultants Ltd 83 Gloucester Place London W1H 3PG Tel: 071 486 4774	Safaris	Rwanda, Zaire, Kenya, Tanzania, Malawi, Zambia, Zimbabwe, Botswana, Namibia, Swaziland, Lesotho and South Africa	300
The Travel Trading Company Trofarth Clywd LL22 8BW Tel: 0492 650225	Wildlife and cultural holidays – 'soft adventures'.	Alaska, Canada, Australia, Thailand, Burma, Borneo, Christmas Islands, Cocos Islands, Turkey, Cyprus	First year of operation

Staff	Environmental policy and initiatives:
	• Has lobbied successfully for the development of less luxurious facilities in East Africa's National Parks, and avoids, where possible, giving custom to hotels that provide unnecessary luxury • One of the partners of the company is chairman of the Yorkshire Wildlife Trust and is also a trustee of the Kenya Wildlife Trust, which he helped establish with Dr Richard Leakey, Director of Kenya Wildlife Service • Keen to uphold National Park regulations even to the extent of reporting other tour companies to the authorities • Company uses vehicles fitted with catalytic converters • The company's five drivers in Nairobi are self-employed; the original driver/guide (now co-director of the Nairobi operation) was given a grant and later an interest-free loan to buy vehicles **Very aware and active.**
4 full time; 1 part time	• Has a long-standing green policy, which it says is well known to clients • Has raised £40,000 over the last 25 years for a number of international conservation projects • Has worked with RSPB, particularly on their 'Stop the Massacre' campaign as well as the Rwanda mountain gorilla project • The company is the UK representative for the Hellenic Society for the Protection of Nature • All tours are accompanied by an expert in the field, such as a botanist/ornithologist, etc **Has a long-standing involvement particularly through environmental organisations.**
2 full time; 1 part time	• Guidelines are included in information for travellers, but these are fairly general • The director is a trustee of a charity involved in National Park development and anti-poaching initiatives • Donates prizes for charitable fundraising events **Aware, but not yet doing very much.**
2 full time	• Supports and donates to Living Earth Foundation • 'Ensure that our properties are "friendly" as far as possible' • Has moved away from luxury holidays because money was not reaching local economies **Very aware of issues, but not actively doing very much yet.**

	Type of holiday	Destinations	Annual no. of customers
Wildlife Travel Ltd (RSNC) Dudwick House Buxton Norwich NR10 5HX Tel: 0603 278296	Specialist birdwatching, wildflower, painting, rambling and wildlife photography holidays	Cyprus, Crete, Greece, Turkey and Majorca, UK (Norfolk Weekends)	200-plus
Zoe Holidays 34 Thornhill Road Surbiton Surrey KT6 7TL Tel: 081 390 7623	Escorted tours in small groups by minibus	Greece	less than 20 to date

NOTE: One company that was set up after we compiled this table and that seems worthy of note is **Sensibility Travel**. It takes small groups to Thailand and has firm environmental principles.
Address: 83c Finsbury Park Road London N4 2JY
Tel: 071 704 0919

Staff	Environmental policy and initiatives:
2 part time	<ul><li>Green Flag member</li><li>Wildlife Travel was set up to raise funds for the Royal Society for Nature Conservation and its associated wildlife trusts</li><li>The Director is the key campaigner for Cretan Lagoons, the focus of a campaign supported by RSPB</li><li>Active supporters and advisers to the Laona Project which aims to use green tourism to protect and enhance the Akamas National Park in Cyprus</li><li>Plans to form the Society for the Protection of the Cretan Heritage, jointly with local Cretans</li><li>Whenever possible uses locally owned hotels, and checks whether the profit benefits the local people</li></ul>**Actively involved in campaigns.**
1 full time	<ul><li>Green Flag member</li><li>Tours are designed to benefit rural areas and to give tourists a better understanding of the way of life and background of the area visited</li><li>Groups are small and accompanied by the proprietor, so activities can be controlled directly</li></ul>**Has not yet done much, but is waking up.**

7
CONCLUSION:
THE PLEASURE PLANET

In terms of environmental concern, tourism is currently where the nuclear power and pesticide industries were in the early 1960s. Most people expected them to bring electricity too cheap to meter and more than enough food to keep all the world fed. Then scientists began to realise their huge environmental costs. We may be some way from the day when the tourism industry causes a disaster on the scale of Chernobyl, but it is now clear that a holiday business that, in effect, promises pleasure too cheap to meter will lead us all to destruction.

Political controversy will rage around the tourism, leisure and sports industries in the coming years. Apart from anything else, the more of us there are, and the scarcer wild areas become, the harder it will be to find suitable sites for major developments. Recently, for example, environmentalists attacked *all* six sites initially proposed for the 1998 Winter Olympics. The International Olympic Committee found itself having to choose between sites likely to affect – for example – a nature reserve in the Caucasus, a reindeer migration route in northern Sweden and a National Park in Japan.

Protecting the environment from commercial interests will always be tough and, despite the attempts of some politicians and developers to paint themselves as Davids against a Green Goliath, the resources of the environmental movement are minuscule when compared with those arrayed against them. So we should all do everything in our power to support local, regional, national and international environmental groups that are trying to ensure that we have a planet left to enjoy. Some of the most active groups are listed on pages 344–65.

Given the scale of the impacts outlined in earlier chapters, it is extraordinary that the industry has not been more directly targeted for attention in the 1990s. But we are now seeing a small number of established groups – including WWF – waking up to the issues while new groups, such as Tourism Concern, begin to highlight the broader social and economic impacts. We should support such organisations and lobby them to do more. Ring them up before going on a holiday to ask for advice on what to do – and what to avoid.

Politicians – local, national and international – are also critically important in all of this. They help to create the climate in which planners and developers operate. In many countries, however, and particularly in regions like Eastern Europe, they now see tourism as the goose that will lay the golden egg. And they tend to think in a very short time frame – usually just as far as the next election. So if there are things you want stopped or started, lobby your MP and MEP.

Maybe the answer to tourism's problems lies with those clever people in California. If the work of Telepresence Research Inc. is anything to go by, it won't be long before instead of going on holiday we will strap on an EyePhone headset, don a DataGlove and immerse ourselves in a 'virtual world' created by computers. And if the addictive effect of primitive arcade games like 'Space Invaders' is anything to go by, the attraction of such virtual worlds will be mind-bending.

But, just as television opened viewers' eyes to places they had never dreamed of going, so Virtual Reality (VR) technology is just as likely to fuel new waves of tourism. It's a virtual certainty that before long tour operators will be inviting us in to experience the latest holiday destination, activity or experience – in their own VR booths. Or, just as they currently send videos to clients, maybe they will send laser disks for the latest VR players.

All the trends point to the inevitable conclusion that more people will want to travel more often. In resort after resort, region after region, the pressures will build to unacceptable levels. *No* may be one of the shortest words in the English language, but ultimately it will probably be one of the most important in making tourism sustainable. More and more holiday resorts and tourism regions will have to follow in the wake of Venice (see page 251) and limit the number of people they allow in.

No one expects the transition to sustainable tourism to be easy. Our survey of tour operators shows that most of the firms responding – and remember that these are among the most thoughtful in the UK – are still at a very early stage in moving towards anything that could be labelled sustainable. Many firms are still sublimely unaware that this is an issue that many of their customers will eventually be insisting is addressed.

Yet tourism can contribute immeasurably to the richness of our lives and to our understanding of the world in which we live. Furthermore, as the small number of 'green' or 'sustainable' tourism success stories shows, there is a tremendous amount this powerful industry can do to help protect the extraordinary environmental and cultural resources it exploits. Just as Dustin Hoffmann was advised in the film *The Graduate* to 'get into plastics', the boom industry of the 1960s and 1970s, so today's young people would be well advised to consider a career in sustainable tourism. We are on the threshold of a boom period in totally new forms of tourism, and those who spot the opportunities in good time could well repeat – or exceed – the astounding success of earlier green businesses, most notably Anita Roddick's Body Shop.

Inevitably, as public concern mounts, we will see some tour operators and others involved in the tourism industry claiming to be earth-friendly. So much the better, as long as the claims are based on real achievements. But, along with campaigning organisations like Friends of the Earth, Greenpeace and WWF, we will all need to cross-check such claims before accepting them at face value.

We believe that the tourism industry is extremely unlikely to reform itself honestly unless its customers decide that they want change – and ensure that their views are heard in every corner of the industry. We are all responsible for the problems that tourism creates. And we can all be part of the solution.

If we are prepared to demonstrate our concern, to challenge the operators, to goad governments and to act responsibly when we are away from home, we will be helping to ensure that our huge appetite for leisure and holidays does not expel us from one Eden after another – until, finally, there is none left at a price we can afford. In short we can ensure that our holidays do not literally cost the Earth!

8
APPENDICES

Main Environmental Organisations

ARK

Room 312, Linen Hall, 162–8 Regent St, London W1R 5TB
Tel: 071 494 0145

Main aim: To involve the public actively in environmental campaigning and initiatives.

Background: Campaigns through distributing information, through projects and through selling 'greener' product lines, under the *Ark* banner. In 1991 launched the Green Travel Bug campaign in association with Manchester Airport, in which people flying from the airport were given a pack with ideas on what they can do as a holidaymaker to reduce their environmental impact.

How you can help: Life membership is £1; Friend of Ark membership is £60 pa.

British Trust for Conservation Volunteers (BTCV)

36 St Mary's Street, Wallingford, Oxfordshire OX10 0EU.
Tel: 0491 39766

Main aim: To enable people to take practical action towards protecting the environment and to improve access to Britain's countryside.

Background: BTCV's Natural Break programme of conservation working holidays involves around 6,000 people in a wide variety of activities, from protecting wildlife habitats to improving access to the countryside. Also organises around thirty international conservation working holidays throughout Europe.

How you can help: Membership £10 pa, for which you get quarterly copies of the news magazine *The Conserver* and an illustrated annual report *BTCV in Action*. You could also go on a Natural Break holiday.

Council for the Protection of Rural England (CRPE)

Warwick House, 25 Buckingham Palace Road, London SW1W 0PP. Tel: 071 976 6433

Main aim: To work for a beautiful and living countryside.

Background: Branches in every county campaign for the countryside through well-informed research and briefing of national and local government and of the media. Very concerned about the impact of tourism in the countryside and wider environment and is consulted by the government and tourist boards on the development of tourism strategy and infrastructure (leisure complexes, holiday villages, timeshares, theme parks, etc.).

How can you help: Membership £12 pa, for which you get three issues of the *Countryside Campaigner* and an annual report. You can also do voluntary work at one of CPRE's regional branches.

Countryside Commission

John Dower House, Crescent Place, Cheltenham, Gloucestershire GL50 3RA. Tel: 0242 521381

Main aim: To look after the countryside of England and Wales – and help people enjoy it.

Background: Has been involved in a wide variety of initiatives to encourage the tourism industry to be more environmentally considerate. Promotes green tourism and has produced, with the English Tourist Board, a pamphlet called *Principles for Tourism in the Countryside*. It carried out research on tourism businesses situated in or near the National Parks, to find out to what extent they support conservation work, and is also investigating ways in which the tourism industry could plough some of its profits back into conservation work.

How you can help: This is a government-run organisation with no membership, so help is not needed from individuals. But the Commission produces a wide range of publications and codes of conduct.

Countryside Commission for Scotland

Battleby, Redgorton, Perth PH1 3EW. Tel: 0738 27921

Main aim: A government agency which promotes landscape conservation, informal recreation and the well-being of rural communities.

Background: Undertakes research and raises understanding and awareness of countryside matters. In 1992 it merged with the Nature Conservancy Council in Scotland to form Scottish Natural Heritage. It contributes to planning decisions some of which relate to tourism projects. It also gives grants to tourism projects. It has contributed to the Scottish Tourist Board's work on tourism and the environment.

How you can help: Does not take membership.

David Shepherd Conservation Foundation

PO Box 123, Godalming, Surrey GU8 4SJ. Tel: 0486 32576

Main aim: The conservation and sustainable management of the earth's atmosphere, resources, natural habitats, forests, rivers, seas, countryside and wildlife.

Background: A fund-raising organisation which donates money to a wide variety of conservation projects and organisations throughout the world. David Shepherd gives public talks every year, and he uses this forum to stress the principles of travelling responsibly.

How you can help: By becoming a Friend of the Foundation (£15 pa).

Earthwatch Europe

Belsyre Court, 57 Woodstock Road, Oxford OX2 6HU.
Tel: 0865 311600

Main aim: To improve understanding of the planet, the diversity of its inhabitants and the processes which affect the quality of life on earth.

Background: Earthwatch gives people the chance to get involved in research work by working alongside field scientists. Anyone aged 17–70 can participate in environmental and conservation projects all over the world. Some projects study the impact of tourism on the environment, including one looking at how the behaviour of lemurs in Madagascar is affected by contact with humans.

How you can help: Become an Earthwatch member (£22 pa), which makes you eligible to join projects, entitling you to the bi-monthly magazine, which includes details of the 130 projects in forty countries that you can help.

Environmental Transport Association (ETA)

17 George Street, Croydon CRO 1LA. Tel: 081 666 0445

Main aim: To campaign for a government transport policy that puts the environment first.

Background: First mass membership body in the UK covering land-based transport (cars, bicycles, coaches, trains) with a clearly defined environmental responsibility. Looks for better transport alternatives that tackle the problems of pollution and congestion.

How you can help: Membership (£20 pa) gives you insurance cover for personal accidents and access to the ETA helpline, as well as a quarterly newsletter, *Going Green*. ETA also offers a road rescue package for environmentally conscious motorists.

Friends of the Earth

26–28 Underwood Street, London N1 7JQ. Tel: 071 253 4248

Main aim: Protection of the environment and promotion of sustainable development.

Background: Campaigns locally, nationally and internationally on a wide range of issues, including tropical rainforests, climate change, depletion of the ozone layer, acid rain, air and water pollution, hazardous waste, recycling, energy, countryside protection, sustainable agriculture and transport.

How you can help: Membership £16 pa, for which you get the Welcome Pack and their regular magazine *Earth Matters*.

Green Flag International

PO Box 396, Linton, Cambridge CB1 6UL

Main aim: To help the tourism and travel industry improve its environmental performance and to advise travellers on what they can do to minimise their environmental impact.

Background: Set up in December 1990 as a non-profit making company, works with the tourism industry, local authorities and national tourist offices on a range of environmental initiatives and projects.

How you can help: By buying the information pack (£5) and by passing on information to them about their members' performances.

Greenpeace

Canonbury Villas, London N1 2PN. Tel: 071 354 5100

Main aim: To force changes in the law to protect wildlife and to stop the pollution of the natural world.

Background: An international organisation which campaigns against the abuse of the natural world through lobbying and non-violent action protests, backed by scientific research.

How you can help: Through membership (£12 pa), for which you get their newsletter. You can also help their campaign to protect sea turtles in Indonesia. Ask for information on who to write to – and what to say.

Living Earth

The Old Laundry, Ossington Buildings, Moxon Street, London W1M 3JD. Tel: 071 487 3661

Main aim: To help individuals respond to and understand environmental issues through education projects.

Background: Specialises in environmental education, raising levels of understanding and knowledge to help people to make positive decisions concerning their environment. Programmes are under way in West Africa, Latin America and the UK.

How you can help: Donations welcome.

Marine Conservation Society (MCS)

9 Gloucester Road, Ross-on-Wye, Herefordshire HR9 5BU. Tel: 0989 66017

Main aim: To protect the marine environment for wildlife and future generations.

Background: Campaigns for cleaner beaches in Britain. It compiles an annual publication, *The Good Beach Guide* (Ebury Press, £5.99). Other campaign targets are to persuade: holidaymakers not to buy products made of coral; governments to establish marine protected areas; and the regulatory authorities to ensure cleaner water for divers. The MCS has published several sets of guidance notes, including the *Seashore Code*, *Guidelines for Divers* and the *Underwater Conservation Code*.

How you can help: Through support and membership (£12 pa), for which you get details of campaigns, diving projects and supporters' network. You can also write to the Marine Conservation Society for further ideas on ways to help.

The National Trust

36 Queen Anne's Gate, London SW1H 9AS. Tel: 071 222 9251

Main aim: To preserve places of historic interest and natural beauty.

Background: An independent conservation charity, which looks after over half a million acres of some of Britain's finest countryside and plays a vital role in preserving our heritage. Owns 560 miles of coastline, and more than 300 historic buildings and gardens are kept open to the public. Enterprise Neptune, set up about 25 years ago, buys up large tracts of the UK coastline and preserves them in their unspoiled state.

How you can help: Become a member (£21 pa), for which you get a membership card entitling you to enter most National Trust properties free of charge, as well as other benefits.

Royal Society for the Protection of Birds (RSPB)

The Lodge, Sandy, Bedfordshire SG19 2DL. Tel: 0767 680551

Main aim: To conserve and protect wild birds and their habitats through campaigns, education and research.

Background: Europe's largest wildlife conservation charity, the RSPB campaigns in many areas relating to tourism.

How you can help: Membership £16 pa. Write to your MP about an RSPB campaign if you feel strongly about it. For more information on what you can do, send for the RSPB's leaflet *I want to help*.

Tidy Britain Group

The Pier, Wigan WN3 4EX. Tel: 0942 824620

Main aim: To promote the prevention and control of litter and to encourage environmental improvement schemes.

Background: Organises theme weeks throughout the year, some of which relate to tourism. 1991 weeks included 'Coastline Week' and 'Tidy Travel Week'. The Clean Watersides Campaign tackles the litter problem in the canals and lakes in North West Britain, which is mainly caused by increased recreational use.

How you can help: Membership £10 pa. You could also set up your own clean-up campaign on beaches, rivers, canals and reservoirs.

Tourism Concern

Froebel College, Roehampton Lane, London SW15 5PU. Tel: 081 878 9053

Main aim: To reduce the negative impact of tourism on local communities and the environment through greater awareness and understanding – and a change in current tourism practice.

Background: Set up in 1989. Aims to get tourism and environment issues on to the international agenda. Activities have included organising a conference for tour operators on the impact of trekking in the Himalayas. A set of guidelines for trekkers will hopefully be distributed via tour operators and airlines.

How you can help: Membership £12 pa, for which you receive a quarterly newsletter, a starter pack with information, free access to information and a list of contacts in the Tourism Concern network. Volunteers are also welcome to help with projects and office administration.

World Wide Fund for Nature (WWF)

Panda House, Godalming, Surrey GU7 1XR. Tel: 0483 426444

Main aim: Conservation of wildlife and wildlife habitats.

Background: An international organisation which works through education, influencing public policy, site protection, species conservation and training. It has been involved in two major campaigns relating to tourism and the environment: working with the Greek Sea Turtle Protection Society to help protect the loggerhead sea turtles of Zakynthos; and working successfully to stop the trade in chimpanzees, used particularly in Spain as photographic models to pose with tourists.

How you can help: Membership £15 pa, for which you receive the quarterly WWF magazine. (If you pay a higher membership rate you get more benefits.)

Youth Hostels Association (YHA)

Trevelyan House, 8 St Stephen's Hill, St Albans, Herts AL1 2DY. Tel: 0727 55215

Main aim: To provide low-cost accommodation to those of limited means to help them gain a greater knowledge and care for the countryside.

Background: The YHA has a network of over 250 youth hostels throughout England and Wales and provides access to many more worldwide. It also offers 'Great Escapes' adventure holidays, special interest and environmental educational activities. The YHA has a full-time countryside officer advising on countryside issues and on participating in conservation projects. David Bellamy has been president of the YHA for over eight years.

How you can help: Membership from £2 to £8.90 pa depending on age. This entitles you to stay in youth hostels and to discounts on some merchandise.

Official Tourist Bodies

Association of British Travel Agents (ABTA)

55 Newman Street, London W1P 4AH. Tel: 071 637 2444

Main aim: To regulate the performance of its members and ensure financial security for their customers.

Background: An environmental committee was established in late 1990, with representation from a number of tour operators with an interest in the environment. An agenda for action has yet to be developed.

Association of Independent Tour Operators (AITO)

PO Box 180, Isleworth, Middlesex TW7 7EA. Tel: 081 569 8092

Main aim: To promote awareness of small, specialist tour operators.

Background: It is aware that the environment is a key issue for the tourism industry. Helped to set up Green Flag International (see page 347) and has worked with ski tour operators to research and provide guidance on environmental issues for company representatives in resorts. They plan to raise the environmental awareness of their members by drawing up an environmental charter – and asking members to donate a proportion of their receipts towards environmental causes.

British Tourist Authority (BTA)

Thames Tower, Black's Road, Hammersmith, London W6 9EL. Tel: 081 846 9000

Main aim: To promote Britain overseas as a tourist destination.

Background: Together with the Tour Operators' Study Group and Thames Television's 'Wish You Were Here . . . ?' holiday programme, the BTA launched the international *Tourism for Tomorrow Awards*, which aim to encourage and promote environmentally sensitive tourism projects. In 1991, fifty schemes from seventeen countries competed for an award. In conjunction with the Countryside Commission, the BTA also published a booklet called *Britain's Treasured Landscapes*, which illustrates the unspoilt areas of Britain while encouraging visitors to respect them by using the Country Code. A similar publication is planned for Britain's coasts and islands. Recently produced a report aimed at UK tourism industry called

'The Green Light: A Guide to Sustainable Tourism', in conjunction with the Countryside Commission and the Rural Development Commission.

English Tourist Board (ETB)

Thames Tower, Black's Road, Hammersmith, London W6 9EL.
Tel: 081 846 9000

Main aim: To promote England as a tourist destination and to encourage the provision and improvement of tourist facilities within England.

Background: Works closely with the Countryside Commission and the Rural Development Commission. Recently staged a major conference on tourism in the countryside called *Shades of Green*. The ETB has produced or contributed to a number of studies and reports looking into tourism, including the 1991 report of the government's Tourism and Environment Task Force.

European Tour Operators' Association

26–28 Paradise Road, Richmond, Surrey TW9 1SE.
Tel: 081 332 0014

Main aim: To represent European tour operators when operating within Europe.

Background: Has worked with the UK government task force on tourism and the environment – and points out the need to reconcile the economic and cultural benefits of tourism with its environmental impact. Focuses on package tour holidays by coach or air and is currently drawing up a green code for tour operators to pass on to their clients, partly in response to an increased number of environmental enquiries from members.

Northern Ireland Tourist Board

48 High Street, Belfast BT1 2DS.
Tel: 0232 231221

Main aim: To encourage tourism – and the provision and improvement of tourist accommodation and tourist amenities – in Northern Ireland.

Background: Has commissioned a study on the Tourist Board and on sustainable tourism in Northern Ireland. Has also helped to promote the *Tourism for Tomorrow* competition (page 369).

Scottish Tourist Board

23 Ravelston Terrace, Edinburgh EH4 3EU.
Tel: 031 332 2433

Main aim: To promote Scotland internationally and to encourage the provision and improvement of tourist amenities and facilities in Scotland.

Background: In 1990 the Board carried out a major review of tourism and the environment, involving other relevant government agencies.

Wales Tourist Board

Brunel House, 2 Fitzalan Road, Cardiff CF2 1UY.
Tel: 0222 499909

Main aim: To encourage tourism in Wales.

Background: Has worked with the Countryside Commission and the English Tourist Board on a guide to good practice by the tourism industry in national parks.

World Travel and Tourism Council (WTTC)

50 Victoria Street, London SW1H 0NH. Tel: 071 222 1955

Main aim: To promote the expansion of travel and tourism to benefit consumers and national economies.

Background: In spring 1992 the WTTC planned to start an annual State of the World Travel and Tourism Environment Report. It is also establishing a World Travel and Tourism Environment Research Centre in Oxford.

World Tourism Organisation (WTO)

Capitan Haya 42, 28020 Madrid, Spain. Tel: 010 341 571 0628

Main aim: To promote tourism and to help developing countries.

Background: An intergovernmental body covering worldwide tourism. Its tourism and environment programme is divided into three main areas: information, increasing the environmental awareness of the tourism industry as well as of tourists and supporting more environmentally sustainable tourism planning and development.

Specialised Organisations and Campaigns

Alp Action

Bellerive Foundation, Rue de Muzy 1, 1207 Geneva, Switzerland. Tel: 010 41 22 7359295

Main aim: To protect the cultural and natural heritage of the Alps.

Background: Started in early 1991. Raises awareness about the destruction of the alpine environment by uniting the media with the scientific and environmental communities – as well as business. Has carried out an extensive reafforestation programme, planting 200,000 trees in six alpine countries.

How you can help: Only corporate sponsors can join Alp Action.

Annapurna Conservation Area Project (ACAP)

King Mahendra Trust for Nature Conservation, PO Box 3712, Babar Mahal, Kathmandu, Nepal

Main aim: To involve local communities in the long-term environmental protection of the Annapurna region in Nepal.

Background: The protected area covers over 2,600 square kilometres. The heart of the programme is conservation education – ACAP believes that, without increasing the level of awareness of both villagers and visitors, lasting environmental protection cannot be achieved. The project includes small-scale conservation and alternative energy projects to improve the local standard of living and to minimise the negative impacts of tourism. Guidelines for tourists are issued and the project is maintained by entry fees to the area and by donations.

How you can help: Through donations and, if you go to Nepal, by paying entry fees to the area and following its guidelines.

Australian Wilderness Society

130 Davey Street, Hobart, Tasmania 7000, Australia. Tel: 010 61 02 34 9366

Main aim: Works to prevent the destruction of wilderness areas in Australia.

Background: Current campaigns are directed at protecting Australia's native forests and the Kakadu wetlands.

How you can help: Through subscribing to newsletter *Wilderness News*, which also entitles you to membership (overseas rate A$68 pa).

British Divers Marine Life Rescue

12 Maylan Road, Corby, Northants NN17 2DR. Tel: 0536 201511

Main Aim: To rescue marine animals in danger or distress.

Background: Projects have included rescue and care of seal pups showing symptoms of seal distemper.

How you can help: Membership costs £10 pa. You can also sponsor the organisation or become an activity organiser.

Care for the Wild

1 Ashfolds, Horsham Road, Rusper, Nr Horsham, Sussex RH12 4QX. Tel: 0293 871596

Main aim: To minimise cruelty to and exploitation of wildlife, and to help protect and conserve endangered species.

Background: Runs an orphan elephant fostering scheme in Kenya, and raises funds to protect forty black rhinos. Also involved in protecting the turtles in Zakynthos, Greece.

How you can help: By becoming a supporter through donations, for which you will receive updates on projects, or by practical help such as handing out leaflets.

Centre for the Advancement of Responsive Travel (CART)

70 Dry Hill Park Road, Tonbridge, Kent TN10 3BX. Tel: 0732 352757

Main Aim: To help people travel sensitively and to be respectful of places and cultures.

Background: Researches and publicises guidelines for sustainable travel alternatives. Has produced the *Credo for the Caring Traveller* and the *Responsive Traveller's Handbook*, available to all members of Tourism Concern (see page 349).

How you can help: By sending comments about travel experiences, particularly information on good or bad tour operators, and on locally organised tour operations.

Coral Cay Conservation

The Sutton Business Centre, Restmoor Way, Wallington, Surrey SM6 7AH. Tel: 081 669 0011

Main Aim: To help the government of Belize manage the coastal marine resources of the Belize Barrier Reef.

Background: Currently establishing a second marine reserve in Belize, where it will be equipping future park managers with information, training and resources. Uses satellite images to map the area and to monitor the movement of different species. Teams of divers are used to do research work, such as charting the reef and tracking pollution under the guidance of qualified marine staff.

How you can help: Takes on volunteers with diving skills – and welcomes people with medical or marine biology experience.

Council for National Parks

246 Lavender Hill, London SW11 1LN. Tel: 071 924 4077

Main Aim: To protect, promote and enhance National Parks.

Background: Has successfully defended National Parks from major tourist complexes, secured important concessions in the Water Act and helped set up the Broads Authority. It also played an active part in a recent review of National Parks. It is calling for a new Act to carry out recommendations of the review panel – and is leading the campaign for more National Parks.

How you can help: By becoming a Friend of National Parks (£10 pa), for which you will receive regular copies of the Friends' magazine *Viewpoint*, the newspaper *National Parks Today* and discounts on other in-house publications.

Cretan Lagoons

Wildlife Travel (RSNC/The Wildlife Trust's Partnership), Dudwick House, Buxton, Norwich NR10 5HX. Tel: 0603 278296

Main Aim: To persuade the Greek authorities to create a nature reserve instead of destroying a bird-rich lagoon in Crete.

Background: A joint project between Wildlife Travel, the RSPB and several interested Greek environmentalists. A third of the site has already been lost and the rest is threatened by plans to build hotels. Funding is being sought from the EC through the Greek Ministry of Tourism. Wildlife Travel take about 150–200 people a year on bird-watching holidays to the lagoon.

How you can help: Write to the Greek Ministry of Tourism to express your concern and tell people about your reasons for going to the lagoons.

Elefriends

Coldharbour, Dorking, Surrey RH5 6HA. Tel: 0306 713320

Main Aim: To protect elephants from poachers and to stop the ivory trade.

Background: Founded and coordinated by the Born Free Foundation. Supports anti-poaching measures in Africa, campaigns and tackles consumer markets for ivory around the world.

How you can help: Become an Elefriend for a year (adult, £12.50), and you will receive copies of *Trunkline*, their newsletter.

European Blue Flag

Lion House, Muspole Street, Norwich NR3 1DJ. Tel: 0603 762888

Main Aim: To improve the standards of the marine and coastal environment.

Background: Started in 1987 by the Foundation for Environmental Education in Europe. EC-wide scheme with three categories: ports, boats and ships, and beaches. Beaches are awarded a blue flag for water cleanliness and for providing adequate visitor facilities and information. In the UK, the Blue Flag scheme is run by the Tidy Britain Group and the English Tourist Board, and is also supported by the Department of Environment, local authorities and water companies.

How you can help: No requirement for public help, but you can help keep the pressure up by lobbying for cleaner beaches.

Europe Conservation

Via Fusetti 14, 20143 Milano, Italy. Tel: 010 39 2 5810 3135

Main Aim: To create a new approach to conservation, encouraging individual initiatives.

Background: International non-profit organisation with branches in France, Italy and Belgium. Raises funds for research and current campaigns include trying to save Polish wetlands from drainage and a whale adoption scheme.

How you can help: Membership costs £5 pa, entitling you to a projects bulletin. Volunteers can participate in wildlife research projects around Europe (contributory costs range from £100–£700).

Friends of Conservation (FoC)

**Sloane Square House, Holbein Place, London SW1W 8NS.
Tel: 071 730 7904**

Main Aim: To end the threat facing the wildlife and habitats of East Africa.

Background: Works closely with wildlife authorities, governments and local communities to provide money and managerial assistance for endangered habitats and species. Provides training for park rangers, information and guidelines for visitors, funds for anti-poaching measures and sanctuaries for threatened wildlife – as well as working with local schools and universities in the area.

How you can help: Through donations, for which you receive a regular *Survivor Newsletter*.

Friends of the Ionian (FoI)

**21a Stanbridge Road, Putney, London SW15 1DX.
Tel: 081 780 0420**

Main Aim: To unite efforts to conserve the environment of the Ionian Islands and to reduce tourism's impact on the environment.

Background: Encourages tour operators to work with Ionian communities, organises monthly island clean-ups and cultural activities such as Greek language courses, Greek dancing and museum visits. Operates in co-operation with other Ionian projects to help protect monk seals and the loggerhead turtles.

How you can help: Membership £8 pa. Donations also welcome. Contact FoI before and after your holiday so you can assist their projects.

Greek Animal Welfare Fund

11 Lower Barn Road, Purley, Surrey CR8 1HY. Tel: 081 668 0548

Main Aim: To promote animal welfare in Greece.

Background: Offers tour operators free copies of a pamphlet *Going to Greece?*, which gives guidance to tourists wanting to help animals in distress.

How you can help: Write and let them know if you see animal cruelty in Greece. The Fund's leaflet *Hints to Holidaymakers* lists organisations in Greece. Membership £10 pa.

InterFace

Moulsham Mill, Parkway, Chelmsford, Essex CM2 7PX.
Tel: 0245 252414

Main Aim: To personalise package tourism and promote creative
alternatives.

Background: Looks at issues in society that affect human dignity.
Organises *Before You Go* weekends for travellers. North South
Travel (Tel: 0245 492882) helps InterFace by offering discounted
air fares worldwide and donating all profits to projects in
developing countries through the North South Charitable Trust.

How you can help: Book your travel through North South Travel.

International Gorilla Conservation Programme

Fauna and Flora Preservation Society (FFPS), 1 Kensington Gore,
London SW7 2AR (written enquiries only, please)

Main Aim: To ensure the survival of the mountain gorilla and its
tropical forest habitat.

Background: Set up in 1978 in Rwanda, as the Mountain Gorilla
Project. Conservation awareness is the key to their approach –
they give hundreds of open-air lectures and seminars in villages,
colleges and schools. The most crucial element of the project
has been tourism based on the carefully controlled viewing of
undisturbed gorilla family life. This has proved to be profitable
for the local people, who now have a vested interest in
conservation. Activity now covers the entire range of mountain
and eastern lowland gorillas in East Zaire, Rwanda and West
Uganda.

How you can help: Through donations to the International Gorilla
Conservation Programme or by supporting the Flora and Fauna
Preservation Society – and by going to see the gorillas in Rwanda,
Zaire and where possible, Uganda (see page 155).

Into The Blue

Cherry Tree Cottage, Coldharbour, Dorking, Surrey RH5 6HA.
Tel: 0306 713431

Main Aim: Part of the Born Free Foundation, Into The Blue aims
to return dolphins from captivity to more natural surroundings and
eventual release into the open sea.

Background: Has flown three ex-dolphinaria dolphins from 'concrete captivity' to a marine sanctuary in the Caribbean. Plans to assist more dolphins as part of an international rehabilitation programme. Recommends that people do not visit traditional dolphinaria.

How you can help: Membership £12.50 pa, for which you receive project updates.

Kasanka Project

Worldwide Journeys and Expeditions, 146 Gloucester Road, London SW7 4SZ. Tel: 071 370 5032

Main Aim: To rehabilitate the Kasanka National Park in Zambia's northern Serenje district and make it work effectively as a wildlife conservation area.

Background: The only privately run National Park in Africa. Tour operator Worldwide Journeys and Expeditions (formerly EcoSafaris) acts as the main agent and a director of the company acts as a consultant and adviser to the park authorities. Started in 1990, the project involves local people in conservation and provides employment and education to demonstrate that poaching is not in their best interests.

How you can help: Join one of its conservation tours, working as a volunteer with scientists in the field.

Laona Project

PO Box 257, Limassol, Cyprus. Tel: 010 357 53 58632

Main Aim: To revitalise declining rural economies by introducing an alternative to mass tourism, preserving traditional, social and cultural values.

Background: Initiated by FoE Cyprus, the project centres on five villages around the proposed Akamas National Park in the Paphos district. Public buildings are being restored and villagers are offered grants and low interest loans to renovate their properties for non-intrusive tourism. Small-scale industry is encouraged, with a key focus on assistance for local agriculture.

How you can help: If you visit the region, stay in Laona Project accommodation, use the facilities in the village where the project is active – and voice your support for the project.

Mountain Agenda

c/o Geographical Institute, University of Berne, Hallerstrasse 12, CH 3012 Berne, Switzerland. Tel: 010 41 31 658019

Main Aim: To raise the position of mountain environments on the political agenda.

Background: The idea is to organise scientists to carry out research on the Alps and other mountain areas of the world. Also planned to use international platforms like the UNCED Conference in Rio in 1992 to focus world attention on mountain conservation issues.

How you can help: Individual membership not available, but donations are welcome.

Programme for Belize

PO Box 99, Saxmundham, Suffolk IP17 2LB. Tel: 072877 501

Main Aim: To conserve the rainforests of Belize while raising the standard of living.

Background: Has bought a 45,000 hectare plot of hinterland, now known as the Rio Bravo Conservation and Management Area, so it can manage it sustainably. Carefully controlled eco-tourism will be encouraged and buffer zones will be established around the reserve.

How you can help: If you buy an acre of rainforest (£25), you will receive a certificate of 'ownership', along with a bi-annual newsletter.

Rio Mazan Project

Development and Environment Centre, 38–40 Exchange Street, Norwich NR2 1AX. Tel: 0603 611953

Main Aim: To help protect the remaining high Andean forests in Ecuador through education and local action.

Background: Project participants are researching current forest uses and looking at land distribution. Will eventually be independently run entirely by Ecuadorians.

How you can help: Membership £7 pa, for which you will receive a quarterly magazine, with news of the project. Donations are welcomed – as are volunteers with relevant skills.

Save the Cairngorms Campaign

PO Box 39, Inverness IV1 2RL. Tel: 0463 85345

Main Aim: To campaign for a proper management policy to guarantee the safe future of the Cairngorms Mountains.

Background: Run by fifteen major conservation and outdoor organisations. Encourages active conservation in the area and increases public interest in – and care for – the mountain range.

How you can help: Write for information about ways to help. Donations much appreciated.

Sierra Club

730 Polk Street, San Francisco, CA 94109, USA.
Tel: 010 1 415 776 2211

Main Aim: To promote conservation of the natural environment by influencing public policy decisions.

Background: Well-known environmental organisation in the USA. Campaigns include National Park and forest protection, Clean Air Act re-authorisation and implementation, and Arctic national wildlife refuge protection. Also provides travel guides.

How you can help: Membership $35 pa, which includes a subscription to the bi-monthly magazine *Sierra*.

Surfers Against Sewage

The Old Count House, Warehouse, Wheal Kitty, St Agnes, Cornwall TR5 0RE. Tel: 0872 55300

Main Aim: To achieve clean seas for all recreational water users.

Background: Currently campaigning for improved sewage treatment before it is disposed of at sea, and for general awareness of waste disposal to avoid the sea and beaches being littered with sanitary towels, condoms, etc.

How you can help: Welcomes help from professionals – doctors, microbiologists and solicitors, for example. Membership £5 pa, for which you receive a quarterly newsletter. You can also help by lobbying your MP and by reporting pollution incidents to the National Rivers Authority as soon as you see them.

Survival International

310 Edgware Road, London W2 1DY. Tel: 071 723 5535

Main Aim: To stand up for the rights of tribal people worldwide.

Background: Campaigns for the right of tribal people to decide their own future and to protect their lands, their environment and their way of life. Works with tribes ranging from the Yanomami in Brazil and the Bhils in India to the Penan in Sarawak and Australia's Aborigines.

How you can help: Membership £12 pa (£3 unwaged), entitling you to a regular newsletter, urgent action bulletins, campaign documents and the *Survival* catalogue of goods – which include tapes of tribal music.

TRAFFIC International

219C Huntingdon Road, Cambridge CB3 0DL. Tel: 0223 277427

Main Aim: To prevent international trade threatening species' survival.

Background: The largest wildlife trade monitoring programme. Much of its work involves helping to enforce CITES (see page 74).

How you can help: Apply for free copies of the TRAFFIC Bulletin, published three times a year. Write for information – or tell them if you think you have come across illegal trade in endangered species whilst on holiday.

Venice in Peril Fund

24 Rutland Gate, London SW7 1BB. Tel: 071 823 9203

Main Aim: To protect Venice and its heritage.

Background: Set up in 1970, the Fund is involved in restoring and conserving buildings. To date has 'adopted' about a hundred buildings, including some churches.

How you can help: Through donations, for which you will receive an occasional newsletter covering the work of the Fund and projects undertaken by the Italian government and other public and private organisations dedicated to the preservation of Venice.

Whale and Dolphin Conservation Society (WDCS)

19a James St West, Bath, Avon BA1 2BT. Tel: 0225 334511

Main Aim: To protect whales and dolphins.

Background: An international charity dedicated to the conservation and appreciation of whales, dolphins and porpoises. Among many other projects, it is leading the UK campaign against dolphin killing by the tuna industry and sponsoring work worldwide to help prevent endangered river dolphins from becoming extinct.

How you can help: Membership £10 pa (£7.50 unwaged and £15 family), for which you receive a bi-annual magazine, *Sonar*, the WDCS newsletter and opportunities to join whalewatching expeditions. It also looks for volunteers for office work and fund-raising.

Wildlife Link

246 Lavender Hill, London SW11 1LN. Tel: 071 924 2355

Main Aim: To help wildlife conservation charities develop and formulate their policies, and to lobby government on their behalf.

Background: The liaison body for all the major voluntary organisations in the UK concerned with the protection of wildlife. Representatives are involved in co-ordinating policy work for wildlife and habitat protection, particularly through meetings with the government.

How you can help: Through donations or office-based volunteer work.

World Conservation Monitoring Centre (WCMC)

Conservation Monitoring Centre, 219c Huntingdon Road, Cambridge CB3 0DL. Tel: 0223 277314

Main Aim: To support conservation and sustainable development through the provision of information on the world's biological diversity.

Background: Collects and disseminates data on the status and distribution of threatened species, habitats, National Parks and the wildlife trade. Information is provided to governments, NGOs, conservation agencies, research scientists, media and the corporate sector, but not directly to the public.

How you can help: Through donations. WCMC does not have a membership.

World Conservation Union

(previously the International Union for the Conservation of Nature and Natural Resources, or IUCN)

Avenue du Mont Blanc, CH-1196, Gland, Switzerland. Tel: 010 41 22 649 114

Main Aim: To safeguard the diversity of the natural world and to promote the sustainable use of natural resources.

Background: The world's largest scientific conservation organisation. Membership includes government ministries, agencies and non-governmental organisations. Active in over 100 countries with over 600 members. Recent projects related to tourism have included hosting a conference on environmental problems in the Alps.

How you can help: No help needed.

Zoo Check

Coldharbour, Dorking, Surrey RH5 6HA. Tel: 0306 712091

Main Aim: To stop the captivity of animals in traditional zoos – and help to keep wildlife in the wild.

Background: Part of the Born Free Foundation, Zoo Check is an active campaigning organisation, carrying out research on the plight of captive wildlife in zoos throughout the world.

How you can help: Membership £12 pa, entitling you to two bulletins and two newsletters. You can also send information and photographs, particularly on foreign zoos, about zoo management, cage sizes, the condition of animals and any symptoms of abnormal behaviour.

Other Useful Addresses

ACTIVITIES

Adopt-a-Cave, 51 Timber Square, Roath, Cardiff CF2 3SH (written enquiries only)

Auto Cycle Union, Miller House, Corporation Street, Rugby, Warwickshire CV21 2DN. Tel: 0788 540519

British Association of Paragliding Clubs, The Old School Room, Loughborough Road, Leicester LE4 5PJ. Tel: 0533 611322

British Association for Shooting and Conservation, Marford Mill, Rossett, Wrexham, Clwyd LL12 0HL. Tel: 0244 570881

British Balloon and Airship Club, PO Box 1006, Birmingham B5 5RT. Tel: 021 643 3224

British Canoe Union, John Dudderidge House, Adbolton Lane, West Bridgford, Nottingham NG2 5AS. Tel: 0602 821100

British Field Sports Society, 59 Kennington Road, London SE1 7PZ. Tel: 071 928 4742

British Gliding Association, Kimberley House, Vaughan Way, Leicester LE1 4SE. Tel: 0533 515939

The British Hang Gliding Association, Cranfield Airfield, Cranfield, Bedford MK43 0YR. Tel: 0234 751344

British Horse Society, British Equestrian Centre, Stoneleigh, Coventry, Warwickshire CV8 2LR. Tel: 0203 696697

British Mountaineering Council, Crawford House, Precinct Centre, Booth St East, Manchester M13 9RZ. Tel: 061 273 5835

British Orienteering Federation, Riversdale, Dale Road North, Darley Dale, Matlock, Derbyshire DE4 2HX. Tel: 0629 734042

British Parachute Association, 5 Wharf Way, Glen Parva, Leicester LE2 9TF. Tel: 0533 785271

British Sub-Aqua Club, Telford Quay, Ellesmere Port, South Wirral, Cheshire L65 4FY. Tel: 051 357 1951

British Surfing Association, T2 Champions Yard, Penzance, Cornwall. Tel: 0736 60250

British Water Ski Federation, 390 City Road, London EC1V 2QA. Tel: 071 833 2855

British Waterways, Greycaine Road, Watford, WD2 4JR. Tel: 0923 226422

British Windsurfing Association, 163 West Street, Hayling Island, Hampshire. Tel: 070546 3595

Cadbury World, PO Box 1958, Linden Road, Bournville, Birmingham B30 2LD. Tel: 021 459 9116

The Camping and Caravan Club, Greenfield House, Westwood Way, Coventry CV4 8JH. Tel: 0203 694995

The Caravan Club, East Grinstead House, East Grinstead, West Sussex RH19 1UA. Tel: 0342 326944

Center Parcs, Rufford, Newark, Nottinghamshire NG22 9DP. Tel: 0623 411411

Centre for Alternative Technology, Machynlleth, Powys SY20 9AZ. Tel: 0654 702400

Circus Society, 52 Wiltshire Road, West Harnham, Salisbury, Wiltshire SP2 8HR. Tel: 0722 29867

Council of National Golf Union, Formby Golf Club, Formby, Liverpool L37 1LQ. Tel: 0704 872164

Cyclists' Touring Club, Cotterell House, 69 Meadrow, Godalming, Surrey GU7 3HS. Tel: 0483 417217

Disneyland, The Walt Disney Company, 1401 Flower Street, Glendale, California 91201, USA. Tel: 010 1 818 544 5383

Disneyworld, Walt Disney World, PO Box 40, Lake Buena Vista, Florida 32830, USA. Tel: 010 1 407 824 4321

Ducks Unlimited, One Waterfowl Way, Long Grove, Near Chicago, IL 60047, USA.

The Epcot Centre, Walt Disney World, PO Box 40, Lake Buena Vista, Florida 32830, USA. Tel: 010 1 407 824 4321

European Cyclists' Federation, c/o Fietsersbond ENfB, Postbus 2150, NL-3440 DD, Woerden, Utrecht, The Netherlands. Tel: 010 31 348023119

Golf Course Wildlife Trust, 1 Hinde Street, London W1M 5RH. Tel: 071 495 8095

Intermediate Technology Development Group, 103–105 Southampton Row, London WC1B 4HH. Tel: 071 436 9761

Jersey Zoo, Jersey Wildlife Preservation Trust, Les Augres Manor, Jersey JE3 5BF. Tel: 0534 64666

The Kite Society, 31 Grange Road, Ilford, Essex IG1 1EU (written enquiries only)

Laser Sport, Building 19, Stanmore Industrial Estate, Bridgnorth, Shropshire WV15 5HR. Tel: 0746 767186

Lawn Tennis Association, Queen's Club, Palliser Road, West Kensington, London W14 9EG. Tel: 071 385 2366

Leptospira Reference Laboratory, Public Health Laboratory, County Hospital, Hereford HR1 2ER. Tel: 0432 277707

London Zoo, Regent's Park, London NW1 4RY. Tel: 071 722 3333

Monkey Sanctuary, Near Looe, Cornwall PL13 1NZ. Tel: 0503 62532

Motoring Organisations Land Access and Rights Association, 45 The Fairway, Brunton Park, Gosforth, Newcastle Upon Tyne NE3 5AQ (written enquiries only)

Museums and Galleries Society, 24 St Charles Square, London W10 6EE. Tel: 081 960 1650

National Anglers Council, 11 Cowgate, Peterborough PE1 1LZ (written enquiries only)

National Centre for Organic Gardening, Ryton-on-Dunsmore Coventry CV8 3LG. Tel: 0203 303517

National White Water Centre, Bala, North Wales LL23 7NU.
Tel: 0678 520826

Natural History Museum, Cromwell Road, London SW7 5BD.
Tel: 071 938 9123

Ramblers' Association, 1/5 Wandsworth Road, London
SW8 2XX. Tel: 071 582 6878

Rare Breeds Survival Trust, National Agricultural Centre,
Kenilworth, Warwickshire CV8 2LG. Tel: 0203 696551

Royal Botanic Gardens, Kew, Surrey TW9 3AB. Tel: 081 940 1171

Royal Yachting Association, RYA House, Romsey Road,
Eastleigh, Hampshire SO5 4YA. Tel: 0703 629962

Sea World, 7007 Sea World Drive, Orlando, Florida 32821, USA.
Tel: 010 1 407 363 2571

Sports Council, 16 Upper Woburn Place, London WC1M 0QP.
Tel: 071 388 1277

Swimming Pool and Allied Trade Association (SPATA), Spata
House, 1A Junction Road, Andover, Hampshire. Tel: 0264
356210

Sustrans, 35 King Street, Bristol BS1 4DZ (written enquiries only)

Weald and Downland Open Air Museum, Singleton, Nr
Chichester, West Sussex PO18 0EU. Tel: 0243 63348

Welsh Canoeing Association, Pen-y-bomt, Corwen, Clywd
LL21 0EL. Tel: 0490 2786

ORGANISATIONS

Audubon Society, 950 3rd Avenue, New York 10022, USA.
Tel: 010 1 212 832 3200

The Bristol Bond, PO Box 753, Bristol BS99 1ZJ (written enquiries
only)

Bund, Arno Behlau, Postfach 300220, 5300 Bonn 3, Germany.
Tel: 010 49 228 400970

CITES Secretariat, 6 rue du Maupas, Case Postale 78, 1000
Lausanne 9, Switzerland. Tel: 010 41 21 200081

Conservation Foundation, 1 Kensington Gore, London SW7 2AR.
Tel: 071 235 1743

Council for National Parks, 45 Shelton Street, London
WC2H 9HJ. Tel: 071 240 3603

Countryside Council for Wales, Plas Penrhos, Frodd Penrhos,
Bangor, Gwynedd LL57 2LQ. Tel: 0248 370444

Earth Island Institute, 300 Broadway, Suite 28, San Francisco,
CA 94133, USA. Tel: 010 1 415 788 3666

English Heritage, Fortress House, 23 Saville Road, London W1X 1AB. Tel: 071 973 3000

English Nature, Northminster House, Peterborough PE1 1UA. Tel: 0733 340345

Environmental Protection Agency, 401 M Street, Washington DC 70460, USA. Tel: 010 1 202 260 2090

European Commission, DG 23, 200 rue de la Loi, Brussels B1049. Tel: 010 322 235 1111

The Forestry Commission, 231 Corstorphine Road, Edinburgh EH12 7AT. Tel: 031 334 0303

Green Party, 10 Station Parade, Balham High Road, London SW12 9AZ. Tel: 081 673 0045

International Primate Protection League 116 Judd Street, London WC1H 9NF

Operation Raleigh, The Power House, Alpha Place, Flood Street, London SW3 5SZ. Tel: 071 351 7541

Reefwatch, Tropical Marine Research Unit, University of York, Heslington, York YO1 5DD. Tel: 0904 430000

Royal Society for Nature Conservation, The Green, Whitham Park Lincoln LN5 7JR. Tel: 0522 752326

RSPCA, The Causeway, Horsham, Sussex RH12 1HG. Tel: 0403 64181

Soil Association, 86 Colston Street, Bristol BS1 5BB. Tel: 0272 290661

US Environmental Defense Fund, 1616 P Street, NW Suite 150, Washington DC 20036, USA. Tel: 010 1 202 387 3500

Voluntary Service Overseas (VSO), 317 Putney Bridge Road, London SW15 2PN. Tel: 081 780 2266

TOURIST ORGANISATIONS/TOUR OPERATORS

Australian Tourist Commission, Gemini House, 10–18 Putney Hill, London SW15 6AA. Tel: 081 780 2227

Biological Journeys, Building 1876, Ocean Drive, McKinleyville, California 95521, USA. Tel: 010 707 837 0178

Breakaway Adventure Travel, 581 Boylston, Boston, Massachusetts 02116, USA.

Carnival Cruise Lines, 3635 NW 87th Avenue, Miami, Florida 33178, USA. Tel: 010 1 305 599 2600

Cunard, 30a Pall Mall, London SW1Y 5LS. Tel: 071 491 3930

DRV (German Travel Agents' Association), Mannheimer Strasse 15, W-6000 Frankfurt, Main no 1, Germany. Tel: 010 496 92739070

Gulf Local Authorities Development Association, 91 Digger Street, Cairns 4870, Queensland, Australia.
Tel: 010 617 70 511 420

London Tourist Board, 26 Grosvenor Gardens, Victoria, London SW1W 0DU. Tel: 071 730 3450

Oceanic Society Expeditions, Fort Mason Centre, Building E, San Francisco, CA 94123, USA. Tel: 010 1 415 441 1106

Tiger Tops, 13 Chapter Street, London SW1P 4NY.
Tel: 071 630 7102

Tourism Authority of Thailand, 49 Albemarle Street, London W1X 3FE. Tel: 071 499 7679

Tourism for Tomorrow Awards, British Tourist Authority, Thames Tower, Black's Road, London W6 9EL.
Tel: 081 846 9000

Wilderness Tours, Jeepston, Nr Hobart, Tasmania 7116, Australia. Tel: 010 6 102 971 384

Wildland Adventures, 3516 NE 155th, Seattle, Washington State 98155, USA. Tel: 010 1 206 365 0686

Further Reading

Books

The Holiday Makers, Jost Krippendorf (Heinemann Professional Publishing, £14.95)
One of the most interesting general books on the tourism industry, analysing present and future patterns of tourism and leisure.

The Good Tourist, Katie Wood and Syd House (Mandarin, £5.99)
A useful introduction to some of the environmental, social and ethical issues revolving around tourism.

The Good Beach Guide, Guy Linley-Adams (Ebury Press, £5.99)
Useful source of information on the state of Britain's beaches, region by region, based on personal reports and inspections. Also gives information on local wildlife and walks, and suggests alternative entertainment for rainy days.

The Rough Guide Series (Harrap-Columbus)
'Green' sections covering wildlife and environmental issues are increasingly included in this mainstream travel guide series.

Periodicals

Holiday Which? and national newspapers (the *Independent* and the *Observer* for example) cover environmental issues, but if you are looking for something rather more provocative, try the Tourism Concern (see page 349) newsletter *In Focus*. Available four times a year to all members or on a subscription basis, the newsletter gives news of projects, conferences, workshops and books.

Also useful are *BBC Wildlife* and *Green Magazine*. Further afield, ask for a sample copy of Natour, described as the 'European magazine for tourism and the environment'. It is produced bi-monthly in both English and Spanish. Annual subscription costs US$55. Details from: Natour, Viriato, 21–28010 Madrid, Spain. Tel: 010 34 1 593 0831.

INDEX